Teacher
decision-making
in the classroom

Routledge Education Books

Advisory editor: John Eggleston
Professor of Education
University of Keele

Teacher
decision-making
in the classroom
a collection of papers

edited by

John Eggleston

Routledge & Kegan Paul
London, Boston and Henley

First published in 1979
by Routledge & Kegan Paul Ltd
39 Store Street, London WC1E 7DD,
Broadway House, Newtown Road,
Henley-on-Thames, Oxon RG9 1EN and
9 Park Street, Boston, Mass. 02108, USA
Set in Press Roman 10 on 11 pt by
Hope Services, Abingdon
and printed in Great Britain by
Lowe & Brydone Ltd,
Thetford, Norfolk
© Routledge & Kegan Paul Ltd 1979;
editorial selection, Preface and
chapter 1 © John Eggleston 1979

British Library Cataloguing in Publication Data

Teacher decision-making in the classroom
(Routledge education books)

1 Decision-making – Congresses 2 Elementary
school administration – Congresses
I Eggleston, John
372.1'1'02   LB1027   78–41187

ISBN 0 7100 0171 1

Contents

Contents

Notes on contributors

PAUL BELLABY is Lecturer in the Department of Sociology, University of Keele.

KEITH DRAKE is Lecturer in the Department of Education, University of Manchester.

JOHN EGGLESTON is Professor and Head of the Department of Education, University of Keele.

DOUGLAS FINLAYSON is Senior Lecturer in Educational Research, School of Education, University of Liverpool.

DENIS GLEESON is Lecturer in Sociology of Education, Department of Education, University of Keele.

MARTYN HAMMERSLEY is Lecturer in the Faculty of Educational Studies, Open University.

ANDY HARGREAVES is Lecturer at the Open University.

DAVID H. HARGREAVES is Reader in the Department of Education, University of Manchester.

COLIN HUNTER is Lecturer in the School of Education, Leeds Polytechnic.

GEORGE MARDLE is Lecturer in the Sociology of Education, Department of Education, University of Keele.

SYLVIA QUIRK is Lecturer in the School of Education, University of Liverpool.

JOHN SUTCLIFFE is Lecturer in the Department of Education, University of Cambridge.

MERVYN TAYLOR is Lecturer in Educational Psychology, Department of Education, University of Keele.

MICHAEL WALKER is Lecturer in Sociology of Education, Matlock College of Education.

RICHARD WHITFIELD is Professor and Head of the Department of Educational Enquiry, University of Aston in Birmingham.

PETER WOODS is Senior Lecturer, Faculty of Educational Studies, Open University.

Preface

The papers in this volume are revised versions of those presented to a working group funded by the Social Science Research Council. The group met for two extended week-end seminars at the University of Keele in September 1976 and March 1977 and engaged in much correspondence and informal discussion. It was comprised of a number of researchers and teachers from schools, universities and colleges who, from sociological, psychological, economic and a range of other perspectives, were concerned to begin the exploration of the reasons for the decisions teachers make in the classroom; some considered decisions, some apparently unconsidered. Yet, considered or not, these decisions significantly affect the lives of all who work in classrooms— children and teachers. In addition to the authors of papers in this volume, the group included Stephen Ball, Edith Cope, Chris Day, Sara Delamont, J. Dennis, Tony Green, J. Harris, Peter Musgrave, Philip Robinson and C.J. Saville.

A central aim of the group was to consider the possibilities for achieving greater understanding of classroom decision-making and all the contributions in this volume were produced in the furtherance of this objective. In order to facilitate consideration by a wider population the group decided to gather the papers together as a book that identified and mapped existing knowledge and indicated where it might be augmented.

All members of the group join me in expressing our warm appreciation to the Social Science Research Council for funding the group, the University of Keele for its hospitality, our publishers for their positive response to our work and Mary McBratney for typing and assembling the manuscript. D.F. Thoburn and F. Parker have commented helpfully on some sections of the book.

Earlier versions of the articles by David H. Hargreaves and John Eggleston appear in *Classroom Decision-Making,* a special issue of the

ix

Preface

Cambridge Journal of Education, 7, no. 1, Lent Term 1977. An earlier version of the article by Peter Woods appears in P.E. Woods, *The Divided School,* London: Routledge & Kegan Paul, 1978. The editor and authors offer their grateful thanks for permission to reproduce some previously published material, and to the Social Science Research Council for permission to publish two papers.

John Eggleston

Chapter 1

Editorial introduction:
making decisions in the classroom

John Eggleston

Teachers are constantly making decisions in their classrooms; indeed, decision-making is probably the central feature of the role of the teacher. Decisions are about lesson content, teaching style, the motivation of the class, the incentives or disincentives to apply, the resources to use, the moments to change course or pace: these and a thousand other occasions in the daily routine of the classroom call for decisions which not only are inescapable but also have vital consequences for the success or failure of the day's work and that in the weeks and months ahead. The decisions involve fine judgments of the capacities of individual children, determination of their needs and evaluation of their achievements. Decisions may even call for consideration of such fundamental matters as the purpose of education and the justification of the whole *raison d'être* of the classroom. In theory, and even to some extent in practice, most of the activities of the individual classroom are a consequence of the decisions of the individual teacher.

Nowhere is the range of the individual decisions of the teacher to be seen more clearly than in the modern progressive primary school. Here the structural features of timetable, curriculum, examination and tradition that appeared to constrain so many teachers' decisions in the past are far less in evidence. The teacher, responding to the needs of the pupils, appears to be able to decide to do almost anything that professional judgment deems correct. A classic example is that of Miss Sanders, a fictional character who appeared in the text of an advertisement for audio-visual equipment in an American educational technology magazine. Underneath a large photograph of Donnie, one of her pupils who has broken his arm, the text reads:

> You're all hanging up your coats at school and in comes Donnie
> with a cast on his arm. Everybody has to see it and touch it and
> write on it. 'How long do you have to wear it, Donnie?' 'Miss

1

Sanders, what makes bones?' 'How can you break your arm
swimming?' 'Will it grow back, Miss Sanders?' This is the teachable
moment. It's the rare moment when you really want to learn. But
your curiosity sure isn't satisfied by seeing just the cast. You want
to see inside. So somebody goes to the film library and brings back
a film selection on bones. You put it in the projector and—wow—a
great movie. This way Miss Sanders can teach you all kinds of things
—more things than anyone would expect her to know—at the exact
moment when you want to learn them. And it's alive, the way
you're used to seeing it.

Even a more traditional teacher in a more conventional establishment than that of Miss Sanders is likely also to exercise a wide range of
decision-making through the working day: in choice of texts, in
'playing' of the examination syllabus, in distribution of resources and
efforts among different children. It may also be argued that in most
schools the decision-making role of teachers is being increased by wider
changes within the system. Curriculum development has meant that the
range of viable and professionally legitimate curriculum contents has
increased enormously. Indeed, an essential part of much modern curriculum development is the emphasis on teachers' choosing from the
materials, resources and programmes available. A whole range of recent
innovations have further reinforced this trend, including unstreamed
classes, independent learning, child centred approaches, project
methods and enquiry groups. All these as well as broader trends such as
the moves to comprehensive secondary schooling and child centred
learning have obliged teachers to exercise more responsibility for what
is taking place in their classrooms because less and less are they able to
refer to some superior, global authority. No authority outside the
individual classroom can possibly make many of the decisions now required of the teacher because no external authority can have access to
the evidence on which they must be based.
 A further consequence of such changes is that teachers are 'freed'
from external supervision in the close detailed way that was possible
when the head, familiar with most curricula in the school, could legitimately visit a classroom and enquire with some precision about the
stage of development reached, holding in mind a clear view of what
would and should have been the 'normal' situation. The point is re-
affirmed by the changing role of inspectors, both DES and Local
Authority, whose role is now seen increasingly as one of adviser rather
than supervisor. Even the terms in which the work of the DES Assessment of Performance Unit are couched makes clear that the concept
of the Unit is to provide information that will assist the individual
teacher in making decisions (Department of Education and Science,
1977).

All this is not to say that the teacher is virtually independent or even autonomous in curriculum decisions. Many others influence that which takes place in the classrooms, not least employers and parents. However, even without such external influences, it may be argued that relatively few teachers exercise autonomous decision-making (Eggleston, 1975). Not only is Miss Sanders a unique entity, she is also a structural phenomenon. She is likely to be highly predictable in her treatment of Donnie's accident; in the things she says about the role of hospitals, the doctors and nurses within them, the importance of accident prevention and much else. Miss Sanders holds her position as a teacher within the established social system, a system within which she has trained to become a teacher. It is unlikely that her decisions in her classrooms, however spontaneous they appear to be, will be capricious; still less are they likely to be disruptive of the social order.

However, should she ever exceed the normal bounds and encourage her class to produce seditious poems or to lobby the local authority that runs her school with banners bearing words of protest, there are well-established ways in which she can be encouraged to discontinue such activities. And as Sharp and Green (1975) point out, there are also subtler constraints. They portray, among others, the position of 'Mrs Carpenter'. Mrs Carpenter is an able and enthusiastic teacher of new approaches in mathematics in Mapledene Junior School. But when she is called upon to justify her new approaches and to make a rational case for their further development, she is 'lost for words'. Sharp and Green offer extended transcripts of interviews, using Mrs Carpenter's confused and wandering arguments to illustrate that she and her kind are handicapped in their capacity to justify effectively decisions to researchers and other external 'authority figures' by the lack of an 'accounting language'. When teachers lack this facility, their decisions are unlikely to remain subordinate to others.

While alerting us to the ways in which teachers act as 'agents of social control', sociologists have also shown us the ways in which teachers' decisions are an important feature of the process of social control. Sharp and Green usefully illuminate this issue in their discussion of Linda. Linda was a girl at Mapledene about whom certain decisions had been made by teachers at an early stage in her career. It had been decided that Linda, for a variety of reasons, had limited capacity and would be unlikely to achieve highly. Sharp and Green illustrate how effectively these decisions had been implemented and how difficult, though not impossible, reversing these decisions was, even in the light of contradictory evidence.

The literature of sociology and social psychology abounds with evidence of the way teachers' decisions about the capacities of children— commonly linked with assumptions about social class background— effectively influences their achievements in school. The well-known work of Rosenthal and Jacobson (1970), though much disputed, carries unmistakable evidence of the consequences of teachers' decisions on individual students. Eggleston (1977) has pointed out how much the teacher's interpretation of children's capacities and needs and the curriculum appropriate for them is a consequence of his own views of the social system and the place he sees the children as occupying.

Yet how do teachers make the decisions and judgments to which we have been referring? Research on teacher behaviour in the classroom has taken two broad courses in the past decade. On the one hand there has been the descriptive/interpretative set of approaches; on the other, the curriculum development/evaluational approaches.

The first course can be traced through the detailed *classroom observation analysis* of writers such as Flanders and Lungdren. To these have been added the more interpretative approaches of workers such as Delamont (1976), Walker and Adelman (1975) and Keddie (1971). An illuminating recent example of this school is that of Delamont (1976):

> Consider the following incident from a lesson on the history of the Napoleonic wars which followed material on British politicians of the period. As soon as the whole group had assembled:
>
>> Evelyn puts up her hand. Mrs. Flodden acknowledges it, and asks what she wants:
>> Evelyn: I've got an epigram about Burke. Can I read it?
>> Mrs. F. says yes 'of course'. Evelyn reads her epigram and gets laughter from the class.
>> Mrs. F. gets Evelyn to write it on the board so anyone who chooses can copy it down. Then announces 'notes on the Napoleonic wars'.

This is an ordinary classroom exchange which, at first glance, had no features worthy of comment. However, it shows, as almost every other exchange shows, who really controls lesson content. As the lesson opens Evelyn makes a contribution relevant to the previous lesson. She offers an epigram. Note that by *offering* it she implies she has no natural right to teach the class, she asks permission. (We can assume that, because Evelyn feels confident enough to offer her epigram, Mrs. Flodden is likely to accept it—not all teachers receive such offers.) Mrs. Flodden grants her the privilege—and then immediately 'colonises' it. She tells Evelyn to put the verse on the board, and so defines it as a piece of information that can be officially recorded. It is not, however, so important that writing it down is compulsory as the notes on the Napoleonic Wars are. By implication, therefore, Mrs. Flodden defines the epigram as marginal to history, the notes are central.

The second course of research on teacher behaviour is concerned not so much with classroom analysis of the teacher's activity as with its *behavioural consequences* for the children. It is more or less visible throughout most Schools Council/Nuffield and other development projects and their specifically evaluative extensions by writers such as James Eggleston, Tawney and Parlett. This may be seen at its clearest in the field of science teaching, in which Kerr (1964) pioneered the examination of the behavioural consequences of teacher decision-making. More recently it has been associated with the Science Teacher Education Project (1974), in which teachers are helped to make their decisions in the light of anticipated behavioural consequences. Sutton (1975), writing of this project, offers a useful illustration of the approach:

> Let us take an example. A teacher heard of an experiment which he thought might be a useful introduction to the topic of floating. An egg sank in one liquid, floated in another, and hung, as if suspended, in another. (The liquids were water and salt solutions of different concentrations.) He gave this experiment to two small groups (each containing four pupils) to investigate: one group was thoroughly absorbed in it, took a lot of the initiative, and made excellent progress: whereas the other group, after initially enjoying pushing the egg up and down, finished up by breaking the egg and spilling the solutions.
> 1 Which of the needs listed earlier do you think the experiment might have been meeting in the first group of pupils?
> 2 Can you explain the success of some small part of your lessons in these terms?

There are some links between study of what teachers do and the study of the consequences of their actions that have been illustrated by the work of Delamont and Sutton. The work taking place at the Centre for Applied Research in Education at the University of East Anglia is one well-known example. But few of the links explore the important middle area: How and why do teachers make decisions in the classroom—about the use of new and existing curricula, about progress, resource usage, selection of information, and much else? The first set of approaches describes what teachers do; the second tends to be concerned with what teachers' options are and the consequences of taking them. Neither course focuses centrally upon the decision-making process itself and seeks to explain it. The papers contained in this volume represent attempts to fill in this middle ground. The SSRC sponsored working group on teacher decision-making in the classroom, comprising psychologists, social psychologists, sociologists, economists and others from schools, colleges and universities, has undertaken a preliminary exploration of initiatives that can illuminate the continuous but often latent processes of decision-making in the classroom—processes that have important consequences for all participants. The range is wide. It includes decisions on curriculum, to whom it is available and on what terms; decisions on the use of evaluation and assessment; the criteria for the grouping of children and, above all, decisions on what are the nature, needs and overall social identity of the children and the adults of the classroom. The work of the group has involved not only the consideration of the processes whereby these decisions are made but also the ways in which they are put into effect and their consequences.

The papers that follow speak for themselves. Each defines its areas of concern, identifies existing knowledge and goes on to indicate where it might be augmented. Sutcliffe and Whitfield commence with a paper that maps the field, presenting in detail the results of their previous research on the nature and incidence of decisions and the complex network of variables that surround them. In the chapters that immediately follow, contributors examine some of these variables in greater detail. Taylor looks at the teachers' implicit personality systems and how they bring to the classroom 'sets of decision rules' by which information about one category of pupils' behaviour implies the placing of pupils in a range of further categories. Finlayson and Quirk consider a closely related issue, the ideology of the teacher and its consequences for the teacher's decisions. Though often hidden, they see ideology not only as a key to much of the teacher's behaviour but also as a source of justification for behaviour.

A number of contrasting but essentially complementary perspectives are offered in subsequent chapters. David Hargreaves develops a phenomenological analysis of classroom decision-making. He returns to the question of the teacher's values, linking them with professional skills in decision-making, and addresses himself to the possibility of change in the light of further knowledge. He concludes:

> If we could explicate the interrelationship between values and skills, as betrayed in decision-making, then perhaps we could provide the experienced teacher with the tools to uncover and to reconstruct his own common sense knowledge, skills and values and thus to change more thoroughly and with self-awareness.

Drake, in contrast, takes a micro-economic perspective in which he uses the classic economist's analysis of choice between scarce means to achieve desired ends. He develops a model based upon the realities of human choice—choice characterised by uniqueness and voluntarism rather than by the crude determinism of classical economics he rejects.

A number of contributors based their papers on detailed studies of life in classrooms. Bellaby considers the range of classroom régimes. Based upon his work in contrasting comprehensive schools, he demonstrates the wide variation of teacher decision-making therein. Yet, he also shows that these differences can produce not only different consequences, but also, in some ways, similar consequences—particularly when the classroom is seen in a macro-perspective as a component of the total social system. Here Bellaby is exploring the key concepts of social control (a central feature of many contributions) at both macro and micro level. Hunter offers a consideration of decision-making based on a case study of a Yorkshire Comprehensive School, whilst Andy Hargreaves looks at strategies, decisions and control in a middle school. In one of the most detailed accounts of interaction in a middle school yet written, he indicates the value of ethnographic approaches to explaining teacher behaviour in the classroom. Woods addresses himself to the familiar realities of the classroom as well, emphasising the immediate importance of survival in the classroom and how this can dominate the decision-making of the teacher. Unless the teacher can 'get it right', there may be no more classroom decision-making for him to do. Woods also offers a valuable reminder of the complexity of factors both internal and external that are always present:

> Teachers are forced by the twin pressures of commitment and structural constraint to accommodate problems and develop survival strategies.

Hammersley assembles a preliminary model of teacher activity, returning again to the underlying issues of social control and social change in the classroom and in society.

The book concludes with contributions by Gleeson and by Mardle and Walker that take up the potential of classroom behaviour as a means not only of social control but also of social change. Using a range of perspectives, both papers outline possibilities for changed decision-making behaviour that provide appropriate extensions to the more limited time perspectives adopted in some of the other papers.

Together the contributions indicate the immense potential of this emergent and fascinating field of study. But the discussions of the group have made it clear that there is as yet only incomplete knowledge of the factors involved in teachers' classroom decision-making, either at the minute to minute level of classroom activity or at the fundamental ideological level that underpins it. How are such decisions made, changed, reified, transmitted and justified? What is known of their consequences—and does such knowledge substantially influence decisions? How are decisions affected by the structural constraints of the school, the profession and the education system? Answers to questions such as these may hold the key to a fuller understanding of the school and of the social structure generally. Not only are there the attractive research prospects that show clearly in most papers; there are, even more importantly, the prospects of fuller understanding of life in classrooms that can enhance the effectiveness and fulfilment of all those who work therein.

7

Chapter 2

Classroom-based teaching decisions

John Sutcliffe and Richard Whitfield

Introduction

While recognising that teachers' decision-making in the classroom is influenced by factors in and decisions of the educational institution as a whole, and that these in turn are affected by policy decisions made at local and national levels, it is most important to recognise that, in the British tradition, considerable autonomy is given to the individual teacher. Studies of the detail of how that autonomy is exercised within the classroom are required if we are to understand and suggest ways in which the structure of teachers' day-to-day activities to promote more effective learning may be modified. Despite a good deal of research into classroom interaction which plots teachers' actions, we know very little indeed about the precursors of those actions—namely, teachers' decisions. If action is to be changed, a prerequisite is to change the patterns of decision-making; furthermore, any directed intervention is only possible through an understanding of the process. This paper outlines a perspective through which such understanding may be gained by means of classroom-based research and describes some recent experimental fieldwork.

It should be noted that whilst the improvement of teacher training procedures constitutes an important reason for our interest in this field, notions concerning 'the effective teacher', containing logical implications for pupils' learning, are secondary to the focus of the present paper. If, as Whitfield (1975) suggested, 'the successful or effective teacher becomes characterised as one who consistently makes sound or appropriate decisions in order to implement a set of desirable intentions concerned with pupils' learning', then the judgment of desirability (by whom and using what criteria?) becomes an additional dimension in order to link teacher effectiveness with teacher decision-making behaviour. Results of investigations of the decisions required of teachers within the classroom may, however, provide a framework for various courses of training, which may include simulations of a variety of classroom conditions permitting practice of decision-making under relatively controlled conditions. The critical incident technique, pioneered in Canada by Flanagan and later used with university students by Crawford and Signori (1961), has found wider, more recent, application in a school context. Studies by McPhail (1967) and Bjerstedt (1969) exemplify its use with adolescents and teachers, respectively. Extensions of the technique into the area of initial teacher training, such as that advocated by Bishop and Whitfield (1972), have yet to be widely applied and evaluated.

The teacher as decision-maker

In 1969 Bjerstedt wrote (p.55),

> A teacher is in his daily work to a great extent a decision maker in a situation of constant social exchange, where the inability to make a decision at the right moment or inadequacy in social relations can easily have an adverse effect on both the harmony and effectiveness —and perhaps not only for the actual situation but also for the future.

In the same vein, Bligh (1972) regarded much of a teacher's work as taking and acting upon a series of decisions. An acceptance of this viewpoint carries with it the implication that part of a student teacher's course should involve a knowledge of and practice in decision-making.

Before any conceptual clarification of teacher decision-making, it is important to examine the meaning of the word 'decision' alone. Examination of some fourteen dictionaries spanning the period from 1755 to the present reveals the phrases most commonly used to define a decision:

(i)   the action of deciding
(ii) settlement, conclusion, judgment, resolution
(iii) the quality of being decided
(iv) making up one's mind

The more recently published dictionaries include a more explicit mention of the notion of choice:

(v)   the choice of a course of action
(vi) the choice arrived at after comparing several courses of action

All human activity may thus be said to involve decision-making, and the decisions, whether implicit or explicit, appear to fall into two distinct classes.

First, there are the non-immediate, contemplative decisions concerning events in the future. Such decisions may be changed before implementation and, whether changed or not, are the result of a conscious thought process at some time past or present. Let us call these *reflective* decisions. The second class of decisions are the immediate instantaneous ones, those which occur as a result of forces perceived as affording no time for reflection. These we can call *immediate* decisions. An immediate decision is similar to the concept of a 'tactical' decision introduced by Dettre (1970), except that he stresses the purely selfish, personal and self-protective components in tactical decisions. Dettre's dichotomous classification of decisions appears to rest on the time taken to effect a change in the behaviour of the subject of the decision rather than on the circumstances in which the decision is made. Bishop and Whitfield (1972) dichotomised teacher decision-making using 'long term' and 'on-the-spot' as category labels; the two concepts are respectively equivalent to reflective and immediate decisions.

In common with others engaged in social interactions, the teacher is required to make both kinds of decision professionally as well as in private life. His reflective decisions are particularly manifest in lesson planning and will encompass aspects of classroom behaviour and role interpretation of both teacher and students. In arriving at such decisions, it is unlikely that all the available alternatives will have been explored by the decision-maker. However, an account of the components giving rise to a reflective decision could be obtained from the teacher, whilst recognising that some or all of the account may be contaminated by the intervention of the investigator. The teacher's reflective decisions are likely to be based on his knowledge of the teaching environment gained via experience and instruction. Indeed, a major part of teacher training is directed towards influencing the teacher's reflective decisions.

Whilst the effect of cultural factors is common to each type of decision, the immediate decision is a more distinctly personal decision. It is less obviously influenced by conventional professional training, although the decision is likely to be expressed in such a way that its expected consequences conform to the norms and tenets of social behaviour. The immediate decision appears to be a function of the interaction of the individual's personality and life style as they impinge on the current social situation—whether in a professional or private context.

Decision-making and decision theory

It is important to distinguish between observable decision-making behaviour and decision theory (sometimes called decision-making) encountered in some psychology courses. Decision theory is an attempt to describe in an orderly way those variables that influence choice. The variables fall into two major groups: first, subjective utility, which is a description of the interweaving of the rewards and payoffs associated with the various alternative choices, and second, the subjective evaluation of the probabilities of occurrence of the consequences associated with each of the choices. Since decision theory attempts to describe how decisions should be made (an inheritance from its roots in mathematics and economics), and since the associated experiments usually involve only two-alternative choices (often concerned with money or a rather artificial game), few of the findings have relevance for the complexities of teachers' work in classrooms.

Shepard (1964) notes that man's perceptual analysis of sensory input is a demonstration of his remarkable ability to integrate the responses of a vast number of receptors. The rules on which this integration is based appear to be both complex and non-linear. He continues by dramatically exposing the contrast between 'the effortless speed and surety of most perceptual decisions and the painful hesitation and doubt characteristic of "higher level" decisions'. Miller (1956) has collected a variety of results to demonstrate the existence of a channel capacity for the higher processes (for example, memory and discrimination). Evidence from a number of sources (Adams and Fagot, 1959; Hoffman, 1960) indicates that man is able to combine a small number of attributes according to simple linear or additive rules. However, non-linear rules or complex interactions among variables seem to evince marked conceptual difficulty. As well as in the fields of learning and memory, the difficulty posed by interactions among attributes is seen when subjects are asked to rate objects or other people on each of several specified dimensions. Osgood, Suci and Tannenbaum (1957) showed that subjects tended to collapse multi-dimensional attributes into a single 'good' versus 'bad' dimension, with a consequent loss of detailed information concerning the pattern of attributes unique to any one subject. Yntema and Torgerson (1961) suggest that a decision based on the utility or worth of an alternative is arrived at by the separate consideration of the values attached to the various attributes of the alternative. In their model the overall value of the alternative is represented as a monotonic function of the separate attribute. Shepard (1964) prefers an amendment to the model in which the desirability of the attribute and not the attribute itself contributes monotonically to the total work.

Having contrasted the difference between perceptual and non-perceptual decision-making, and having sketched the wealth of evidence indicating man's inability to process data based on interrelated variables (the work of Aitchison is particularly germane, see Taylor *et al.*, 1971), the complexity of an investigation of the process preceding the arrival at a decision is revealed.

As Wilson and Alexis (1962) point out, decisions shape as well as mirror the environment. They reject the 'closed' decision model for being too rational, restricting alternative outcomes and minimising the weight given to the environment of the decision-maker when arriving at a decision. In contrast, the 'open' decision model with which we shall be concerned in examining classroom decisions accents the individual's ability to control his behaviour. It is assumed that most human behaviour is learned and is therefore the outcome of conscious and unconscious selective processes at all perceptual levels. Such a model necessarily reflects the limitations of human cognition as well as the complexity of the individual's total environment. Particularly for reflective decisions (open model), criteria of satisfaction (which can be defined in terms of one's aims or goals) replace the optimisation criteria of solutions obtained within the closed system. The open model can be extended to emphasise cognitive processes in decision-making; for instance, by postulating a hierarchical system of decisions, the model incorporates adaptive behaviour. Each successive decision is an attempt to improve the outcome in the light of new information resulting from the weighting of selected consequences of the preceding decisions.

Definitions

It is central to this paper to characterise what is meant by a 'teaching decision' for a teacher in the school setting. While the distinction between 'immediate' and 'reflective' decisions mentioned earlier can be thought of in terms of the time lapse between perception by the teacher or an observer of a decision situation and an action in response to that perceived situation, we need some exploration of the total class of human decisions.

The diverse literature on decision-making curiously circumvents any definition of a decision even though decisions are widely recognised as being an important characteristic of human activity. Dictionary definitions (i) to (iv) previously given are somewhat circular in their attempts to clarify a decision, whereas (v) and (vi) introduce the concept of choice. More practically, a decision may be defined by describing how to recognise that a decision is taking or has taken place, or by defining the situations in which decisions are likely to occur. Such a basis is unlikely to give rise to a dictionary definition; rather, it will stipulate several propositions, each of which must be satisfied for the term 'decision' to be used in the context of teaching.

Limitations of defining a decision in terms of choice and choice points

Implicit in the concept of decision is that of choice. However, choice implies a conscious awareness within the individual of available alternatives, which in turn implies an ability to discriminate among them. Decisions may be made without a conscious awareness or weighing of options, even, for example, for such overt acts as writing on the blackboard. Since decisions are not always consciously monitored, a definition of decision-making which encompasses the notion of choice is both inappropriate and unnecessarily limiting. Similarly, a definition which involves the notion of a choice point as the instant of choice is unhelpful. For instance such a definition might be:

If at least two individuals respond differently to the same environmental stimuli then the stimuli have given rise to a choice point at which a decision may have occurred. A decision is the manifestation of choice at or following a choice point.

However, choice is a function of the individual's conscious state at the time of his choice (including that part of his history that is able to be recalled or which is recognised as pertaining to the situation). Differences in the conscious states of two individuals may be manifest as different responses to the same environmental stimuli without either individual's having a choice of response. Hence, observation of such a situation would erroneously suggest the occurrence of a behavioural choice point.

Further, an individual must have recognised the existence of two or more alternative responses in order that a choice may be made. Yet all behavioural acts may be said to follow from choice points since the alternative of not making the act is always available. For example, the individual may be precluded from considering the alternative as a result of institutional prescriptions. (An act is defined as a voluntary movement—that is, under voluntary control; hence reflexes, bodily movements compelled by force and those occurring during sleep or in a state of diminished consciousness are not included.) A third objection to a definition of a decision being based on a concept of a choice point is that the choice point does not necessarily identify the decision point. A decision point is either coincident with or subsequent to a choice point. Yet it is the decision point that is to be identified.

Decisions and behavioural acts

Decisions are observable in so far as they give rise to observable behaviour. And therein lies a problem. It is the change in the ongoing behaviour that indicates the translation of a decision into an act. Yet a decision may be made to continue an on-going stream of behaviour in the light of available alternatives, or to postpone the implementation of the decision as a behavioural change for a period of time. For instance, an individual may decide to ignore stimuli impinging upon him from the environment, resulting in no change in his observable behaviour; another person in a comparable situation may fail to perceive the stimuli. If, in the former case, the person's on-going stream of behaviour is uninterrupted then the observation of behaviour will not reveal the existence of the decision. Thus it is necessary to supplement the recording of behavioural acts with other observations in order to be aware of these no-change or 'null' decisions. The supplementary observations must also attempt to distinguish between null decisions and the failure to perceive stimuli both between and within individual decision-makers.

Intention and decision

Hirst (1971) defined teaching in terms of the intention of the teacher (to bring about pupil learning) and Whitfield (1975) suggested that decisions are the bridge between intention and action. Despite their logical consistency, such descriptions remain unhelpful for empirical work. Such models not only require the identification and verification of intentions, they incorporate further semantic problems. For instance, it can be misleading to say that a given act is intentional. If in the course of teaching there are necessary consequences to an act originating in the teacher, then the act is intentional only with regard to those consequences that are foreseen as being highly probable. (The foresight of the certainty of a consequence of an act is not always equivalent to intention because of the reasonable possibility that a person intent on something might be bluffing.) The consequence need not be the end itself, but an intermediate stage in the satisfaction of another desire. Further, a particular physical act (pressing on the accelerator pedal whilst driving a car) may be *both* intentional (to increase the speed of the vehicle) and unintentional (colliding with a pedestrian) according to the *result* that is under consideration.

The foregoing avoids the consideration of motives as being either conscious or unconscious by defining intentional acts in terms of consequences. Any qualification of decisions by way of intention restricts consideration yet again to conscious decisions and the methodology for mapping these to introspective techniques. Further, if a result is *not* brought about by conscious intention, then it is concealed from awareness and is therefore regarded as involuntary; hence it is not an act (as defined) and so cannot be said to be intentional. Thus, the addition of an intentional component not only fails to clarify the definition of a decision but also limits the scope of any categorical system.

The word 'motive' is no more helpful, for motive can be defined as the intention with which the intentional act is done. Also, it is important to differentiate between intention and desire in so far as there are passive desires such as contentment which would not be classed as intentions. Intention is the desire that prevails and issues in action. Not all the desires of the teacher within any one lesson are manifest as acts during that lesson.

The strategy of the proposed definition of a teaching decision

It is desirable that a definition should enable the concept it describes to be more easily recognisable. Further, in both the physical and social sciences, the most usable and useful concepts are those which prescribe their own testing operations, give criteria for their application and suggest means for their measurement. We require a definition which is logically consistent, empirically testable and empirically quantifiable.

In order to achieve these requirements, a general definition of a decision is given. This is followed by a definition of teaching which, in turn, gives rise to a definition of a teacher. Thus, a teaching decision is defined by marrying the three components.

A 'decision' has been made by an individual whenever he himself or one or more observers acknowledges the availability of at least one alternative behaviour to the one observed at a given instant of time. The realisation of the existence of an available alternative need not have taken place by the time the behaviour is observed for either the individual or the observer(s). If the observed behaviour consists entirely of spoken words, then a different phrasing or a repetition of those words does not constitute an alternative response. However, a subsequent rephrasing of words uttered previously may indicate a subsequent decision. It is a necessary condition that the decision involves, or has involved in the individual's previous history, the higher cognitive processes. Learned reflexes and behavioural acts selected without conscious awareness at the instant of response constitute decisions provided that conscious processing of alternative responses can be said to have taken place at some time in the past history of the individual.

'Teaching' may be defined operationally as follows: An individual is teaching whenever, whether solicited or not, he undertakes to explain, show or state by way of instruction relationships inherent in or between one or more symbols to at least one other person. (A symbol is a stimulus representing and standing as a substitute for something else, by possession of analogous qualities or by association or other relationship including convention.)

If, *in addition*,

(i)   the individual is allowed or required to *control* the method and content of the instruction (subject to accepted social constraints, whether implicit or explicit) for a particular subject or group of subjects, *and* if this control is acknowledged by those to whom any instruction is addressed, *and/or*

(ii) the individual is permitted to *modify*, change or otherwise control the behaviour, individually and collectively, of those volunteering or assigned to him for instruction, *and/or*

(iii) the individual is allowed or required to *evaluate* verbal and physical behaviour of those persons assigned to him, against some value system accepted by him or imposed upon him by external agencies at the time of the evaluation,

then the individual is defined to be a 'teacher'.

It is seen, then, that teaching, as defined, occurs in a social context and involves the interaction of two or more persons. Each individual generates stimuli which, together with those arising from the surrounding environment, impinge on the other(s). Inherent in the definition of a teaching decision is the perception of at least one of these stimuli by participants and/or by observers.

A 'teaching decision' is thus 'a decision made during the execution of the professional responsibilities of the teacher', as outlined. This definition is somewhat similar to that proposed by Dunkin (1976), who defined teaching behaviour as 'acts performed towards another or others in contexts where the expectation is that the latter will learn as a result.' As he has pointed out, the definition does not require that the performer of the acts be formally designated as a teacher or that the acts have behind them a direct intention to promote learning. Indeed, it is not necessary that learning, whether the desired learning or not, result from the teaching behaviour. Thus, this definition also avoids making inferences about teacher intent.

To summarise, our model of a teaching decision thus far has four stages within the defined role of the teacher:

(i) environmental stimuli (observable)

(ii) perception of the stimuli by the individual, setting up a response need

(iii) the filtering and interpretation of the stimuli, giving rise to a decision to act or not to act

(iv) behaviour, if the decision was one to act

Further, teaching decisions are seen to be those occurring within one or more of the three areas of *control, modification* and *evaluation* defined to be the professional responsibilities of the teacher.

Because we are focusing on teachers' decision-making behaviour, it is not necessary at this stage to consider any aspect of the learning taking place in the classroom. Indeed, learning becomes relevant to teacher decision-making only when the *quality* of the decisions is under examination. Such evaluative work is seen as logically subsequent to an investigation of the properties and antecedents of teaching decisions.

Classes of teaching decisions

A classification of teaching decisions is necessary in order to describe, analyse and interpret teaching behaviour. In the introduction we named the poles of a first dichotomy in such a classification as 'immediate' and 'reflective'. A category consisting of 'null' decisions has also been shown to be appropriate, and this gives rise to a second dichotomy dependent upon whether the decision manifests itself as an act or not; the poles of this dichotomy we term 'action' or 'no action' (null). The discussion of teacher intention gave rise to a third dichotomy involving the awareness or lack of awareness of the whole or part of the decision process by the teacher.

Trial analysis of videorecordings of secondary school lessons have revealed the need for a fourth dichotomy. Consider a decision by the teacher to summarise verbal information by means of a written list on the blackboard. (This might be an out-of-lesson reflective decision or a within-lesson immediate or on-the-spot decision.) Having decided to form such a list, each addition to it is interpreted not as a separate decision but rather as continuing steps in the execution of the original decision to form the list. However, the teacher's decisions to accept or reject material suggested by the pupils for inclusion in the list are separate teaching decisions (probably immediate). The continued addition to the list over time is an example of a 'composite' decision, which is to be contrasted with a 'simple' decision in which there is no repetitive element or temporal extension.

To summarise, therefore, the basic distinction is the one drawn between immediate and reflective decisions. The primary concern of our initial researches has been with the immediate decisions—that is, with those *decisions which occur in response to observable environmental stimuli and which are perceived by the teacher as requiring an immediate response.* It is the pupils' interactive behaviours, giving rise to environmental stimuli within the classroom, that are the determinants of the teacher decision-making process in which our research interest lies. Immediate decisions may be consciously monitored or there may be no conscious awareness of the process by the teacher; they may give rise to an observable act by the teacher or they may be no-change decisions, where there is no observable interruption in the ongoing stream of observable teacher behaviour. Also, immediate decisions may be of the 'composite' kind outlined above.

This summary serves to distinguish the subset of immediate decisions from the set of teaching decisions. Figure 2.1 illustrates the relationship among ten subsets of decisions formed by the four dichotomies described in the summary above. Our empirical research has to date concentrated on the striped areas in Figure 2.1 whilst noting the relative frequency of the observed reflective decisions. The dichotomies

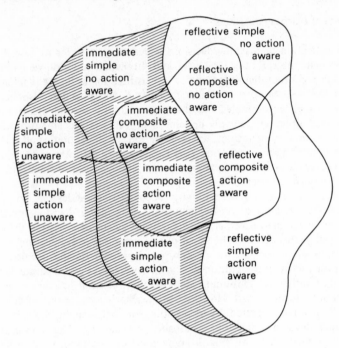

Figure 2.1 A map of some categories of classroom teaching decisions

shown in the figure are: immediate/reflective, aware/unaware (of the decision process), action/no action by the teacher (no-change 'null' decision) and simple/composite (the decision gives rise to one or more similar actions, separated in time).

In addition to this classification, the *content* of the decision itself gives rise to another classification system, as follows:

(i) immediate decisions associated with the subject matter; the lesson content;

(ii) immediate decisions associated with apparatus and other aids; appropriateness of illustrations; timing of introduction;

(iii) immediate decisions associated with pupils' behaviour;

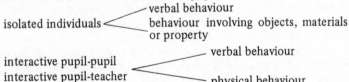

isolated individuals < verbal behaviour / behaviour involving objects, materials or property

interactive pupil-pupil / verbal behaviour
interactive pupil-teacher \ physical behaviour

(iv) immediate decisions by the teacher associated with the amendment of the teacher's behaviour.

Classification of classroom stimuli which are precursors of the relevant teaching decisions

It has been emphasised that the immediate decision is consequent upon observable environmental stimuli (or a single stimulus); thus, *the stimuli serve as a means for indicating the imminence of the decision point*. Since decisions as defined are contingent upon stimuli, it becomes necessary to specify those sub-groups of stimuli which trained observers are to monitor from among the multifarious array of stimuli which any lesson presents. These sub-groups then become part of the observer test criteria which are subsequently described. We therefore stipulate the following subsets of stimuli of interest:

A *Pupil centred stimuli*

These comprise any perceived auditory, visual or tactile stimulus emanating from the pupil and regarded by the observer as containing a component of *either* attention-seeking *or* communication, or both, however conventionally or unconventionally manifest. Such stimuli may be directed towards the teacher or towards another pupil. Specific categories are:

A1 cues suggesting pupil *understanding* or cognitive grasp

A2 cues suggesting pupil *misunderstanding* or cognitive confusion

A3 pupil behaviour indicative of specific *co-operation* with teacher's wishes

A4 *disruptive* pupil behaviour, including cues suggesting boredom

A5 *other* pupil-based stimuli suggesting attention-seeking and/or communication

(Note A1/A2 and A3/A4 are, respectively, components of two bipolar constructs; categories here may be subsequently collapsed if desired.)

B *Distractor stimuli* (not directly pupil caused)

These include any visual or auditory stimulus which emanates from *either* within the classroom (internal distractor) *or* outside the classroom (external distractor) and which is perceived by the observer as distinct from the ongoing level of background stimulation. Distractor stimuli within the classroom may accompany those in class A or they might be quite distinct from that class.

C *Materials-based stimuli*

These consist of any visual, auditory or tactile stimulus associated with inanimate material within the classroom and perceived by the observer as being under the teacher's direct control. Of prime concern in this class are stimuli associated with classroom materials, visual aids and apparatus.

The categories of stimuli and associated teaching decisions are recorded during videotape analyses of lessons using Lesson Immediate Decision Observation Matrix (LIDOM) forms A and B shown in Figure 2.2.

LIDOM Form A
Record each stimulus (as defined) with a tick; more than one tick can be placed in a box.

Time (minute of lesson) Stimuli classes	1	2 -------------------- 39, 40
A. Pupil centred		
A1 Understanding		
A2 Misunderstanding		
A3 Co-operation		
A4 Disruption		
A5 Other attention/ communication		
B. Distractors (internal/external)		
C. Materials-based		

LIDOM Form B
Record each decision (as defined) with a tick; more than one tick can be placed in a box.

Time (minute of lesson) Decision types	1	2 -------------------- 39, 40	
All			
No change			
Composite			
Possibly reflective			
Decision with unseen stimuli			
Heart rate maxima (subsequent analysis of chart record)			

Figure 2.2 Lesson Immediate Decision Observation Matrix (LIDOM) forms A and B

A summary of the postulated stages in teacher decision-making

The sequence, within the individual, immediately before and after a teaching decision is now listed:

(a) observable classroom stimuli which may or may not be perceived by the teacher; by implication, such stimuli are perceived by the observer (e.g. pupil's hand raised whilst group work is in progress)

(b) assuming recognition of the stimulus by the teacher, a conscious or unconscious response on the part of the teacher (if conscious, it may take the form, for example, of an implicit or explicit threat to the teacher's self-perceived status, role or integrity)

(c) the filtering and interpretation of the stimulus by the teacher leading to a decision which may or may not result in an act

(d) observable discontinuity in the behaviour of the teacher if the decision results in an act (e.g. teacher visits the pupil and group to which his attention was called in (a)).

This sequence is applicable to both immediate and reflective decisions. In the latter case, the time scale of the sequence (a) to (d) is much longer. In the case of a learned (or 'conditioned') response by the teacher to a particular incident or situation, section (c) is by-passed. Indeed, in the case of immediate decisions, there may be no conscious awareness of this part of the decision process.

The LIDOM observation schedules and their associated instructions allow for the recording of observable classroom stimuli independently of the perception of the stimuli by the teacher. Hence, the total number of incidents ignored or not perceived by the teacher may be recorded.

Figure 2.3 shows the temporal sequence of teacher decision-making

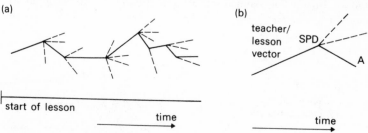

Figure 2.3 A representation of the sequence of teaching decisions during a lesson and of events at a decision point

during a lesson. The nodes represent decision points (D); the dotted lines indicate alternative teacher options perceived by either the observer or the teacher (or both) which were not chosen at the time. Thus the continuous line represents the teacher-lesson vector. On either side of the nodes are, respectively, perception (P) of a decision situation provoked by a stimulus (S) and any action (A) resulting from a choice, so that the temporal sequence for each decision is S, P, D, A. (Null decisions cannot of course be indicated by a node in this diagram.)

Design and methodology

Our work concentrates on the categorisation and quantification of the immediate decisions made by teachers in the course of their normal classroom teaching. The realisation that a decision could give rise to no observable change in behaviour on the part of the teacher raises the problem as to how such a null decision might be monitored. Indeed, it is important to distinguish between the teacher who makes a null decision and one who fails to perceive the classroom event that would be likely to give rise to a null decision had the perception occurred.

In the absence of observable teacher behaviour, one way to monitor null decisions would be to request and direct introspection whilst the teacher is viewing his or her video-recorded lesson. Such a technique might be expected to isolate some if not most of these decisions. Further thought about the nature of classroom interaction between the pupils and the teacher indicated that many kinds of classroom incident may be interpreted by the teacher as a challenge to one or more facets of his value system. Indeed, some incidents may appear to the teacher to challenge the authority vested in him or to conflict with his perceived role. Thus, the idea arose that one might expect to find a variation in teacher stress throughout a lesson consequent upon the decisions associated with the classroom incidents which occurred during the lesson. Figure 2.4 summarises the pupil/teacher relationship in this context.

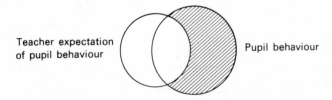

Figure 2.4 Diagram showing the interrelation between teacher and pupil classroom behaviour. Teacher stress is related to the shaded area, which represents the pupil behaviour not consistent with teacher wishes and expectations

The value of a measure of teacher stress lies in its potential as a more objective technique of identifying null decisions. If a sufficiently sensitive measure of stress could be found, and given that it could be validated against other decision categories, then it would be reasonable to suppose that a comparison between a record of teacher stress and a videotape of a lesson given by the teacher would reveal decision points where there was no observable change in teacher behaviour.

Obvious physiological correlates of stress are increased heart rate and decreased skin resistance. Preliminary work, the availability and reliability of compact, unobtrusive and lightweight apparatus, the relatively long latency of changes in skin conductance and the variation in conductance with the temperature of the immediate environment pointed towards the use of heart rate as the more reliable correlate of teacher stress.

Apart from the reliability of verbal responses when collecting data by way of introspection, there are other problems associated with self-analysis of videorecords. Individuals respond somewhat differently to seeing themselves in particular roles. Indeed, Linard (1973) has shown that some teachers become anxious, others aggressive. Thus, to ask teachers to introspect whilst watching a playback of a recent lesson is likely to lead to greater unreliability of data so collected, without first acclimatising the teacher to the process. Hence, a structured interview with the teacher was preferred to a wholly introspective technique, with the interview taking place as soon as practicable after the recorded lesson but without any viewing of the lesson by the teacher.

To summarise, the data to be collected from each participating teacher consisted of videotaped recordings of particular lessons, heart rate records for the same lessons whenever possible and the teacher's responses to the interview questions. After the collection of data had begun, it became possible to investigate teacher stress in a small number of teachers using sound recordings copied directly from the lesson videotapes. The Dektor Psychological Stress Evaluator displays inaudible frequency modulations of the human voice. Components of these patterns are said to be related to the psychological stress in the speaker at the moment of the utterance. A fuller discussion is given by Smith (1975). Each teacher was given a written undertaking that the videotapes would be treated as confidential material and used for no purpose other than that directly related to our investigation.

The teachers

A design based on the comparison between a group of inexperienced teachers and a group of experienced teachers has two distinct advantages. First, a university department of education usually contains a group of

23

trainee teachers soon to become probationer teachers. Second, if there are differences between the two groups of teachers then, subject to other controls, such differences may be related to the experience variable; on the other hand, if no differences are revealed between the two groups, then the groups may be coalesced in order to produce a larger sample of teachers. It was thought practicable to have twenty teachers in each group. Because the investigation was fundamentally concerned with pupil/teacher interaction, it seemed necessary to use a matched group design where the personality and attitude variables were controlled between the two groups.

A number of instruments for measuring personality variables were considered. From these, two appeared to have greater reliability and validity than the rest: Cattell's 16PF (Cattell, 1957) and the EPI (Eysenck, 1969). Statistical tests based on data collected from some 466 students in both a college and a department of education suggested that the EPI had the greater construct validity.

Similarly, two attitude questionnaires were subjected to analysis. They were Opinions about Education (Oliver and Butcher, 1968) and the Minnesota Teacher Attitude Inventory (Cook, Leeds and Callis, 1951). Again, the MTAI was preferred by virtue of preliminary statistical tests based on the teacher trainee responses.

Whilst the statistical analysis was taking place, the heads of some sixteen Cambridgeshire local authority secondary schools were contacted in order to explain the nature of the investigation and to request permission to approach the school staff for experienced teacher volunteers. By means of several visits to the schools of cooperative heads a pool of some 65 experienced teachers (35 male, 30 female) was accumulated. All the volunteer teachers completed the EPI and MTAI questionnaires and were informed that, with a probability of roughly one third, they might be asked to take a further part in the investigation—and that this part would involve the videotaping of actual lessons. Each teacher was told that there would be an opportunity to withdraw at that stage if it was so desired. By this time, a new intake of postgraduate certificate students had become established in the Cambridge Department and 132 of them completed the same two questionnaires at a group session.

Matching the two groups of teachers

In order to pair the inexperienced and experienced teachers, a computer program was written which calculated the generalised distance between each experienced teacher and all inexperienced teachers on the basis of their personality and attitude scores. Although it is known that attitude scores may change over time and with training (see Herbert and Turnbull,

1963), the assumption was made that a teacher's score relative to his group mean score would not change significantly with time and training. Further, the generalised distance measure is able to take account of the intercorrelations, however small, among the four component scores of the EPI and the MTAI. The computer program ended with an ordered listing of the ten inexperienced teachers who were the smallest distances away from each experienced teacher. The only constraint imposed on the matching procedure as outlined was that each matched pair of teachers should be of the same sex. By this procedure twenty experienced teachers were chosen as the smallest distance away from an inexperienced teacher on personality scores and on attitude towards pupils, thus producing forty participants.

Videotaping procedure

It seemed preferable to allow the probationer (inexperienced) teachers to settle into their first teaching post (which could, of course, be anywhere in the country) before requesting them to videotape any of their lessons. Consequently, most of the videotaping took place in their third and fourth terms of full-time teaching. In this context, an experienced teacher was defined as one who had had at least five years continuous full time teaching experience; in practice, most had much more than this minimum level.

Preliminary videotaping trials took place with local experienced teachers who were known to have no closely matched inexperienced teachers. This gave an opportunity to optimise the positioning of the equipment in various shapes of classroom and to overcome a variety of technical problems. Figure 2.5 shows the chosen layout for each classroom. The stationary video camera, on a monopod about seven feet high and with a wide angle lens, is placed in one corner (depending

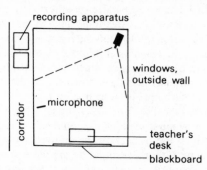

Figure 2.5 Plan showing the typical arrangement of apparatus for classroom videorecording

25

upon the prevailing light) at the back of the room, with the microphone towards the front. The recording equipment and the operator are outside the room, usually in a corridor. With a minor rearrangement of desks or tables (where possible), the camera's field of view encompasses up to thirty pupils.

Whereas an early prediction had been made about the inhibiting effect of the video camera on the teacher, the preliminary work, augmented by conversations with teachers who took part, indicated that pupils were inhibited in terms of the confidence with which they made verbal contributions to the lesson. This effect on pupils was still reported by some teachers on the sixth videotaping session with the same pupils. The teachers were reluctant to admit any effect upon themselves on any occasion.

The main data collection

Originally it had been planned to videorecord each participating teacher and class six times in an attempt to control for the effects of the presence of the camera and microphone in the classroom. For practical reasons (time and amount of travelling) and primarily because some slight pupil inhibition was reported by some teachers on the sixth occasion, it was decided to undertake only four recording sessions with each class.

On the first two occasions the equipment was set up in the classroom but no actual data collection took place—although some test recordings were made, the tapes being subsequently re-used. The teachers assumed that both occasions were normal videorecording sessions. On the third and fourth occasions full recording took place, and one of these two recorded lessons was randomly selected as the data for that teacher. Such a double-blind technique was used to prevent the possibility of cues being given inadvertently to the teacher or the pupils, or both. Because it was important to interview the teacher as soon as possible after the lesson which became that teacher's data, requests were made to teachers to choose classes which they taught twice on the same day, or classes which were separated by no more than half a day if on successive days. Further constraints imposed were that the pupils should be in the fourth form (age 14–15) and that the lessons should not take the form of practical work sessions—that is, there should be an amount of teacher-pupil interaction reflecting whatever style of teaching the teacher saw as appropriate to that part of the syllabus. It was constantly emphasised before the first of the four visits that no different quantity or quality of lesson preparation was required and that no evaluation of any lesson was intended at any stage of investigation.

Lessons given by thirty-eight teachers (19 experienced, 19 inexperienced) have been videorecorded and follow-up interviews have been conducted. For various technical reasons just under half of these lessons have full heart rate data corresponding to the lesson; this is sufficient for the required comparison. In order to check on the general reliability of the EPI and MTAI questionnaries, each teacher who had participated in the videorecording completed the questionnaires for a second time as did a random sample of teachers who were not sufficiently well matched to take further part in the investigation. The test-retest reliabilities were 0.87 and 0.83, respectively.

Data analysis

The major part of the analysis centres on the videotapes. It has been mentioned earlier that observation matrices (LIDOM (A) and LIDOM (B)) were prepared on which to categorise the stimulus that gives rise to a teaching decision and the decision itself.

Following the definitions given previously, a set of rules by which an observer on replaying the videotape may identify an immediate decision made by a teacher can be given:

1 Is the person teaching?
2 Is the person a teacher?
3 Do you, the observer, perceive an environmental stimulus (or stimuli), as defined, emanating from some part of the classroom environment external to the teacher?
4 Does the teacher act in such a way that you consider the act to be in response to the environmental stimulus perceived by you?

A yes response by the observer to each of the four questions is a necessary and sufficient condition for a positive identification of an immediate teaching decision.

It was felt that provision should be made for the observer to record a teaching decision (as perceived by the observer) where no prior stimulus was actually perceived, although its prior existence was assumed. Such a category allows for the fallibility of the observer and, particularly in the case of direct observation of a lesson, takes into account the variation in the level of observer attention over time. Items in this category could be followed up via teacher introspection and could give valuable information associated with the categorisation of the stimuli that give rise to teaching decisions. Similarly, using the categories shown in Figure 2.1, the teaching decisions themselves were classified. Superimposed on that classification is a second one dependent upon whether the content of the decision is associated with class management, lesson content or the wider classroom environment, such as materials, apparatus, aids or interruptions other than by pupils within the classroom. In addition, the videotape records allow the measurement of the latency between the classroom stimulus and the onset of the act consequent upon the teaching decision. More general measures of interaction are also available, such as the proportion of time the teacher is teaching (as defined). All such classifications and measurements permit a comparison to be made between the two groups of inexperienced and experienced teachers.

Once the teaching decisions have been pinpointed on the videotape, the significant fluctuations in the heart rate record may be compared in terms of their probability of occurrence within a very small time interval of the observed decision point. In this way it seemed feasible to use heart rate monitoring as a means of isolating the 'key' teaching decisions in a lesson in addition to indicating some null decisions. Comparisons between the stress shown by the heart rate record and that from the voice analysis were thought to be especially relevant for those decisions which were categorised by the content of what the teacher was saying at the time. Other information is available from the teachers via the three major sections of the interview: first, lesson aims, intentions and preparation; second, teacher decision-making and third, teacher stress.

Perhaps the most concise way to indicate the scope of the analysis of the data collected is to list under five headings some of the main *hypotheses* which are currently being investigated.

(a) *Observer consistency and reliability*

Are different observers able to identify teaching decisions consistently and reliably? Are teachers able to identify their own teaching decisions reliably and consistently? Is there agreement in the identification of a teaching decision between the teacher and other observers?

(b) *Comparisons between experienced and inexperienced teachers*

Are there differences in the numbers of immediate or reflective decisions per lesson (or other time unit) between the two groups of teachers? Are there differences in the proportions of decisions allocated to the different decision categories between the two groups? Are there differences in the proportions of stimuli allocated to each category for the two groups? How does the latency of the decision change with experience?

(c) *Classroom stress levels*

Are there observable peaks in the teacher's heart rate during the lesson and are these attributable to stimuli associated with teaching? Is the overall level of heart rate during a lesson different when the records of matched pairs of experienced and probationer teachers are compared? Does the presence of a video camera and microphone affect the teacher's mean heart rate? Is there a difference in the teacher's mean heart rate in the classroom compared to his mean heart rate in school or outside school altogether? Does the increase in heart rate correspond with the occurrence of a teaching decision? Is it possible to identify the 'no-change' decision? Is the speed of an immediate decision related to the level of arousal and personality of the teacher in the situation?

(d) *Effects of attitude and personality*

Are the numbers of expressed available options associated with a teaching decision, the frequency of occurrence of different kinds of classroom stimuli and levels of classroom arousal, related to personality, experience, attitude (to education), age, sex, length of training?

(e) *Classification of teaching decisions*

Can immediate decisions be distinguished from reflective decisions and, if so, is the primary option of a reflective decision the one chosen in a comparable immediate decision situation by the same teacher? Are the relative frequencies of kinds of teaching decision related to the age of the class, its composition by sex, the subject being taught, sex of the teacher, the time of day, etc.? Do teachers classify their own teaching decisions? If so, why? What categories and criteria do they use? Is the classification idiosyncratic? If they do not classify, can they reliably use an imposed classification? With what frequency are immediate decisions transformed into reflective decisions? What are the personal correlates of these frequencies? Are there any differences in the frequencies of immediate and reflective decisions related to one or more personality variables and the teacher's attitude to education? Are the respective frequencies of any categorisation of teacher decisions related to the personality or attitude or experience of the teacher (or their interaction)? Can composite teaching decisions be distinguished from other decision-making behaviour? To what extent is the teacher aware or unaware of the decision process? What proportion of the teacher's decisions are classified as 'no-change' decisions?

Results

Analysis of the data is still continuing, but some answers to the questions posed above are given in the following summary.

A small proportion of teaching decisions occur which have no observable classroom stimuli associated with them (the null decisions). Such decisions are identified by changes in the teacher's behaviour (often changes in verbal content), most commonly with a change in the flow or continuity of the lesson. These tend to occur more frequently in the case of experienced teachers.

By defining reflective decisions to be those which have a longer latency than immediate decisions, the two categories can be easily distinguished. The latency of the decision following an observable classroom stimulus is shorter for inexperienced than for experienced teachers. This more rapid reaction may reflect the greater insecurity of probationer teachers at the start of their careers. The proportion of immediate to reflective decisions is also greater for the inexperienced teachers, and experienced teachers far more frequently convert potential immediate decisions into reflective ones. This may be possible because they have fewer problems of class management (see below). Composite decisions occur more frequently, too, for experienced teachers, probably reflecting their greater ability to plan, structure and summarise the lesson content.

Differences between the teacher groups in the overall categorisation of the stimuli giving rise to teaching decisions are also evident. Although the proportions are in the same relative order (classroom management, lesson content and environmental stimuli), a higher proportion of stimuli is associated with classroom management problems in the case of the inexperienced teacher, whilst environmental problems (especially associated with materials and aids) show a slightly higher proportion for experienced teachers. The class management difficulties of the probationer might have been predicted (particularly by those involved in teacher training), whilst additional awareness and use of materials are likely to be a function of the amount of teaching experience.

The heart rate data suggest that certain classes of stimuli (giving rise to a teaching decision) can be monitored in this way. For both groups of teachers class management problems, pupil challenges to teacher accuracy and classroom interruptions (particularly by an adult) result in a detectable increase in teacher heart rate. The teacher's arrival in the classroom can be seen on the heart rate trace in some cases, by comparison with the same individual's previous heart rate level. Inexperienced teachers tend to have a slightly higher heart rate in the classroom than do experienced teachers, a finding which is in line with studies of lorry drivers and airline pilots.

The analysis of the teacher's voice trace suggests that most commands given by the teacher (whether experienced or not) produce an increase in teacher stress, irrespective of the forcefulness of the command. Many requests, some of which may sound particularly gentle, can be identified as easily as the more loudly expressed directions. Occasionally, an ungrammatical sentence spoken by the teacher can show up in the voice trace as stressful to the teacher, possibly at the instant of teacher realisation.

The proportion of time spent teaching the whole class is slightly higher for the experienced teacher. It is likely that there are subject differences here, though an analysis among subjects is outside the scope of this study. However, in the interviews the experienced teachers generally reported spending more time on lesson preparation than did the inexperienced teachers; perhaps the two findings should be considered together, for the one could have a bearing on the other. Similarly, the experienced teachers more often reported being aware of their aims and intentions during the lesson; if true, then one would predict a difference in the categorisation of teaching decisions between the two groups of teachers. For instance, the interaction between the aims of the teacher (if only as perceived by the pupils) and the pupils' classroom behaviour is such as to be likely to reduce the frequency of class-management problems, especially where the teacher's aims are clearly understood.

None of the teachers who took part in this study was aware that their classroom decision-making behaviour was under investigation. When the notion of teaching decisions was introduced in the structured interview, all teachers readily agreed that teaching consisted of decision-making processes. In response to a particular question, the categorisation of teaching decisions which the teachers suggested was almost identical to that devised in the study itself. The three areas were clearly separate in the minds of the teachers taking part. By contrast, no experienced teacher reported classroom teaching as being a stressful situation, although the heart rate records indicate otherwise. The most commonly reported source of stress was concerned with role conflict resulting from demands made by others in the school hierarchy as well as from duties and expectations not directly associated with classroom teaching itself.

Although teachers said in the interview that they were aware of the decision-making process whilst teaching, it seems unlikely that this is true for the immediate decisions. Indeed, the variety of options used in comparable classroom situations by the inexperienced teachers precludes their rational consideration of choice without a necessary reflection time which would be identifiable on the video tapes. This suggests that teaching experience is synonymous, in this context, with the learning of what works best for that person in the classroom; the mechanism may well be by way of the behaviouristic model.

It has not proved possible to discover whether the presence of the video camera and microphone affected the teacher. Self-reports suggest that the teacher quickly adapted to the presence of the instruments to the extent that they were unaware of their presence in the classroom. In contrast, the teachers commented that the pupils took longer to adjust and were subdued in the early (trial) recording sessions. The investigation of comparisons between trained observers and teachers in identifying and classifying teaching decisions from a small sub-sample of the videotapes has not yet been completed; nor has work on the interrelation of teacher decision-making and teacher personality, attitude, sex, age and length of training.

Clearly, the work outlined here is merely a beginning and further developments suggest themselves. The two classroom observation schedules (concerned with lesson stimuli and teaching decisions) need further refinement as do techniques for measuring teacher stress in natural classroom settings (see Kyriacou and Sutcliffe, 1977, 1978; Roy and Whitfield, work in progress). The interaction of pre-lesson and within-lesson decisions could in itself be the subject of several studies. Indeed, the model of teaching which we have developed is extremely suggestive, and we now briefly lay out some of its potential implications.

Potential extensions and applications

Our interest in teacher decision-making arose initially from a desire to improve teacher training programmes. Improving a teacher training programme is synonymous with improving the professional effectiveness of the entrant to teaching. Unfortunately, there are few, if any, agreed criteria of professional effectiveness in teaching, and half a century of research on teacher effectiveness and evaluative issues in teaching has produced little to guide the teacher trainer anxious to devise training curricula on a more rational basis. It seems that the training community remains at a stage in which there is a loose professional identification of 'the experienced master teacher' whom the student is to emulate, and the range of both general and subject-specific teaching skills (such as questioning, reinforcement, blackboard writing, demonstrating, lesson preparation) which the student should acquire. Training courses with a bias to each of these views have been aptly described (Stones and Morris, 1972) as (i) modelling master teachers and (ii) mastering teaching models. In the UK at the present time it may be said that approach (i) to the development of professional skills is now being increasingly supplemented by approach (ii), arising from analyses of teaching and their implementation in, for example, microteaching. However, the extensive utilisation of concepts and methods inherent in American performance (or competency) based teacher education with its roots exclusively in behaviouristic psychology seems, perhaps fortunately, remote.

Perhaps all too slowly teacher trainers have realised the limited value of attention to the charismatic master teacher (however important he obviously is in his particular context) on the one hand, and to lists of ideal skill-based upon particular and often ill-identified teaching styles and methods on the other. We believe that viable research on teaching effectiveness (which necessarily involves valuative statements) is contingent upon, and must therefore await, improvements in:

(a) the *description* of teacher behaviour
(b) the *analysis* of classroom interaction and
(c) the short and long term *assessment* of crucial pupil and teacher behaviours

In short, we need to be able to describe the actual teaching/learning encounter with more sophistication and precision *before* we can make evaluative judgments about teaching in terms of its effects upon pupil behaviour (e.g. Rosenshine, 1971). Diagnosis must precede curative treatments through training. Moreover, the descriptions we seek must be of representative samples of teachers teaching representative samples of pupils in representative natural rather than contrived environments.

Despite this plea for adequate description before evaluation, in the practical world of teacher education, programmes and certification are on-going and evaluative judgments are continually being made, albeit in the absence of much illuminative research. It would be concealing to pretend that our focus on describing teaching in terms of different kinds of decision-making did not originate from notions of effective and desirable teacher behaviour which can now be more explicitly declared, even though they are not a part of our present research.

Implicitly, we have rejected as inadequate or incomplete existing models of teaching. Nuthall and Snook's (1973) three basic models of teaching ('behaviour control', 'discovery–learning' and 'rational'), whatever their merits, are not general enough for a description of a wide range of teaching acts, so that their application in both research and training is restricted. Nevertheless, the desire for an appropriate and general model remains, and our decision-making model is, we believe, more comprehensive and embracing than any of the ,other alternatives; so far only Shavelson (1973, 1976) at Los Angeles has indicated a similar conceptual framework in his writings, though the unpublished work of Heilen in Bjerstedt's group at Malmo is also relevant. Preece (1977) has speculated about the application of catas-trophe theory to problems of classroom discipline and his paper is also compatible with the model presented here.

In terms of the decision-making model of teaching, *the effective teacher in our society* is possibly one who possesses the following interacting qualities:

1 A stable value system, promoting consistent rather than erratic behaviour in very similar situations.
2 Cognitive flexibility, and thus able to generate a variety of options in decision-provoking situations possessing surface similarity but having significant differences.
3 Warmth and empathy (affiliation) in relation to other persons.
4 Sensitivity in use of pupils' ideas.
5 The ability and sufficient motivation to create a variety of class-room materials and activities.

6 A manner which is demanding of pupils in terms of their attention and resource for learning.

In summary, the effective teacher is stable yet flexible, warm and sensitive, creative and demanding. It is of interest that factors 2 to 5 seem to reach significance in a number of process/product studies reviewed by Rosenshine (1971) and are related to Ryans's (1960) scales. Within these qualities there are elements of rationality, child-centredness and control which are, individually, more central elements in other models of teaching.

A desirable early application of the basic studies of interactive teacher decision-making must therefore be in the field of professional *teacher training,* both initial and in-service. The Science Teacher Education Project (1974) made some use of the interactive decision-making concept in the context of limited descriptions of school situations. The DES sponsored Teacher Education Project (see Kerry, 1977) is also making use of such descriptions to develop class control skills in trainee teachers. *Simulation* through case studies, card descriptions, role play and critical incidents is likely to be an important tool and contrasts with the teach/reteach process of micro-teaching. (Micro-teaching seeks to simplify units of teaching so that component teacher skills may be separated and individually improved through early feedback and repetition. While the value of this is not denied, the reteach element is contrived rather than natural. The concept of 'practising pedagogical decision-making' is not primarily intended to rehearse specific actions for future teaching situations, but to promote sensitivity, awareness and flexibility towards the unpredictable encounters and challenges within teaching.)

Training in interactive and immediate decision-making (both inside and outside the classroom) necessarily aspires to improve the quality of teaching. Hence the training application cannot be divorced from aspects of the *evaluation of teacher effectiveness.* Concurrent study of the evaluation of teachers in the classroom along dimensions such as those already referred to is thus inevitable, and this should have implications for teacher selection and professional certification. Relation of such evaluations of teachers to specific pupil cognitive gains would be an important separate study.

Aspects of *pupil behaviour* in which there is a natural concomitant interest are their perceptions of teachers' decision-making. We believe that it is of fundamental interest to explore the relationships between patterns of teacher decision-making, pupils' perceptions of these, and their attitudes to the subjects being taught. Necessary also is exploration of relationships between pupils' attitudes towards both specific subjects and school in general and the imposed school rule systems which are part of the whole school and teacher decision network. Such considerations indicate that teachers, even in their own classrooms, are not totally free agents; the constraints upon their decisions and/or the supports provided by the social context norms and/or explicit institutional rules undoubtedly affect the classroom stimuli which a teacher encounters and the decisions which the teacher makes in response. Research-based statements about these undoubtedly complex interactions would assist our understanding of the whole process of schooling and teaching and would enable institutional rule systems to be devised in ways which might reduce pupil alienation and disruption in classes in ordinary schools. The extent to which teachers' decision-making patterns are related to important individual or group *pupil input variables* such as age, sex, IQ, perceived ability, personality and socio-economic background is also of interest, and would seem to present few fundamental problems of data collection.

Another related series of applications of the decision-making concept is concerned with particular *pedagogical issues.* The concepts of a teaching *method* or a teaching style have been particularly difficult to define empirically with reliability (e.g. Bennett, 1976; Eggleston, Galton and Jones, 1976); nevertheless, educators still find the terms useful for descriptive purposes. Teaching 'method' and 'style' are multi-variate concepts, and it is possible that more adequate empirical specifications of these could be obtained from patterns of teachers' decisions; cluster analysis of interactive decision sequences would seem to be the most appropriate tool for this sphere. A dichotomy between 'demanding' and 'easy' methods may be worth exploring—the former being conceptualised by the need for a number of different skills and consequent increased stress levels; demanding methods may be too stressful for those teachers unsure of their requisite skills and will in these cases produce avoidance behaviour.

A vital pedagogic consideration in many subjects is the extent and nature of practical work, in particular that performed by pupils—for example, in the workshop, laboratory or gymnasium. Knowledge of the effects of practical work variables upon teachers' decisions and the interactive behaviour which practical and/or demonstration work produces is vital to an understanding of teaching in these contexts. As yet we know little of the detailed character of the additional demands which such parameters place upon teachers, and it is certainly clear that when a teacher decides to use apparatus (or audio-visual aids, etc.) the demands of the situation take on new dimensions. A further pedagogical application is in the field of teacher decisions and strategies which are prompted by the perception of a pupil error or conceptual misunderstanding in specific subject areas such as mathematics, science, geography and art; here interest would be focused more towards the remedial teacher strategies rather than the 'external' objective assessment of pupils' cognitive abilities.

Finally, studies are suggested which explore the relationships between

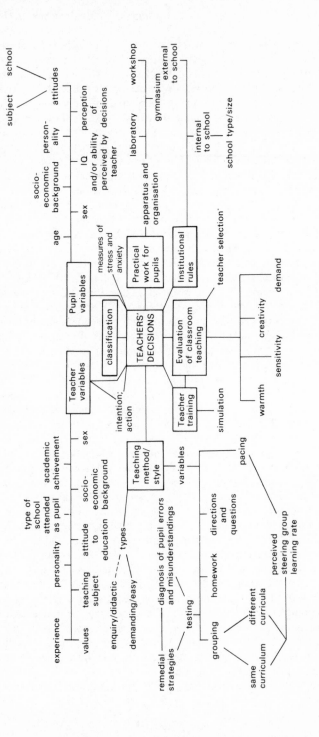

Figure 2.6 A map of relevant concepts and experimental variables for research into teachers' decision-making within the classroom

teachers' *values,* their *intentions* when faced with critical incidents, and their actual classroom *actions.* Why teachers do what they do and the degree of rationality in their decision-making are issues of continuing interest, but ones for which reliable empirical criteria will be difficult to obtain.

The foregoing areas of interest and application are summarised in Figure 2.6, a map of concepts and experimental variables. The extent and complexity of this map should ensure that interested researchers are kept busy in the field for many years to come. It is at least possible to speculate that decision-making within the classroom is more complex than that at other points of the educational system where records are frequently required to be kept within group management processes and where the actors have both less professional privacy on the one hand and more peer protection on the other.

Acknowledgment

We wish to thank the British Petroleum Company Limited for their kind support of much of the work described in this paper over the period 1972-6; in particular, Mr J. Ball (Manager, BP Educational Liaison) has, we believe, been farsighted in suggesting that resources be allocated to this important area, which is of relevance not only to school classrooms but also to many other interactive situations in which teaching is involved.

Chapter 3

Teachers' implicit personality systems:
an exploratory study

Mervyn Taylor

One of the most important elements of decision-making in any social situation is the categories which individuals create in order to understand the behaviour of other people, for these represent base-line data on which inferences are made and decisions and actions taken. These derived inference networks or expectancies are necessary for the prediction of the behaviours of other people so that their surprise value is minimised; for the teacher, in his task of controlling pupils' cognitive and social behaviour, these networks may be especially important. So although it is not necessary to go as far as William James in conceptualising teaching as an act of warfare, nevertheless, like the general, the teacher must be one jump ahead in anticipating the likely consequences of interactions among pupils, between them and him, and between pupils and the learning material in the classroom.

Although there have been a relatively large number of investigations into the way we perceive other people, most person perception research has been concerned with indirect perceptions in which the stimulus person is fictitious or absent, so that only a conception, as opposed to a perception, of him is actually made. Inherent in this approach is the utilisation of cues which have been so simplified that conclusions based on this kind of evidence must be applied with great caution to interactive and more natural situations (e.g. Argyle and McHenry, 1971); even where research procedures have involved social interaction prior to the subjects making perceptual judgments, the situations so devised have frequently been somewhat forced and artificial (e.g. Bronfenbrenner *et al.*, 1958). Particularly important in the context of person perception research is the distinction made by Ryle (1949) between episodic and dispositional judgments which, when combined with Brunswick's (1956) distinction between overt and covert judgments, produces a useful framework with which to classify perceptual information (see Figure 3.1).

	Episodic	Dispositional
Overt	He is doing his maths exercises.	He always does his maths exercises without talking to his neighbour.
Covert	He is finding his maths exercises difficult.	He is not very good at maths but is always hard-working.

Figure 3.1 Classification of perceptual judgments (after Warr and Knapper, 1968, p.9)

In an interactive situation episodic judgments feature more prominently than in one involving indirect perception, since the participants need to monitor each other's moment by moment behaviour in order to mesh the interaction. The relationship between episodic and dispositional judgments is an intimate and interactive one, partly because it is from episodic judgments that dispositional qualities are inferred but also because the dispositional qualities provide a contextual framework for the interpretation of on-going episodic behaviour. It is this latter feature of the perceptual process which has been the focus of much of the classroom research into labelling and self-fulfilling prophecies, and a rather deterministic standpoint has been adopted by many researchers, who claim that teachers' dispositional judgments of their pupils influence the pupils' episodic behaviours to such an extent that these are modified to conform to the dispositional labels given to them. It is only recently that the other side of the equation has attracted research attention, notably from D.H. Hargreaves (1976) in the context of classroom deviancy. When asked to conceptualise their pupils, primary school teachers do so in terms of covert dispositional judgments (Nash, 1973; Thompson, 1975), though a few overt attributes are often used to distinguish coloured children, for example, or pupils who are handicapped in one way or another. An interesting question in the context of the decisions made by teachers concerning their pupils involves the kind of relationship networks which exist among the teacher's various covert dispositional categories, since location of the pupil in any one category has implications for his location in other categories used by the teacher, and it would seem a useful task to chart the probability texture of the teacher's internal cognitive model used to explain and predict the pupils' behaviour in class.

The degree of relationship between the contents or attributes of perception may be just as important in influencing classroom action as the nature of those attributes alone, for individuals may show substantial differences between what they say and what they do; thus, although many attributes may be employed by a teacher to describe his pupils, giving the impression that an articulated or finely discriminating network is being used, in operational terms, when the different labels are actually applied, there may be very little difference between them and hence the judgmental framework may be collapsed into one or two evaluative dimensions. Bieri *et al.* (1966) and Adams Weber (1969) have suggested that the degree of articulation of the conceptual system will influence the social interactive skills of the individual, though clearly, the relationship between perception and action is complex and cannot be explained in terms of a simple deterministic model. For example, a teacher who possesses a cognitively complex framework for judging his pupils may not have other personal qualities which will enable him to maximise that information; on the other hand, it is difficult to envisage individuals with a monolithic, or undifferentiated system maximising the individual potential of their pupils.

It will be discerned that we are involved with what have been termed the implicit or lay theories of personality which teachers have of their pupils, and the emphasis of these approaches contrasts sharply with that of many personality theorists who, in devising their instrumentation, have deliberately sought to create relationships between dispositional dimensions which are orthogonal, or independent of each other (Eysenck, 1964; Cattell, 1967). The two main approaches to the understanding of lay theories are typified, first, by Asch (1946), Bruner *et al.* (1958) and Wishner (1960), who ask individuals to predict the degree of relationship between one trait, for example, intelligence, and a number of other traits, such as awkward, aggressive, considerate etc.; the advantage of this approach is that the direction of inference can be ascertained, though naturalness is sacrificed to experimental methodology. However, the second approach, involving correlational techniques, is able to utilise more representative contexts, though there is the attendant loss of being able to specify the direction of the trait relationships. Todd and Rappoport (1964) do report a high correlation between the two approaches, though factor analysis reveals quite different structural relationships in the two approaches, which may serve to illustrate that well-known fact that the very act of making conscious a judgment changes the nature of that judgment. The great advantage of the correlational technique is that it allows one to investigate the implicative networks of people in an oblique way, and so facilitates the production of a more realistic sample of inferential judgments.

Both the inferential and correlational approaches to the understanding of individuals' implicit personality systems imply a statistical, linear or additive, as opposed to a clinical, interpretive or intuitive model of explanation, and the particular stance adopted here is similar to that of Sarbin, Taft and Bailey (1960), who propose a probability model with the syllogistic inference providing the basic linkage between the postulate or construct system based on previous experience and the event of instantiation.

The study

The empirical investigation consisted of an examination of the structural relationships between teachers' attributes used to describe their pupils, and was undertaken on an opportunity sample of 24 men and 24 women teachers distributed among 18 different primary schools in the English Midlands. The children, whose average age was 9 years 8 months, numbered 1,491 (765 boys and 726 girls) and were in classes of mean size 31.79.

The individual teachers' perceptions of their pupils were obtained using the full context form of the repertory grid, which differs from the minimum context form in that instead of sorting triads of pupils, all the pupils' name cards are spread before the teacher, who is then asked to group together all those pupils who are alike in some way, yet different from the remainder; when a clear indication of the construct label has been elicited from the teacher, the cards are mixed again and arranged according to some other criterion, and this process continues until the teacher's repertoire of constructs has been exhausted. A full description of the process is given in Kelly (1955, p.224). The repertory grid technique is not without its problems and Kelly's assumption that it samples a person's natural everyday thinking processes seems problematical since so many individuals find it an extremely difficult and taxing procedure; also, the status and nature of personal constructs obtained by the different elicitation procedures, and their relationship to the traditional of the category, are not at all clear (Taylor, 1976b). The big advantage of the repertory grid, however, is that it does allow one to make systematic comparisons of individuals' operational definitions of other persons. To this end, therefore, after the personal constructs had been elicited from the teacher, all the children in the class were rated on the teacher's constructs after they had been transformed into seven-point scales, which were then aligned according to the pole at which the teacher preferred the pupils to be located. All of the teachers' constructs were subject to content analysis and grouped into seven superordinate categories as shown in Table 3.1. Full details and descriptions of the categories, together with a consideration of the effects of sex and degree of formality of the teacher on the nature and number of constructs elicited, can be found in Taylor (1976a). What of the structures, as opposed to the contents, of the teachers' perceptions of their pupils? There have been many different indices used to give a quantitative measure of the overall complexity of grid structures, often termed cognitive complexity (see Bonarius, 1965), though the term 'structural complexity' will be used here to distinguish it from complexity of grid contents, here called 'construct complexity'. Structural complexity is here defined in terms of the amount of variance accounted for by the first factor extracted from the subject's repertory grid. This measure was originally developed by Kelly and has been used by Jaspars (1964), Campbell (1960) and Flynn (1959); a similar measure has been used by Bieri *et al.* (1966), who consider this index superior to that using the number of factors extracted from a grid because there may be too few factors to give a reliable measure. Essentially, this structural complexity index of a grid shows to what extent an individual is using a high or low probability inference system in processing social information. To obtain this data for the sample of teachers, all the grids were subject to principal component analysis (Slater, 1965), and the percentage variance explained by the first factor was taken as the measure of structural complexity— the lowest variance being the most complex, indicating a low probability system. The range of percentage variances obtained was very large, with the most complex score being 29.93 and the least complex 89.56, showing that the degree of structural complexity varied enormously within the sample. A correlation coefficient was calculated to ascertain the degree of relationship between structural and construct complexity data and a Spearman rank coefficient of $r = +0.26$ ($t = 1.88$; n.s.) was obtained, which was taken to indicate that the relationship between structural and construct complexity was so small that the two could be regarded as virtually independent. This would support Seaman and Koenig's (1974) view that although a person might use a large number of constructs to evaluate another person, he may be using them all so similarly in practice that they could be regarded as mere words rather than as meaningful concepts.

TABLE 3.1 Frequency and percentage of constructs employed in each category by 48 primary school teachers

	Construct category	N	%
1	Academic achievement	195	43.72
2	Personality characteristics	88	19.73
3	Behaviour and relationship with teacher	69	15.47
4	Home background	38	8.52
5	Interests and hobbies	30	6.73
6	Physical	15	3.36
7	Miscellaneous	11	2.47
	Total	446	100.00

Ingleby and Cooper (1974), employing a research design which involved supplying six constructs to 13 teachers on which they rated a sample of 156 children in infant schools, found that in their principal component analysis the first factor accounted for an average of 66 per cent of the total variance. They claimed on this evidence that little additional advantage would be gained by giving teachers more dimensions on which to judge their pupils, the implication being that teachers have relatively high probability systems on which decisions about pupils are based. It is suggested here, however, that such a high percentage variance may be the result of using supplied as opposed to elicited constructs, which would have the effect of simplifying the teacher's degree of structural complexity. In the present investigation using elicited constructs, the cumulative proportion of total variance on the first factor was 57.79 per cent, thus indicating a more complex pattern than that obtained by Ingleby and Cooper (*ibid.*).

More important, perhaps, than attempting to establish an absolute level of structural complexity is ascertaining whether or not, and to what extent, complexity varies systematically between different people and different situations, and therefore it was decided to make a comparison between different groups of teachers. The measures for structural complexity were ranked for all teachers combined and then a comparison was made of the separate rank totals for the men and women using the Mann–Whitney U test. A U of 255 (p. < 0.33) was obtained, which showed that, unlike construct complexity (Taylor, 1976a), there was no significant relationship between the sex of teacher and structural complexity.

A second area for comparison was that between high and low dogmatic teachers, since previous research (Steiner, 1954; Steiner and Johnson, 1963; Foulkes and Foulkes, 1965; Warr and Simms, 1965) had indicated a relationship between the degree of dogmatism and the organisation of implicit personality systems in ways which minimised inconsistencies in the evaluative judgments made of other people; hence, it was hypothesised that high dogmatic teachers would show significantly less structural complexity than low dogmatic teachers.

Results from the Rokeach Dogmatism Scale (Rokeach, 1960) previously administered to the sample of teachers provided the basis for the comparison. The mean scores, given in Table 3.2, show a relatively low level of dogmatism for the group as a whole; mean scores for male and female teachers were similar.

TABLE 3.2 Means and standard deviations of male and female teachers' scores on the dogmatism scale

	Mean	SD
Male (24)	140.17	19.49
Female (24)	142.21	28.82
All teachers	141.19	25.17

A Spearman Rank correlation of −0.08 was obtained between dogmatism and structural complexity, thus giving no support to the hypothesis that high dogmatic teachers have high probability inference systems.

This lack of relationship between the two dimensions was surprising but may be accounted for by several different explanations. The first would be that structural complexity is relatively independent of many of the more conventional personality and attitudinal measures and thus represents a way of information processing which justifies its categorisation as a distinct cognitive style. Second, the lack of relationship might be due to the relatively low dogmatism scores of the teachers, who would not exemplify, to a sufficiently noticeable extent, the cognitive characteristics of the highly dogmatic individual. A third explanation might be that in the classroom situation, where the teacher knows the children well, judgments are less stereotyped, and thus the influence of dogmatism on social perception may be reduced.

Although a measure of grid differentiation like that of structural complexity used here represents the overall relationships between the traits used by individuals to judge others, it only loosely approximates to the phenomenon of co-judgment, described by Warr and Knapper (1968) as occurring when the possession of a desirable attribute is assumed to imply the possession of other desirable attributes, and when the possession of an undesirable attribute is assumed to imply the possession of other undesirable attributes, since co-judgment is meaningful only where traits are semantically different and, of course, this may not be the case in a grid with elicited constructs. Also, a disadvantage with a global measure like structural complexity is that it treats all constructs within a grid as functionally equivalent, whereas in practice not all constructs will carry the same weight or be of equal importance in the individual's conceptualisation of the social world. Hence, teachers would be much more likely to regard the dimension of 'hard-working—lazy' as more important than whether or not a pupil participated in out of school activities. In the structural complexity index such qualitative distinctions are ignored. For this reason, another exploratory analysis was carried out, this time on the strength of relationships which existed among the three major dimensions which had emerged from the content analysis of the teachers' constructs— that is, the academic, behavioural and personality characteristics of the pupils which accounted for 79 per cent of all constructs used.

To ascertain the correlation among these three areas of the teachers' grids, the constructs were grouped in each individual's grid according to the taxonomy given in Table 3.1. The element (pupil) totals for each group of constructs was obtained and this was divided by the number of constructs to give an average evaluative score for each pupil on behaviour, personality and academic characteristics; then within each grid correlations were calculated among the three dimensions. The requirement for this analysis was not an overall correlation across the teachers and elements grouped together but, rather, an average correlation of each teacher's individual grid correlations. This was achieved by transforming all individual correlations to Fisher's Z coefficients, obtaining their arithmetic mean, and then transforming this figure back to correlation coefficients (Guilford, 1956).

TABLE 3.3   Average correlations between teachers' academic, behavioural and personality perceptions of their pupils

	Academic	Behaviour
Academic		
Behaviour	0.68	
Personality	0.57	0.53

Table 3.3 shows the average correlations between these groups of constructs used by teachers to describe the academic, personality and behavioural attributes of their pupils. The highest correlation obtained was +0.68 between academic and behavioural characteristics, indicating a very high degree of co-judgment; even the relationship between academic and personality traits was higher than that between behaviour and personality characteristics, and if this is representative of most teachers in primary schools, then it would lend some support to the view that the pupils' academic characteristics influence, to an unsupportable degree, the way in which teachers see their pupils as persons.[1]

TABLE 3.4   Average correlations for male and female teachers' perceptions of their pupils (male teachers top right; female teachers bottom left)

	Academic	Behaviour	Personality
Academic	—	0.72	0.58
Behaviour	0.63	—	0.58
Personality	0.56	0.48	—

TABLE 3.5   Average correlations for high and low dogmatic teachers' perceptions of their pupils (high dogmatism top right; low dogmatism bottom left)

	Academic	Behaviour	Personality
Academic	—	0.64	0.59
Behaviour	0.71	—	0.49
Personality	0.55	0.57	—

Sex of teacher and its relationship to correlations within grids

The method of obtaining average correlation coefficients was identical to that already described above, and the teachers were divided into male and female groups. The results are given in Table 3.4 and show modest differences between the sexes in the pattern of correlations. Although no significant differences between male and female teachers had emerged on the structural complexity dimension, the correlation between academic and behavioural perceptions which male and female teachers had of their pupils did show some variation. Men teachers perceived a closer relationship than did women teachers between a pupil's academic characteristics and his behaviour in class. This finding is consistent with previous results indicating greater female sensitivity to teacher-pupil relationships and male teachers' greater concern with the academic characteristics of their pupils.

Dogmatism of teacher and its relationship to correlations within grids

In this case the teachers were dichotomised into the 24 most and 24 least dogmatic according to their score on the D Scale, and correlations were obtained from both groups. The results are shown in Table 3.5. A somewhat confused pattern is revealed with low, not high, dogmatic teachers showing a greater degree of association between the perception of academic and behavioural and of academic and personality characteristics; this is contrary to the relationship between perception and dogmatism previously reported in the literature (Warr and Simms, 1965; Steiner and Johnson, 1963). A further analysis was therefore undertaken and separate results were obtained for male and female teachers in each of the high and low dogmatic groups. These results, in Tables 3.6 and 3.7, show that the relationship between dogmatism and

TABLE 3.6 Average correlations for male and female high dogmatic teachers' perceptions of pupils (male teachers top right; female teachers bottom left)

	Academic	Behaviour	Personality
Academic	–	0.72	0.63
Behaviour	0.55	–	0.62
Personality	0.57	0.36	–

perception was different for male and female teachers. For male teachers dogmatism did not influence the already high correlations between academic and behavioural perceptions, though in the case of the other two correlations, between the perception of academic and personality and

TABLE 3.7 Average correlations for male and female low dogmatic teachers' perceptions of their pupils (male teachers top right; female teachers bottom left)

	Academic	Behaviour	Personality
Academic	—	0.71	0.55
Behaviour	0.73	—	0.55
Personality	0.55	0.59	—

of behaviour and personality characteristics, correlations did increase with higher dogmatism scores. However, with female teachers high dogmatism was generally associated with lower correlations and low dogmatism with higher ones. Thus, it would appear that the unexpected results obtained in Table 3.5 are largely due to the effect of women teachers. A possible explanation may lie in Yamamoto's paper (1969), which reported that high dogmatic teachers placed more emphasis on pupils' social traits such as courteousness, obedience and considerateness, while low dogmatic teachers gave priority to work orientated characteristics such as curiosity, memory and competitiveness. In the case of women teachers, therefore, who display lower co-judgment scores than men teachers between academic and other characteristics of their pupils, low dogmatism leads to greater attention to work orientated characteristics of their pupils and thus an increased co-judgment correlation.

Conclusion

This exploratory study has attempted to chart some common features of the implicit personality systems which primary school teachers have of their pupils, and to ascertain how personal characteristics of the teachers affect these systems as represented by repertory grids. The results show that, on average, teachers may have probability systems which are more articulated than previous research has indicated and that the complexity of these systems is independent of the complexity of the contents of repertory grids. The findings also indicate that the importance attached to academic perceptions of pupils appears to vary according to the sex of the teacher, with male teachers, more often than female teachers, appearing to overestimate the influence of academic success and failure in their views of children. Similarly for male teachers, the more authoritarian personality does show a tendency to minimise dissonance between the various traits they use to judge pupils. However, the relationship between dogmatism and perception was not a simple linear one, for in the case of female teachers, lower authoritarianism was associated with high probability systems—an unexpected finding, illustrating the interactive influences of the situation and the characteristics of the teacher.

The relatively high correlation between academic and personality attributes of pupils may be due to the teachers emphasising the ascription of personal, as opposed to situational, explanations of the pupils' actions. This may be a direct result of the relatively mono-chromatic nature of the school experience, which nearly always involves the carrying out of normative tasks; thus, the situation tends to be taken for granted—only a relatively few personality constructs are used to explain pupil behaviour, and those that are used seem to be closely tied to the situation. There seem to be many personality characteristics of pupils which are not rendered socially visible in the class-room environment. The tendency to overestimate the role of personal, and underestimate the role of situational, factors in the understanding of other people's behaviour is a universal feature of person perception, but it is in marked contrast to the way in which we attribute causality to our own actions, which are considered to be the responses to external events of some kind. Perceiving children in a greater variety of social situations might diminish this tendency to locate causes in pupils, though again this need not be the case. Hovey (1977), examining whether or not changes took place in teachers' perceptions of 7-year-old pupils after a visit to a week-end centre, found considerable differences in the teachers' willingness to modify their views of pupils after seeing them in a different environment. One pupil in particular, seen as a troublemaker in school, was admitted by all the teachers to be much better behaved and responsive on the school trip; on returning to the normal school situation, he was perceived much more favourably by one of the teachers while another saw no reason to change her perceptions of him, taking a 'too good to be true' attitude.

Implicit personality systems represent sets of decision rules by which information about one category of pupil behaviour implies, with varying degrees of probability, the location of pupils in other teacher categories—a feature of human information processing which was regarded by early research workers such as Thorndike (1920) and Ich-heiser (1949) as aberrative and which needed to be eliminated if judgments of other people were to have any validity. The view of the co-judgment phenomenon today is that it not only is an inevitable process but also greatly facilitates human interaction by reducing the amount of cognitive strain in processing social data while at the same time reducing the uncertainties of social interaction. A covert dispositional judgment, together with its attendant inferential network, can thus be seen as a very powerful and economical way of encoding a vast amount of information, encapsulating the past and predicting the future behaviours of any individual. The effects which these teacher categories have on the creation of new pupil behaviours is a vexed question, but it must be remembered that inferential networks are systems of probabilities, not certainties. Thus, there has to be maintained a balance between confirming and disconfirming feedback in the application of constructs to explain present and to predict future actions of others. Teachers vary, just like other people, in their need to extort validational data to support their judgments and maintain their cognitive systems. What does emerge from studies such as that reported here is that not only does differential access to information affect the perceptions, and therefore the decisions which teachers make concerning their pupils, but that also there is always differential utilisation of such information by the individual teacher himself.

Note

1 The direction of this relationship from academic to personality variables and not vice versa, as has been suggested by Finn (1972), was established by an analysis of variance procedure not described here.

Chapter 4

Ideology, reality assumptions and teachers' classroom decision-making

Douglas Finlayson and Sylvia Quirk

The relationship between ideological formulations and the decision-making of teachers in classrooms is not a problem which has received much attention in the educational literature. This paper seeks to demonstrate that it is a problem of considerable importance and one which merits examination.

The concept of ideology

The concept of ideology has been widely used in the literature of many disciplines. As a result it has been used in many different senses (Plamenatz, 1970). It is possible, however, to distinguish two main usages:
  (i) philosophical analyses of the concept which raise issues about the nature of truth, rationality and knowledge
  (ii) analyses in which the concept is part of a theoretical scheme for the investigation of complex phenomena
Unfortunately, these are often compounded in the literature. In this paper the treatment of the concept will be in terms of the latter usage.

A great many of the usages which employ ideology as part of a theoretical scheme treat it as a concept, as a phenomenon that is susceptible to definition. A fairly common definition is that it refers to sets of ideas which are intended to act as a guide to and justification of the actions of groups and individuals. Apter (1964), for example, says 'ideology helps to make more explicit the moral basis of action', while Bendix (1970) says, 'in an ideological context, ideas are linked to action'.

Writing specifically in the context of an organisation, Minar regards an ideology as 'a set of ideas that interprets an organisation to relevant audiences in the social world'. Krause (1969) develops the notion that ideological ideas are intended for audiences when he distinguishes the 'proponents' of an ideology, namely, those groups or individuals who create, develop and promulgate the material from the 'target' groups for which the ideology is intended. From the point of view of the pro- ponent group, the ideology or set of symbols is intended to persuade the target groups to accept either an action or a condition, to persuade them either to passivity or to activity. This persuasive function is re- garded by Minar (1961) as its most important function. 'Persuasion is the key. Thus, by definition, when "ideas are weapons", they consti- tute an ideology whatever their other characteristics.' While Krause suggests that communication and persuasion processes are aspects of ideology, the direction of that process is defined as one-way, from the proponent group to the target group.

Functional theories of ideology

At the societal level of analysis, two functional theories, the 'interest' and 'strain' theories, have been advanced about ideology (Geertz, 1964). In the first, symbolic expressions of ideas are examined in relation to the perpetual struggle for advantage and power which goes on in society. In the second, ideology is held to be a symptom of, and a remedy for, the chronic mal-integration of society and social groups. Incorporating 'interest' theory, strain theory gives a pervasive role to ideology in the correction or creation of socio-psychological tension. Ideological ideas are said either to deny (or minimise) conflict or to legitimise it.

At the individual level of analysis, ideology is also frequently assumed to play a positive functional role in relation to people working in organisations such as schools (Sharaf and Levinson, 1957). Following Minar, an ideology relating to a school can be regarded as a series of reality assumptions about that school. By associating these assumptions with the group concept of norms, Minar goes on to assert that these reality assumptions make the work of the school understandable and acceptable to the social audiences to which they are addressed, amongst whom will be the teaching members of staff. This function is one that is frequently claimed for ideologies.

Functional views of this nature have associated with them simplistic common-sense models of man (Coulson, 1972). The acceptance of a set of ideological ideas is dealt with using the rather vague and nebulous notion of socialisation. Individuals are said to internalise the norms, values and goals that correspond to social expectations. As a result of this process the individual members of an organisation are said to be motivated to conform to shared norms; they want to do what they are supposed to do. Hence, individual people are defined as socialised actors.

Conformity to norms is said to be the result of an individual's beliefs and motives: individuals are held to believe that conformity is good and nonconformity is bad.

The normative aspect of ideology at the level of the individual is often discussed in terms of 'commitment'. Minar (1961), for example, regards ideological beliefs as implying commitment for individuals and groups to a 'belief in' something with at least an ultimate even if unconscious normative element, and Bendix (1970) adds that 'commitment to action demands that we take a stand and make our own view of the world a matter of principle'. Eastman (1967) has suggested that ideological beliefs are held tenaciously, and he contrasts this with the way scientific theories are held, 'not tenaciously . . . but rather tentatively and provisionally'. When a theory is held with the assumption that 'all the evidence is in' (i.e. when there is no further need for evidential feedback), he suggests that it is in the process of becoming an ideology. The prescriptive element of ideologies, if regarded as guides to individuals as to how they ought to behave in face of a highly problematic social reality and without which they would not know how to act, is a prima facie reason for the tenacity with which they are held.

Some contributions from the psychological literature are consistent with this view of man as a socialised actor. According to these views, it is suggested that individuals, particularly when they have to come to terms with highly complex social phenomena, are dependent on relatively simple images of the world as the basis of prediction about appropriate social actions in those situations. Constituting a part of their belief and attitude systems, these images allow them to understand and structure their environment and give meaning to what would otherwise be an unorganised chaotic universe and to allow objects and situations to be evaluated according to whether they assist or hinder the achievement of desired goals or the avoidance of undesired events (Katz, 1960; Kelvin, 1969).

This conceptual treatment of ideology, the authors claim, should be regarded as 'the ideology of ideology'. It reduces phenomena which are essentially highly complex social and psychological processes to the status of a symbolic definition. By treating these processes in a definitional, as distinct from a dynamic way, their complexity is hidden, and the nature of social and individual experience is presented in terms of how it ought to be as defined, rather than how it is in reality. Nevertheless, the normative approach to ideology is the one which has the widest currency in education and which many proponent groups in education use to guide and justify their actions in relation to teachers.

In this paper, it is argued that the assumptions implicit in the definitional approach to ideology require to be recognised by members of both proponent and target groups. One of the most basic assumptions in the definitional approach is the notion that individuals can be regarded as 'socialised actors'. A number of areas of research can be used to throw serious doubt on the feasibility of such a notion. The first two involve the concepts of attitude and norm which are also basic planks in the definitional approach to ideology. The concept of attitude refers to an attribute of individuals whereas the concept of norm refers to an attribute of a group. The main conclusion to emerge from forty years of attitude research is that there is no consistent relationship between attitudes and behaviour (Wicker, 1969). Studies of what an individual says he does, likes to do, or should do show that these expressions of attitude are unrelated to what he actually does. A number of reviews of the field interpret the lack of relationship in different ways (Harding *et al.*, 1969; Ehrlich, 1969)—that transient situations are usually used in studies, not behaviour in long-lasting relationships, or that we know little about the relationship in that the contrary findings are explained by inadequate methods and poor conceptualisation.

One recent study of norms that cannot be dismissed on these last grounds is that of Cancian (1975), who points out that 'previous studies of norms or values of particular communities have not been based on a systematic description of the actors' normative beliefs, in large part because of the absence of methods to produce such a description'. Rejecting questionnaire, interview and observational methods of analysing norms because these are based on the investigator's assumptions and not on a careful description of the actors' beliefs, he used in his own work a method from ethnoscience to elicit and analyse normative statements from a community of Mayan Indians. No relationship was found between their statements of the community norms and their actual behaviour. Cancian puts forward the view that norms are not personal beliefs but perceptions of how to demonstrate to themselves and to others that they are a particular kind of person.

Argyris's work (1965) in organisations also shows that the link between norms and behaviour is not through the notion of commitment or belief. By means of interviews and participant observation in industrial firms he showed that individual members of these firms perceive clearly what the prevailing norms in these firms are. The majority of members' behaviour did, in fact, conform to the norm, but without either conviction or commitment. Thus the motivation for their conformity cannot be assumed.

According to Homans (1958) and other social exchange theorists, it is rewards which determine behaviour, be they material or in the form of social approval. Hence, perception of what the norms of significant groups are for teachers permit these norms to be interpreted as 'the rules of the game'. For this reason, when any major educational development is launched by government, local authorities or by some authority figure in the school some teachers may be motivated to act or conform on a behavioural level by the rewards associated with the development or by the wish to be seen by others as a certain kind of person. The career prospects of teachers represent an important example of the first motive; the wish to present a competent professional image to various audiences represents an example of the second.

While such considerations are highly relevant to the view of teachers as socialised actors, they fall short of any analysis which regards teachers as professional decision-makers. We view the concept of self as central to the process of decision-making. To take this view is to go beyond the social interactionist position which sees the self as a social by-product of interactive behaviour, an outcome of the process of socialisation, and to treat the growth and development of the self as a process in its own right. For this purpose, the distinction drawn by Horrocks and Jackson (1972) between role-playing and role-taking is a crucial one. In the former, a teacher would be behaving as he feels he is expected to behave, but the behaviour would not represent anything he believes himself to be. In the latter, his behaviour would be a manifestation and implementation of a hypothesised identity, representing an observable product of the self-process. The role a teacher takes, as distinct from one he plays, thus must bear a functional role to his needs, to the way in which he would wish to behave and to his system of values. Hence, comprehensive reorganisation would have been accepted by many teachers because of their belief that such an organisational strategy would contribute towards the creation of a less divisive society and provide greater equality of opportunity for the children in it[1] —beliefs which were part of their value system and their views about the kind of society which ought to exist. Equally, the Plowden ideology (Plowden Report, 1967) would be regarded by many teachers as a charter consistent with their concern to change the focus of educational endeavour away from the influence of selection and assessment procedures and to direct attention on the development of the children themselves. In so doing, the Plowden Report can be said to represent a symbolic infusion of warmth and humanity into the primary, infant and nursery schools. Because the comprehensive and Plowden ideologies provided identities which many teachers could readily accept, the development of their own selves could be manifested in their taking the roles provided by those ideologies.

Another major assumption of the definitional approach to ideology is that ideological formulations have positive functions. But while they may serve some positive functions, it may be, and indeed probably may be, that negative as well as positive outcomes may be associated with their use in education. In order that such an evaluation can be made, an empirical approach requires to be taken to the whole problem of ideology in education. The value of such an approach has already been demonstrated in a study of administrators done by Lunsford (1968), in which he relates the content of the ideology to the functions it is intended to serve in the organisational context of a university. He points out that in universities, as in the schools, where goals are broad and vague and the formal relationships somewhat ambiguous, officials have greater need of the 'normative power' of shared ideals and purposes than do the leaders of other organisations such as business firms or prisons. They have special needs for those 'socially integrating myths' that help to hold the loosely co-ordinated organisation together and give its members a sense of mission. By focusing attention on such unifying myths of common purpose, Lunsford maintains that the administrator is likely to help the university pursue goals more effectively and to build up his own authority as a leader. The task, however, is difficult because the administrator in a university, like most other executives, is in danger of being overwhelmed by a mass of detailed decision-making which reduces the effective time he can devote to analysing the complex problems of university structure and purpose. His increasing isolation from faculty and students further reduces his knowledge of the problems that concern his 'audience' or target groups who will read his message. Thus, the internal looseness and diversity of the large university, which make the job of the university ideologist so important, also make it more difficult.

Lunsford points out the negative consequences that are inseparable from the positive advantages of formulating organisational goals in ideological terms. Such formulations, designed to create a feeling of unity or purpose in an essentially diverse group of scholars, will tend to be of an abstract nature. Only abstract statements will reconcile the diversity of orientations among scientists and humanists, 'applied' and 'basic' researchers, teachers and researchers, to name only a few. Ennobling references to concepts such as 'a liberal education' and 'the search for truth' have as their great virtue their general acceptability to all sections of the university. Their abstractedness can be interpreted by different interest groups in whatever way they choose. At the same time, such abstractness necessarily detracts from their usefulness in determining institutional priorities which lie at the heart of many of the problems of decision-making in university, such as how limited resources are to be shared amongst various competing departmental demands.

To help resolve the conflicts which are associated with such decisions, Lunsford suggests that the tendency will be for another myth to be created, viz: that decision-making by administrators is essentially a rational process and not influenced by social pressures. Such a view is a distortion of the political nature of much of the decision-making in any organisation and, in the light of that experience, the myth that social pressures are relatively unimportant factors in determining how decisions are actually made will come to be seen as serving *only* to rationalise decisions made on other grounds or to express the narrow interest of the decision-making group. By propagating such myths the executive may well be describing his own genuine attempts to find an apolitical consensus and his hope of encouraging others in that direction. But he is doomed to failure in every case when the stakes are high and the consultation is less than 'free and open'. Should the administrator go on to believe his own myth of impartial rationality, and should that rationality be questioned and it be suggested that power relations and group pressures do influence decisions, his response may be one of indignation. In those circumstances some administrators might feel that the only course of action open to them would be to deny the conflict and to reaffirm their own good will and rationality. Lunsford concludes that such a declaration has inherent in it the seeds of further potential conflict which may terminate in the authority of the administrator himself, the very thing which it is designed to bolster, being called into question. Hence, the extent to which proponents of ideologies come themselves to believe that these formulations do reflect reality may well add to their socially derived difficulties at a time when the ideas are intended to be making a constructive contribution to handling their problems.

This point is generalised by Lunsford when he maintains that the way in which the content of administrators' ideology serves their function is by providing a set of verbal symbols which allow the proponent group to redefine the situation which they regard as one of conflict. They tend to structure the situation symbolically as they would like to see it rather than as it is. Lunsford carries his analysis far enough to examine possible consequences of this tendency.

In his paper, Lunsford restricted his analysis to the consequences which ideological usage might have for the proponents of an ideology. In this paper, we propose to adopt a similar approach to the use of ideology in education, but to focus on the problems which such usage raises for the target group of teachers as well as indicating some of the unintended outcomes which it creates for its proponents. In the course of the discussion, questions will be raised about the relationships between the reality assumptions that are offered to teachers by proponent groups, the social context within which these are offered, the complexity of the social environment with which they have to deal, and the reality assumptions that they themselves as individuals have and use to deal with that complexity. To raise issues of this nature is to accept Moscovici's (1972) view that 'systematic social psychology must be renewed and redeveloped so as to become a real science of those phenomena which are the basis of the functioning of a society and the essential processes operating in it. . . . The central and exclusive object of social psychology should be the study of all that pertains to ideology and to communication, from the point of view of their structure, their genesis and their function.'

Perhaps the greatest contribution that a systematic social psychological treatment of ideology in education could make, would be to examine some of the complexities of the social processes involving teachers and those groups and individuals who seek to influence and inform their decision-making in the classroom. By ignoring these complexities, the authors suggest that definitional approaches to ideology mask rather than illuminate some of the basic problems connected with educational change and development.

Ideology in education

Normative views of ideology, it is maintained in this paper, are of special import to education and specifically to teachers in schools and classrooms for a number of reasons:

The first is that they are most likely to refer to complex social phenomena, about which it is difficult, if not impossible, to obtain confirmatory empirical evidence and yet in relation to which action of some kind is required. Examples of such phenomena involve decisions about how to organise schools, about what teachers should aim to achieve, about how to train teachers, about how to teach children, about what to teach children.

In relation to all these issues the paucity of consistent empirical evidence is striking. One reason for this is the difficulty of carrying out empirical investigations whose designs and conceptualisation are sufficiently complex to match the complexity of the real-life social phenomena to which they are intended to relate. Gage (quoted in Biddle and Ellena, 1964), as long ago as the early 1960s, commented on the overwhelming quantity of research dealing with teacher competence yet was unable to draw any conclusions about what would constitute competence in teachers, while Passow (1966) has described the research literature dealing with ability grouping as a 'maze'. The number of variables that need to be considered, the difficulties posed by interaction effects, and the limitations of statistical generalisations in relation to the particular case are all intractable problems. These problems are identifiable within the statistical research tradition. The constraints of that very tradition, however, are questioned by those who regard it as inappropriate to the treatment of the dynamic phenomena of social interaction (Parlett and Hamilton, 1972).

Given the equivocal nature of much of the evidence, therefore, many educational issues require to be resolved by value judgment, as for example, if and to what degree a school should have mixed ability groupings. The recommendations about EPA schools contained in the Plowden Report (1967) is another example of such a decision. In spite of the empirical evidence, which claimed to demonstrate that schools had little or no influence on pupils' achievement, considerable resources were allocated to schools in educational priority areas in an attempt to improve the standards in them. The basis of that decision was again a value judgment, not a simple, rational application of empirical evidence. The late Anthony Crosland, then Secretary of State for Education, was quite explicit about this in connection with the reorganisation of secondary education along comprehensive lines when he said (Kogan, 1971), 'Our belief in comprehensive education was a product of fundamental value judgments about equity and social division. Research cannot tell you whether you should go comprehensive or not—that's a basic value judgment.' Bilski (1973), after studying the way in which both the main political parties approached the issue of secondary school organisation, concluded that 'the policies were influenced by the moral principles and the ways and means of achieving them advocated in the Labour and Conservative ideologies'.

Husen (1968), the Swedish researcher, commenting on his wide experience in connection with school reform in his country, says 'In retrospect I am fully aware of the weaknesses and failures in our attempts to bring research to bear on our school reforms'. One might even ask whether some of the major policies on school structure would have been much different had there been no research at all prior to the decision!

The second aspect of the normative notion of ideologies is that their content embodies a value judgment about what aspects of the situation, say a school or classroom, the groups creating and propagating the ideology consider to be important. If one looks at the ideas which are circulating in our society about schools and classrooms, many differences are observable. Definitions that have emanated from centrally located groups within the education system such as the DES and local authorities, for example, refer to organisational or structural considerations such as type of school, the structure of pupil groups within the school or class, organisation within the classroom, staff structure, timetable characteristics, existence and composition of committee structures. The Schools Council, on the other hand, regard schools and classrooms as places where curricular material is used. Other groups have picked other features of school experience for their attention. Within the classroom, behaviour patterns such as praise or modes of teaching considered to be appropriate to certain kinds of pupil learning may be the focus of concern.

At the same time as particular features of the school and classroom are selected for inclusion in the ideas defining schools and classrooms, certain outcomes are also selected. In relation to the comprehensive reorganisation plan, these were essentially social in nature. The expressed intention that Crosland and the Labour Party had in introducing the reorganisation was to reduce the inequalities and divisiveness in society.

Within the classroom, selected outcomes might refer to pupil behaviour and classroom discipline, as in the case of mixed ability grouping, or to pupil learning, as with discovery learning methods.

Third, in the formulation of the ideas about schools and classrooms, the features of the schools and classrooms which the creative and proponent groups have selected come to be associated in the definition with the outcomes that have also been selected. A systematic example of this kind of school definition is the report of an international conference (Yates, 1966) on grouping in schools. In that report, organisational and classroom characteristics are explicitly linked with specification of individual and social goals.

In symbolically linking organisational and behavioural strategies with specified outcomes the proponent groups are expressing their own normative belief that the implementation of the strategies ought to lead to the outcomes which are specified. Hence, when they seek to persuade others to their view, these outcomes are likely to be specified in advance of the implementation of the behavioural or organisational strategy as part of justifying their implementation. In that context, they will be presented as gains or outcomes to be anticipated if the behavioural or organisational strategies are implemented. If the ideas about comprehensive reorganisation are taken as an example, an empirical question of great complexity—What are the outcomes of organisational change for different schools, in different areas, and for various groups of teachers and children?—is symbolically presented as a claim that if you make all schools comprehensive, then a number of consequences will follow.

To link symbolically organisational or behavioural strategies with specified outcomes is to express a 'theory' about the relationship between the strategies and the outcomes. With regard to schools and classrooms, such symbolic linkages thus represent simplified views of these complex social environments—if x, then a, b or c. In this way, these symbolic formulations reduce the uncertainty and ambiguity of these environments: their formulations suggest appropriate actions to achieve the specified outcomes. Schools and classrooms in these symbolic formulations thus are defined as predictable environments. Such formulations, in which outcomes are anticipated, are in marked contrast to the widespread uncertainty about educational outcomes which one derives from considering the research literature in education. Yet, in ideological symbolic formulations, the probabilistic nature of these outcomes, and the qualifications which it is necessary to include in order to make them consistent with the complexity of the environments to which they refer, are seldom given emphasis.

The link between some desired outcome and the implementation of certain organisational or behavioural strategies thus can be regarded as the first major reality assumption that an ideology in education might make. This assumption, if accepted, symbolically cues a significant measure of goal displacement. The attention of educationists who accept the desirability of achieving the outcome is diverted away from the problem of what actually happens when any organisational or behavioural strategy is implemented to the problem of how the strategy is to be implemented.

The fourth normative aspect of ideology refers to its association with recognisable groups or organisations. These groups or organisations serve to provide social validation, as distinct from empirical validation, for the adoption or implementation of the behavioural and organisational strategies held to be linked to the outcomes which these groups value. The strategies, as distinct from the outcomes which they are intended to produce, thus come to be recognised as a legitimate basis of action·by the groups and organisations.

Dill (1964) has suggested that the power available to groups and organisations and the expectations of expertise associated with them would be likely to influence the attention directed towards them. On this basis one might anticipate that national and local government groups such as the DES and education officials, inspectors and advisers at national and local levels might be expected to provide social validations for the assumptions which teachers use as guides in their work. In addition, academic groups, college of education groups, research workers and curriculum developers might claim that their expertise could provide such validation, and head teachers or senior teachers might claim that their experience, position and expertise could serve to justify the strategies they advocate.

The social validation of organisational and behavioural strategies represents a second reality assumption about schools. These strategies then come to have the status of what schools and classrooms ought to be like.

A fifth consequence of the association of ideology with groups and organisations is that the resources, rewards and sanctions which these groups have available to them can be utilised to implement the behavioural and organisational strategies which they have socially legitimated. Within the education system, organisational strategies can most readily be implemented by national, local and school-based authority figures. Hence, secondary schools can be built and reorganised according to certain structural criteria which allow them to be designated as comprehensive, age-related criteria can be used to fill newly constructed or redesignated middle schools, and schools can be built according to building and architectural criteria which are described as open plan. Within schools, timetables and staff structures can be modified in a manner consistent with the organisation of systems of pastoral care, team teaching, integrated days and integrated studies, and pupil allocation to classes can be changed to create groups of mixed ability.

Such organisational or structural implementations are the physical con-comitants of the initial symbolic formulations which provided the ideological justification for them. Once in existence, however, these organisational structures become the school and classroom contexts within which many thousands of pupils and teachers are required to function.

Curricular and behavioural strategies are also promoted to a con-siderable extent in education. 'Nuffield Science' is a phrase that is synonymous with much curriculum development work designed to promote scientific thinking in pupils, while the Plowden Report, written for the pre-secondary stages of education, can be regarded as a vast mine of curricular and behavioural strategies said to contribute to the socially acceptable though dauntingly all-embracing 'development of the whole child'. When such strategies are regarded highly by national and local groups such as the DES, Schools Council and local authorities, schools and teachers who seek to implement them tend to be rewarded, either materially through the allocation of additional resources or pro-fessionally through promotion to posts of greater responsibility. Schools willing to try out Nuffield Science thus could be given financial assist-ance to purchase some of the equipment considered necessary and per-haps to improve the accommodation, while teachers who had intro-duced these strategies into their classrooms might find their promotion chances of becoming heads, heads of departments, or national or local advisers considerably improved. The expectations of their employing authorities presumably would be that, in their promoted roles, such teachers would continue to advocate the practice of such strategies either in schools when they might have authority over other teachers, at conferences organised to promote the strategies, or in the educational press. In this manner, the resources of the educational system can be brought to bear to promote strategies which have been accorded social legitimation by their association with valued outcomes.

The final consequence of the associations of ideologies with groups or organisations is that the phenomena of group dynamics and organi-sational maintenance can operate in relation to them. Once strategies which are socially legitimated achieve the status of norms these dy-namic phenomena act in both a supportive and a defensive way in the course of the day to day social interactions that take place within the schools. Amongst staff who subscribe to the assumptions, strong feelings of solidarity and identity can develop which are communicated to others who come into contact with them. Members of such staffs might also be described as disciples, and their schools as exemplars of a wider movement which is seeking to propagate the ideologies to which they individually subscribe, whether these are 'the open-plan school', 'the comprehensive school', 'mixed ability grouping' or 'pro-gressive methods' of teaching. Dynamic forces of this nature can provide useful support to individual teachers who may encounter difficulties in the course of implementing the strategy or strategies.

At the same time these group dynamic forces can also be brought to bear on individual teachers who do not accept the reality assumptions about schools which are symbolised in the ideology. Social pressure of this kind acts over and above any persuasive function which the content of the ideology itself may be said to have or rewards which may be associated with implementation.

When such a state of affairs prevails in any school, the definitional conception of an ideology can be said to have been realised. Consensus about the reality assumptions as to what the school ought to be will then be seen to prevail. Such a state, however, can by no means be assumed. Whether it does or not is an empirical matter, not a definitional one and will be influenced, for example, by the values that the staff in that school hold, by the presence of other ideologies amongst the staff, pupils and parents, by the way authority is exercised in the school, and by the skill with which the teachers implement whatever strategies they advocate.

Where two or more ideologies are in competition in a school, the challenge to any one ideology is of a social nature. The proponent groups in their interactions will reflect the phenomena associated with in-groups and out-groups. The assertions and counter-assertions of the supporter of the Black Papers and Progressive Education represent clashes of this kind and are manifestations of all the biased and distortion phenomena associated with such groups. Both sets of assertions have their base in the legitimacy provided by social reference groups. They are, however, different reference groups, reflecting different sets of values. What criteria are to be employed in resolving such issues? Issues of this kind, when they become socially polarised, tend to become intractable and to be resolved by considerations of power and resources.

Just as group and organisational dynamics can support and sustain an ideology, so also can they act in defence of the reality assumptions associated with an ideology. In particular, they can operate to defend the assumption that the outcomes, initially used to justify the implementation of some organisational strategy, actually do occur. Any attempt to test such outcomes by empirical means represents a challenge to the prestige and esteem of the group or organisation which provided the social legitimation for the implementation of the strategy. How do proponent groups in education react to such empirical tests? There is little direct evidence available in this country about such a question, but various studies reported in the political and organisational literature have clearly illustrated the importance of information in organisations and the constraints which operate in relation to access to, and the communication of, information. Because of these constraints, Wilenski

(1967) concludes, after reviewing the literature in the field, 'that the verbal environment of an organisation—captured in felicitous slogans—can for years remain impervious to evidence'. In the next section of this paper, some of these constraints in education will be examined and their influence on the communication process discussed, particularly in relation to the decision-making of teachers in the classroom.

Ideology and teachers' decision-making

Given the normative nature of ideologies in education which advocate and justify organisational and behavioural strategies on value grounds, and which have associated with their implementation, maintenance and defence a variety of social forces which were referred to in the previous section, it is not surprising to come across evidence that the actual outcomes associated with implementation of particular strategies may well be rather different from those which were initially used to justify their introduction. With regard to the organisational strategy of the integrated day, for example, one researcher (Bealing, 1972) has concluded that the alleged occurrence of a primary school revolution associated with this notion is open to considerable doubt.

The detailed evidence of a case study of an Australian purpose-built community school (Fitzgerald *et al.*, 1976) further illustrates the lack of correspondence between the symbolic assumptions of ideology—in this case, the ideology of participation—and the reality of events in a particular school. The ideology of participation in this case study was intended to refer to parents and a variety of community groups in the decision-making of the school and to the participation of the students in decision-making about the nature and frequency of the learning activities in which they engaged at school. The crucial appointment of the headship of the school was given to an individual who appeared to be an ardent devotee of the ideology of participation. In his previous position within the central state administration he had, for example, continually advocated it in the schools in the state (albeit unsuccessfully). Following his appointment he continued his advocacy of it through frequent exposure on the media and in extensive tours throughout Australia. Through such activities he was able to raise considerable resources for the school and to attract wide publicity to the school. Operationally, however, the implementation of the ideology in the school created very serious problems for students, staff, parents and the community. The head seemed able to respond to these problems only within the constraints of the ideology to which he was committed, with the result that at the end of two years parents had refused to participate further in the work of the School Advisory Committee, students had withdrawn from the staff-student meetings and many members of the staff had become disillusioned about the whole idea of participation and expressed their feelings by moving away from the school.

The authors of this Australian study refer frequently to the great gulf that exists between the ideology about participation and the reality of the school. The paper by Colin Hunter (Chapter 8), which contrasts the ideology of the head of a school with case study material illustrating what the school is really like, provides further evidence of this gulf.

For some, such findings might be seen as additional evidence of the problematic nature of the education process. For ideologists, on the other hand, such findings represent a challenge to the meaningfulness of their ideology, a threat to the verbal environment which they create for their school and a disturbance to their belief in the link between strategy and outcome, an essential element in their theories about what schools ought to be like.

To make explicit the gulf between the verbal environment of schools (with their assumptions about what schools ought to be like) and the reality of what the schools are like is to create a very real threat to the individuals and groups who propagate the ideologies and hence is likely to lead them to react in a defensive manner. Two examples of such a reaction will be given. The first is a written statement from the international conference on grouping in schools which has been referred to earlier (Yates, 1966). The second is a comment of Lady Plowden's (Television Education Debate, chaired by Robin Day, BBC 2, 4 February 1977), chairperson of the Plowden Committee, the group responsible for the Report containing some of the ideological material referred to in this chapter. Lady Plowden was participating in one of the early television discussions contributing to the Great Debate in Education; Shirley Williams, the Secretary of State for Education, was one of the principal speakers. Lady Plowden's comment was in response to a question about the effect of her Report on the educational standards in primary schools. Thus, this second example contains a social context likely to reinforce any defensiveness on the part of the individual with the organisational and social defensiveness referred to in the previous section.

As part of the report of the international conference on grouping in schools, Yates (1966) presents the views of the study group about teachers' reactions to the trend towards more flexible grouping systems and the introduction of mixed ability grouping. They maintained that teachers 'stand between, so to speak, the demands and suggestions made by the community through its official spokesmen and the pupils for whose benefit any proposed changes in forms of grouping are intended. They may, and often do, argue on the basis of their professional expertise against the viability of some of the plans that are put forward.' He goes on to point out that the study group have been 'impressed by the predominantly conservative nature of the teachers' reactions to most proposals for change in grouping practices'. The two reasons that are given for such resistance to change refer to the threat to status such changes imply and the limited experience that most teachers have had. Even if one admits that there may be some substance in these reasons, the study group seem to disregard completely the notion that the professional expertise of teachers might be relevant to the evaluation of the grouping strategies under discussion.

The study group go on to recognise the importance of the attitudes of teachers to the success of any changes in grouping practices in schools and their involvement and full consultation in the planning of these changes. From further comment, however, such involvement and consultation does not extend to any evaluation of the grouping changes themselves but is limited to a discussion of teachers' willingness to participate in what might be considered to be appropriate skill training.

Another example of excluding teachers from participation in any evaluative discussion of the desirability or feasibility of implementing organisational strategies is found in the policy-making decision about comprehensive reorganisation (DES Circular, 1965). Discussions with their formal associations were restricted to matters of status and salary. Their associations were formally excluded from any discussions of the policy decision about whether to go comprehensive or not. Teachers working in schools where curriculum changes are allegedly taking place have made similar comment. Shipman (1974) describes how the curriculum team, in their rush to produce materials, failed to support the teachers' initiatives and began to dictate the terms on which local support should operate. Inevitably, the teachers seriously questioned the nature of their involvement in the curriculum work and began to see their participation as peripheral to the real decisions being made elsewhere. It is interesting to note that in some ideological formulations teachers are symbolically excluded from consideration. The Plowden Report, for example, which presents the primary and middle school ideology in some detail, is entitled 'Children and their Primary Schools'.

From the discussions to date, it would seem that advocates of particular organisational, curricular and behavioural strategies in education tend to restrict the access of practising teachers to the initial decision-making stages of the ideological process, to blame them for the slow progress of the strategies in schools, and to deflect criticism associated with the outcomes of the strategies towards teacher groups.

Lady Plowden's reply to criticisms about standards in primary schools shows a similar tendency to attribute the blame to teachers. Unwilling to modify any of the recommendations in her committee's report, which emphasised the individuality of each child and egalitarianism, she explained away the gulf between the assumptions of the ideology and the realities of the classroom situation by arguing that the responsibility for the outcomes must lie with the teachers. She pointed out that the teachers had been young, inexperienced and in many cases mediocre; that many were in their probationary year and were part of a large turnover of staff in the schools.

These comments recognise neither the complexity of the task which the Plowden recommendations pose for the teachers nor the high level and variety of skills which teachers must have if they are to implement the recommendations successfully. The public arena in which Lady Plowden spoke made such admissions and recognitions difficult to express. The context of the Great Debate on Education is a political one, in which government expenditure requires to be cut. This has prompted an alternative ideology which suggests that cuts in educational spending are associated with quality in education. This alternative ideology, whose main political advocate was listening to her comments, placed Lady Plowden in an ideological bind: claims that more teachers, more in-service training of teachers and smaller classes were necessary concomitants of the successful implementation of her committee's recommendations were not made, for they were clearly inconsistent with the alternative ideology.

In terms of her own beliefs, Lady Plowden's comments would seem to exclude any possibility that a relationship might well exist between the high turnover of teachers and the recommendations of her committee. Such a possibility, while it might be associated with an intolerable amount of cognitive dissonance on her part, is nevertheless consistent with the increased complexity of the teachers' task and the high level of skills which the recommendations imply.

This final point is another commentary on the gulf between the verbal environment of what the school ought to be like according to the ideology and the reality of what it is like. For teachers and pupils this gulf represents a mismatch of assumptions about the school—a problem of fundamental importance because of the consequences for them which follow from it. In the remainder of this section, the way in which ideology contributes to that problem, particularly in relation to classroom decision-making, is explored and, in the process, some of the negative if unintended outcomes of ideology in education will be made explicit.

One of these stems from the way in which the ideology is symbolically expressed. Geertz (1964), in contrasting ideology with science, maintains that in the latter the style tends to be spare, restrained and analytic and seeks to maximise intellectual clarity, where in the former the style tends to be ornate and vivid and is designed to motivate action rather than to maximise clarity.

It is of interest to note how many educational ideologies, though they may be ornate and perhaps somewhat lengthy in formulations, are reduced, either by the media or by their proponent groups, to a neat

codified package or even to a slogan. The outcomes which are anticipated as a result of introducing some strategy often become the substance of such slogans—as, for example, 'discovery learning', 'integrated
studies', 'the integrated day', 'participation', 'the community school'.
Slogans of this nature thus can be regarded as symbolic cues for these
outcomes and hence may, in themselves, be contributing towards their
own acceptance amongst teachers who value the outcomes so labeled.

The lack of clarity exemplified in these rather vacuous slogans can
be said to make the ideas so expressed more likely to be acceptable to
a larger audience. The reason for this claim is that lack of clarity in
formulation requires that audiences to whom the ideas are addressed
interpret what the symbolic expressions mean. Provided that the
members of the audience are sympathetic towards the outcomes either
symbolised in the slogan or advocated by the ideology, they can impose their own interpretation of the means which it is suggested will
bring about that outcome. Hence, the illusion of consensus amongst
members of the target group can be fostered in a manner similar to the
unifying myths that Lunsford described in relation to university administrators.

In an attempt to come to grips analytically with the way in which
symbolic ideological formulations are expressed, Naish, Hartnett and
Finlayson (1976) have identified a series of indices which might reasonably be used to justify a particular expression of a set of ideas being
described as ideological in nature. Based on a number of philosophical
criteria, the indices can be grouped according to whether they manifest
a lack of clarity in the expression of the ideas or whether they can be
regarded as being likely to serve some persuasive function. A full
account of these indices and examples of their occurrence in govern-
mental and other kinds of educational literature can be found elsewhere.
In this paper only general comments will be made about the implications
which the lack of clarity and the persuasive expression of ideological
formulations have for the target group teachers.

While a lack of clarity in ideological formulations may serve some
useful persuasive function, it brings serious consequences for classroom
decision-making, where the symbolic formulations have to be translated into the behaviour that constitutes classroom practice. One of
these is that many interpretations of what the formulations mean, in
practice, will be possible. The comprehensive school ideology, as an
organisational strategy for effecting social change, demonstrates this
point well. Data collected by the NFER about the way in which the
schools designated as comprehensive were actually organised made any
generalisation about them very difficult indeed (Monks, 1970): so
much so, that it was virtually impossible to say what a comprehensive
school is. The Ford Project (Elliott and Adelman, 1975) amply demonstrates the multiplicity of interpretations placed upon the codified

ideology represented by the slogan 'discovery learning'. The work of the project was done with a group of teachers, all of whom wished to implement this form of teaching in their classroom practice. Yet a great diversity of interpretations of what the behavioural strategy meant for teachers and pupils emerged. These two examples illustrate well the problem which practising teachers have in seeking to identify the reality assumptions about what their schools and classrooms are in fact supposed to be like when these are symbolised in ideological form.

Another problem for classroom decision-makers stems from the proliferation of assumptions that can be made about the classroom. Even if one stays within one ideology, say that of Plowden, the number and range of goals and strategies which can be advocated for pre-secondary school teachers constitutes an alarming degree of role over-load. The broad aim for schools put forward in the Plowden Report refers to the all-round development of the child. Education is expected to contribute to the intellectual, emotional, social, moral, aesthetic and spiritual development of every child. Given the complex way in which all these aspects of development require to be interpreted in the light of the personality structure of each child and bearing in mind his cultural and home background, the comprehensive fulfilment of the teacher's task according to the ideology becomes virtually impossible.

Nevertheless, to these expectations for teachers have to be added all the curriculum developers' expectations which are contained in various government reports and pamphlets on middle schools. Some of these will be mentioned briefly. According to the Bullock Report, the teacher must attend to every aspect of literacy from oracy to creative and grammatical prose and poetry; in maths, recent developments require a whole new field of specialist competence to deal with structural and other material designated as modern maths; in science, the Nuffield programme requires expertise across a broad front in order that scientific thinking can be encouraged in the pupils; in music, innovatory programmes such as Kodaly, designed to encourage participation and composition, demand further expertise; art work now extends to pottery, collages, stump art, three-dimensional sculpture, and impressionist painting as well as drawing. One could go on with other areas where expertise is demanded: drama; physical education, including dance, free movement, and swimming; environmental studies, in which various aspects of history, geography and social studies are expected to become integrated; humanities and moral education—not to mention extra-curricular activities such as running clubs, meeting parents, visiting homes and taking part in community activities. This list of expectations, all held by various groups of ideologists, perhaps will convey the totally unrealistic overload of expectations directed towards teachers. It would seem inevitable that selectivity on the part of teachers and schools is necessary and that some of these goals will not be achieved or even attempted by some schools and some teachers.

Amongst the many and diverse expectations for teachers which emanate from various ideological groups are many unresolved conflicts. These can lie within particular curriculum areas, as for example, English and maths. How is the promotion of creative writing to be reconciled with accuracy in spelling and grammatical expression, or the promotion of modern maths with the speed and accuracy of computational skills which some maths teachers feel are necessary if their pupils are to do themselves justice in fields such as physics? They can also occur between curricular areas, between curricular and pastoral expectations, and where resources are limited.

A further kind of conflict arises when teachers find themselves constrained by administrative or other organisational considerations. If, for example, a school has no hall or gym, then it is difficult to respond to expectations that one should encourage creative dance. These problems become even more complex when viewed within a school context involving numbers of pupils, numbers of rooms and timetabling issues. More general still are the constraints which national considerations such as the availability of finance impose upon teachers. On what is the available money to be spent? This decision is seldom taken by teachers, yet it is they who are subjected to the consequences of such decisions in relation to the problems of responding to ideological demands.

Given the plethora of expectations which can be directed towards teachers, it is easy for any group seeking to evaluate the work of the schools to select a certain goal or series of goals for special attention, according to their particular system of values and according to the prevailing climate of the time. The Bullock Report did this about standards in reading, the Prime Minister did it about general standards, and the parents of Tyndale School did it about the standards in a particular school. These instances reflect a general concern about standards— merely one goal chosen out of the multiplicity of ambiguous and conflict-laden goals described earlier. How this concern is communicated to teachers and what effect its expression will have on teachers is problematic because, as the enquiry into the William Tyndale School clearly shows, the accountability of teachers for the priorities they give to the range of ideological expectations directed towards them is an important issue, as is the role of HMI and local advisers in relation to this problem.

The work of Taylor and Reid (1971) is useful in showing the relative influence of such groups in primary teachers' decisions about what is taught in their schools. Such groups were rated, along with other outside groups which might be regarded as having status or expertise of various kinds—academics, researchers, journal or article writers, administrators—significantly lower than groups within the school by their sample of teachers drawn from a variety of primary schools. The head was judged to have the most influence, followed by colleagues, pupils, deputy head and then formal and informal groups of staff. Professional colleagues within the school were rated higher than teachers in other schools, indicating the importance of the social context of the particular primary school in any decisions about what is to be taught.

At the same time as this study raises the issue about the extent to which teachers attend to proponent groups concerned with the initiation of change, it also gives some indication as to the way in which some of the problems of ambiguity, overload and conflict are involved for teachers. It may be that Taylor's findings—which emphasise the importance of sources within the school for influencing what is taught, with the head the most important source—are reinforcing the view that the head is the gate-keeper to the school and that his mediation in any decision-making process, and specifically those which involve ideologies communicated to the school, is a factor which must be borne in mind. This emphasis on influential figures located within the school is consistent with the role which leaders in conflict-laden and ambiguous situations are expected to play: they serve to define the situation for the group in order that it can function. Hence, how the head interprets or evaluates the reality assumptions of central and local administrators, national inspectors, local advisers or any other group is perhaps what teachers attend to. This is not to say that they accept his assumptions, but merely that they attend to them.

For those teachers who wish to take the role provided by an ideology, the problems of ambiguity, overload and conflict are perhaps particularly acute. For them, their classroom decision-making and practice and the outcomes which are consequent upon these are of crucial importance to their evaluation of themselves as teachers and to the validation of the identity which has been hypothesised for them by the ideology. Hence, lack of clarity about role expectations and the problematic nature of their outcomes make these teachers particularly vulnerable to feelings of personal inadequacy where implementation of the ideological strategies does not appear to lead to the predicted outcomes. Where, of course, the classroom process does have outcomes which they perceive to be consistent with their needs and value systems, the experience is rewarding for them as individuals, and their belief in themselves as teachers is confirmed. The ambiguous nature of ideological formulations for teachers who accept them as a basis for their role identity, however, considerably increases the risks associated with the taking of such a role and brings sharply into focus the problem of their own professional competence and the role of authority figures such as their head teacher, HMI and local advisers in relation to the ideological process.

Teachers and their professional organisations lay strong emphasis on the assertion of professional competence. The proponents of ideological formulations share this view and where competence is in doubt in relation to an innovation—as with the introduction of more flexible methods of grouping—the 'solution' to this problem is frequently seen as merely acquiring appropriate skills through training experience. This view will not be challenged in this paper but merely reported as a common way of reacting to problems of professional competence.

The potency with which teachers project the professional image of competency is well illustrated in the Australian study (Fitzgerald *et al.*, 1976), where teachers projected this image so effectively that parents were discouraged from any involvement in decision-making about the school. Feeling inadequate in relation to the professionals, parents are disinclined to participate actively in the work of the school. Other groups for whom the studied portrayal of competence is likely to be used, because of their significance for teachers' career prospects, would include head teachers, HMI and local advisers.

When used in relation to such groups, the projection of the teachers' professional image can perhaps best be regarded as a 'counter-ideology' brought to bear by the teachers' professional group in their own defence against groups whom they perceive as threatening in one way or another.

It is in this connection that the distinction made earlier—between the alleged guiding function of ideology, which has been the focus of discussion up to now, and the justificatory function which ideology might serve in relation to whatever classroom practice teachers employ —is useful. Ideological formulations come to be recognised as providing a socially validated rationale for whatever behavioural or organisational strategies they are associated with.

This function of ideology as 'justification of activity' is exemplified in Brown's discussion (1969) of the help which ideological ideas can give to an individual to deal with conflict in terms of 'defence against critics'. He quotes an example, perhaps more familiar in the USA than in Britain, of reporters drawn into 'a series of informal contractual relationships with those who exercise control of both events and news'. Such a situation suggests that there is as much bargaining as reporting in the job. An ideology which defines the reporter's role as one of 'watch dog', stressing the maintenance of social distance between the reporter and his source, might serve as a useful defence against critics who emphasised the 'political' character of the job. Its ideas serve to help the reporter to present himself to others outside his sphere. For this purpose Brown claims that practitioners have a closely textured set of verbal statements which are all-embracing so far as their professional selves are concerned. He analyses a brief reply by a media practitioner at a joint practitioner-educationist conference to illustrate how the statement was particularly apt for that audience in minimising potential or actual conflict with another interest group. He goes on to suggest that, had the audience been one of Members of Parliament, the speaker would have stressed some of the same points, while introducing others more specifically appropriate to the occasion. From the all-embracing statements relating to their professional situation, they select those most suited to their audience.

In the exercise of this skill, an individual chooses from amongst a total range of available statements those considered appropriate to the particular audience he is addressing. To the extent that he is exercising judgments about the statements, the individual must be regarded as an active decision-making agent, not a passively reactive one, as the normative associations often linked with ideological usage would suggest. Hence, one might legitimately ask about the extent to which the exercise of skill in selecting ideological ideas for particular audiences is synonymous with the notion of 'commitment'. Commitment need not necessarily imply the flexibility and adaptability which the selection of appropriate ideas would suggest is necessary. It could be interpreted as rigid adherence to a certain set of ideas, as appeared to be the case with the head of the Australian community school mentioned earlier. Conversely, the flexible adaptation of ideas deemed to be appropriate for an audience might be considered an aspect of manipulation.

The justificatory role that ideological formulations might play in any interactions between teachers and members of groups whom they might perceive to be threatening would be considerable. Teachers might well 'baffle a parent with science' or rehearse the entire ideological rationale known to be advocated by whatever group of teachers, advisers, or inspectors that happen to constitute the audience at any particular time.

Such verbal exchanges which take place before audiences have little or nothing to do with the real decision-making problems which teachers who accept an ideology and are seeking to implement it are likely to have because of the ambiguity and conflict likely to be associated with it. For an individual teacher to make these problems explicit, in a climate where justificatory and counter-ideological activity predominated, would be synonymous with a declaration of professional incompetence. Hence, many of the basic classroom decision-making problems associated with ideologies may remain hidden from public view. While this is consistent with the maintenance of the professional image of competence, dovetailing as it does with the ambiguity of the formulations of proponent ideological groups, it actively inhibits genuinely evaluative and constructive discussion of the real problems for classroom decision-making and practice which ideological and counter-ideological exchanges tend to mask.

Questions arising

It is unlikely that ideological activity in the education system will be reduced. The diversity of interest groups and value systems on the one hand, and the complexity of the educational process on the other, are probably sufficient guarantee of that. And given the motivational function of the propagators of ideologies, it is unlikely that the lack of clarity or the persuasive nature of ideological material will diminish.

At the same time, the extent of the gulf between the normative assumptions made about schools in the ideologies and the realities of the classroom which this paper has sought to explore and analyse cannot be ignored. In relation to that gulf, a number of questions can be raised:

(i) To what extent are HMI, local advisers, head teachers and teachers aware of the functions of ideology?

(ii) What effect will raising the level of awareness of the negative as well as the positive aspects of ideology have?

(iii) How will the groups mentioned in question (i) react to increased awareness of the ideological process in education?

(iv) What consequences will increased awareness have for the relationships which develop amongst the groups?

(v) In the short term, how do teachers react to the gulf between ideology and the reality of the classroom?

It is not suggested that clear and definitive answers are likely to emerge in relation to these questions. Rather, they are posed in order to focus attention on issues that are of some significance in any consideration of educational change and development and which, up to now, have been largely ignored in the Great Debate.

Note

1 These outcomes were the initial justifications offered by A. Crosland, the Secretary of State for Education, who implemented comprehensive reorganisation (see Kogan, 1971).

Chapter 5

A phenomenological approach to classroom decision-making

David H. Hargreaves

Common sense suggests that the decisions made by teachers in school are of different kinds or levels. At one extreme are the highly general decisions which affect the structure and culture of the school in profound ways. Many curricular decisions, such as whether or not to introduce an integrated social studies, and organisational decisions, such as whether to stream or to adopt mixed ability grouping, are of this kind. At the other extreme are the multitudinous and fleeting decisions which every teacher makes daily in the classroom, often without much conscious deliberation, such as whether to pose the question to John or Mary, whether to tell Tom to stop talking, whether to explain a problem to an individual pupil or to the whole class. My concern in this paper is with these ubiquitous, transient and mundane decisions that pervade the experience of every teacher.

The present analysis of such decisions is phenomenological. By this I mean simply that my focus is on the teacher's *experience* of such decision-making rather than on, say, the origins, sources, causes, consequences or effectiveness of the decisions, all of which are legitimate topics for a social scientific analysis. My assumption is that many of these routine decisions by teachers take the form of what Alfred Schutz calls 'cookery-book knowledge' or recipes which provide 'typical solutions for typical problems available for typical actors'. That is to say, the problems about which the teacher makes the decisions are recognised as familiar and regularly recurring ones which arise in familiar circumstances in the classroom and relate to familiar persons, pupils. It is these qualities of similarity and regular occurrence, combined with relative ease and speed of disposal, which permit us to call these decisions 'routine' ones. Occasionally, of course, these decisions do not flow so readily and become a cause for hesitation, reflection, postponement, and even anxiety, but this is not normally the case.

In thus demarcating somewhat artificially one class of decisions (see Sutcliffe and Whitfield (1976) for an elaborate typology of decisions), we must recognise that most of these decisions have not always been routine for teachers but have become so through experience. For the student or inexperienced teacher they are a frequent source of deliberation and puzzlement. This often leads to a cumulative anxiety, since the immediacy and constantly shifting nature of classroom events demand that most classroom decisions be made 'on the spot' in response to those events: only a few decisions can be postponed for systematic consideration at a later stage. In the experienced teacher, then, the knowledge on which the teacher bases the decision is essentially *tacit* and need not be processed in a very conscious way. Were it otherwise, the decision could never be made quickly and easily. The teacher's experience is one in which the decision is made as it were 'instinctively' or 'automatically', freeing the teacher's conscious mind to cope with other matters.

One consequence of this is that it is rather pointless to ask the teacher, after a routine decision has been made, what were the contents of his mind at the time of the decision. In a real sense, there is little that he can report of substance except that 'It seemed the right thing to do in the circumstances' or 'I did it almost without thinking'. We cannot expect the teacher to provide what is of the essence of such decision-making, namely its subconscious components. What we can do is to ask the teacher for a *commentary* upon the decision after the event, for instance by reporting back to him what he did or by showing him a film of his actions. This commentary would consist of a *rationalisation* of his conduct in two senses. In the first sense, the commentary can consist of a justification of the decision in which the teacher seeks to render it socially acceptable to the person who asks for the commentary, whether it be a researcher, a student, or an inspector. In so doing the teacher may adjust his account to what he sees as the values, expectations and interests of him who asks for the commentary. This may tell us relatively little about what lies behind the decision. In the second sense, the commentary can consist of the teacher's methods of rendering his decision as a rational action—that is, his means of understanding his action as having purposes or intentions (goals) which are to be realised through particular understandings of events (knowledge) and through particular actions (means).

Although in practical methodology these two kinds of rationalisation are not easily distinguishable, my assumption is that the latter form constitutes a legitimate source of uncovering the common sense knowledge which becomes tacit in the decision-making itself. The use of commentary is one method, however flawed, by which the tacit can be made into a matter about which one can speak. My own experience in the use of such commentary by teachers suggests that they do not always find this easy to do, that much depends upon the questions one asks, and that any single commentary tells one about only some of the elements involved.

I have reported some of my work on decision-making by teachers with reference to deviance/discipline aspects of pupil conduct elsewhere (Hargreaves, Hester and Mellor, 1975). Here I want to draw out the more general implications of that analysis for a model which can be applied to a much greater variety of routine classroom decisions (see Figure 5.1). At its simplest, the decision can be divided analytically into two elements. The first is the 'problem' about which the decision has to

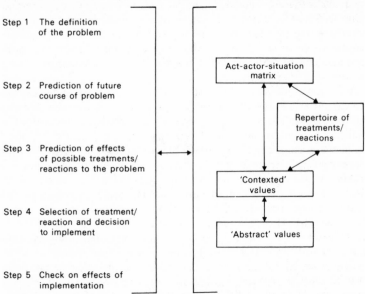

Step 1 The definition
of the problem

Step 2 Prediction of future
course of problem

Step 3 Prediction of effects
of possible treatments/
reactions to the problem

Step 4 Selection of treatment/
reaction and decision
to implement

Step 5 Check on effects of
implementation

Act-actor-situation
matrix

Repertoire of
treatments/
reactions

'Contexted'
values

'Abstract' values

Figure 5.1 A schematic model of decision-making: skill consists in the rapid decision-making by which each step in the decision-making chain 1–5 is systematically related to the act-actor-situation matrix, the repertoire of treatments, and the contexted values

be made. This problem is the state of affairs which calls for some action from the teacher (though the action may consist of taking no overt action) and where more than one possible reaction is available (for choice between alternatives is the essence of decision-making). The second element is the selection and execution of the preferred response to the initiating problem. These two elements are closely tied to each other. The events that constitute the problem requiring the decision can be divided into three:

The act: what is being done by the relevant person(s),
usually the pupils but sometimes also the teacher himself, and *how* is it being done?

The actor(s): who is doing the act and *why* are they doing it?
The situations: where and when are the actors doing what act?

The definition of the problem (and its solution, as we shall see later) rests upon the teacher's understanding of the act-actor-situation matrix. The apparent simplicity of this matrix masks the extremely complex interpretive work undertaken by the teacher, for no two teachers would even define the same event in precisely the same way. Certainly, they would often come to similar definitions of the event, but there would never be an exact equivalence between teachers; and there would be greater divergences between teachers over whether the event constituted a 'problem' over which a decision should be made. But my interest is less in the differences in the interpretational work of teachers, important a topic as that is, and more in common structures in their common sense knowledge. For teachers share a wide range of definitions of acts as certain kinds of acts which they feel they can recognise without difficulty—working hard, looking bored, fidgeting, talking out of turn, being cheeky, concentrating, and so on. Such acts can be recognised (interpreted) 'at a glance', and this recognition rests on a highly skilled capacity to code quickly.

Yet the act is interlocked with the actor. The meaning of the act depends in part upon the actor who is performing the act. Act and actor are like figure and ground in Gestalt psychology: each can be understood only in relation to the other for each is part of the other and the whole is more than a simple addition of two elements. Just as teachers typify acts as certain kinds of acts, they also typify pupils as certain kinds of persons, with particular qualities and attributes, with a particular psychological make-up and a particular history and biography. The act which the pupil commits can be understood by the teacher only by locating the act within his typification of the pupil as a person. Telling support for this is provided for the fact that we draw on our knowledge of a person in order to formulate his motives for an act, and once certain motives are imputed, the meaning of the act is transformed by this attachment of motives to it. The meaning of a pupil's breaking of a test-tube in a science lesson is conditional upon whether the teacher believes it was done by accident, through carelessness or as a deliberate act of destructiveness, and the ascription of such motives depends, *inter alia*, on what the teacher knows of the person who broke it.

Both act and actor are further interpreted in the light of the situation in which they are embedded. The meaning of 'running' as an act changes according to whether the pupil is running in the playground or in a busy corridor—and the meaning of the latter changes if the teacher believes the running is motivated by a desire to inform the authorities that a serious accident has just taken place. Similarly, talkativeness as a pupil attribute is understood differently when it occurs in a classroom examination as opposed to in a meeting of the school debating society. My illustrations are intentionally simple but they do betray the enormous complexity of the linkages in the act-actor-situation configuration by which events are interpreted as 'normal' or 'correct' or as a 'problem' which requires a decision.

In disciplinary matters in classrooms one of the most common problems arises when a teacher defines a pupil act as being a relatively minor breach of the rules and as being slightly disrupting, as when a pupil is talking when he is not supposed to be. The decision posed by this problem for the teacher is whether to take no overt action or whether to intervene immediately, the latter choice clearly involving the further issue of selecting an appropriate form of intervention. The evidence suggests that the decision taken by the teacher rests in part upon his capacity to predict, based upon his common sense knowledge, whether (a) the act will simply 'peter out' of its own accord in a few moments, or (b) the act will tend to persist if left untreated, so that the pupil will go on talking rather than working for the rest of the lesson, or (c) the act will escalate, either by becoming 'shouting' rather than 'talking' or by spreading to other pupils who are not currently talking. If the teacher opts for prediction (a) and decides to ignore the act but in fact (c) occurs, then the teacher has clearly failed to 'nip it in the bud', which is a central element in disciplinary skills. If on the other hand the teacher predicts (c) and decides to intervene when, without that intervention (a) would have ensued, then the intervention was unnecessary and itself disruptive. The teacher's capacity to make the correct prediction, and so to make the right decision, rests upon a clear understanding of the kind of talk that is taking place, the identity of the person who has initiated the talk and the identity of the person who is listening, and the situation in which that talk is occurring, including all the preceding events of the lesson, and even of previous lessons.

Let us suppose that the teacher decides to intervene against the pupil who is talking. There is an enormous range of possible treatments for this minor act of deviance. The teacher may merely look rather hard at the offending pupil or he may without speaking prowl around in close proximity to him. At the other extreme the teacher may make the pupil come to sit at the front or even send him out of the room. How does the teacher choose from this vast range of alternative treatments? Again the teacher's typification of the pupil and his understanding of the situation play a significant role in the making of this decision. Part of his knowledge of a pupil consists in the capacity to predict how the pupil is likely to respond to different treatments ('I only need to look at Kathleen' versus 'Once Kevin starts talking he won't stop until I bring him to the front') in different situations ('Martin always takes a few minutes to settle down after PE' versus 'When we're doing geometry Margaret will do anything rather than work').

These two features—the teacher's capacity to predict the future course of pupil acts and his capacity to predict pupil reactions to treatment—are but two elements in that enormous complex whole which we will call the teacher's common sense knowledge of life in classrooms. But these skills are by no means the whole of the story; they are embedded and affected by the teacher's *values*, within which I include not only the teacher's ideology and pedagogical style, but also his more diffuse social values. Thus, in my study of decision-making in relation to disciplinary events I sought to show that teachers feel constrained not only by the need to keep the lesson flowing with minimal disruption but also by a set of moral considerations of social justice, such as making the punishment fit the crime and distributing time equitably among different pupils. Teachers may share common skills but nevertheless reach different decisions because they take into account, or assign different weights to, certain social values. Decisions are made partly on the basis of social skills and partly on the basis of certain value commitments: both are encapsulated and rapidly processed in every routine classroom decision. The distinction between skills and values is, once again, an analytical one. Though the teacher may temper his decision in the light of his own moral considerations, part of his skill in predicting the pupil's response to his act consists in knowing what values of morality and justice the pupil will draw upon to evaluate the teacher's act.

My own work has concentrated upon decisions made by teachers with reference to infractions of the teacher's disciplinary code, but I believe that the same general approach can be taken to decision-making in any and every aspect of classroom life and by pupils as well as teachers. One would expect a focus upon, say, curricular decisions in the classroom, covering such matters as the pacing and sequencing and use of different pedagogical structures within a single lesson, to expose rather different facets of the teacher's common sense knowledge, and so different skills and values. We would then have to relate the different aspects together since we have no good *a priori* reason for expecting a lack of continuity and coherence between 'disciplinary' and 'curricular' areas of decision-making—they are merely convenient keys to unlocking different doors into the room of the teacher's common sense knowledge. An interactionist approach, in the tradition of Mead, Burke and Blumer, or a more phenomenological approach, in the tradition of Schutz, Garfinkel and Cicourel, permits a variety of models and analyses, but all would share, I believe, a fundamental concern with the act-actor-situation matrix at the heart of human action, and all would see decision-making as an artful, skilled accomplishment in which values have a place.

From this point of view, decision-making is not to be regarded as a separate entity, artificially fractured from the rest of action. Rather, it is one way of looking at, or finding a point of analytical access to, action itself. At present we know surprisingly little about the skills of teaching, especially where the skills are essentially social in character. And most of the work on values is dislocated from the practice of teaching, mainly because the methods of obtaining and assessing values, such as tests, questionnaires and interviews, are themselves divorced from practical action. Sharp and Green (1975) have examined the disjunction between the values that 'progressive' teachers profess (to researchers or to their colleagues) and their classroom practice. As social scientists we ought to *expect* this to be the case, for the disjunction between values and action, theory and practice, words and deeds, is a well-known and widespread phenomenon (Deutscher, 1965). The reason may be relatively transparent. When teachers are asked to display their values (to researchers, parents, colleagues, etc.), they doubtless feel constrained by that situation to express their ideals and to assert a strong degree of coherence, consistency and integration among those values. Practice will not be a simple reflection of those values because practice arises in a different situation which has a quite different structure and set of constraints.

I have argued that practice can be analysed in terms of the teacher's understanding and definition of the situation (the act-actor-situation matrix) and his understanding of the skills he possesses to cope with the situation as it has become defined. Values do not disappear at this point; rather, the values are related to emergent nature of the situation and the teacher's skills for handling it. The 'abstract' values (as expressed in tests, questionnaires and interviews) become 'contexted' values. It is this contextualisation of values which is a highly complex phenomenon, partly because contextualisation often involves a *selective* application of values and partly because in application values frequently *conflict* with one another. For instance, the realisation of one value might be seen by the teacher, in the light of his skills, necessarily to involve undermining another value. In other words, when values are contextualised, they are often experienced as *dilemmas*, as my own work and that of Berlak *et al.* (1975) suggests. What from one point of view can be described as 'inconsistency' is from this point of view a natural, rational and inevitable feature of action.

Values are embedded in teachers' classroom practices; but because there is no simple correspondence between 'abstract' values and everyday practice, it is a research task to analyse precisely how values are, often tacitly, embedded in action. Here is the significance of classroom decision-making, for it is in decision-making that all these features find their point of articulation.

My claim is that through an examination of the common sense knowledge, skills and values of teachers we can provide a basic model of teaching, and an important method of achieving this is through the collation and analysis of teacher commentaries. Such an analysis would yield important practical as well as theoretical insights, because if we can speak about what in the experienced teacher is subconscious and taken for granted, then there exists the possibility that we can *teach* this knowledge to the novice teacher and speed up the process of skill acquisition which in its natural development occurs slowly and painfully. The weakest point in teacher education—the move away from the concept of teacher training is significant—is still the provision of the student teacher with classroom skills by which he can make quick and effective decisions. We give good preparation in curricular matters, but many skills are left to the student to pick up, naturally, we hope, on teaching.

It is the perennial complaint of student teachers that there is too great a gap in their training between theory and practice; and as long as we can give no reasonable account of how values are embedded in practice, it will continue to be a valid criticism.

An equally important task is the facilitation of change in the experienced teacher. It is relatively easy to change the values to which an experienced teacher will claim a verbal allegiance. Perhaps the disjunction between espoused values and classroom practice, as examined in the work of Sharp and Green and others, indicates the readiness of teachers to change their values as well as their difficulties in transforming their action in line with their values. As long as the relation between skills and values remains at a tacit level, must we not expect values to change in relatively superficial ways?

If we could explicate the interrelationship between values and skills, as betrayed in decision-making, then perhaps we could provide the experienced teacher with the tools to uncover and to reconstruct his own common sense knowledge, skills and values and thus to change more thoroughly and with self-awareness.

It is a high hope for a research programme; but there are relatively few alternatives open to those who decide to make a career out of helping new and inexperienced teachers to be better in the exercise of their profession.

Chapter 6

Decision-making in the classroom:
a microeconomic analysis

Keith Drake

Johnny is singing to himself as he works. The teacher may respond by reflex: 'Be quiet, Johnny.' Alternatively, he may resolve Johnny's behaviour into a decision problem. He could tell Johnny to be quiet. This might help Johnny's neighbours to work and deter other potential songbirds. Or he could leave Johnny alone because he is actually working for once. The teacher does not want to antagonise and so distract him. Johnny's neighbours have not told him to shut up, which they might have done had he been annoying them.

A true reflex action is, by definition, of no interest in decision analysis. If no alternative action is perceived, no choice is possible. The non-reflexive response is to structure the choice into alternatives of action and inaction. The action alternative may be characterised as involving a combination of four estimates of subjective probability. The teacher estimates the probability of his admonition antagonising Johnny, with the separate but contingent probability that this will reduce Johnny's effort. He also estimates the probability of Johnny's singing reducing the effective effort of his neighbours. He further estimates the probability that such an admonition will deter other pupils from similar distracting behaviour.

The inaction alternative hinges upon the same set of probability estimates. Whichever alternative is selected, it will follow from two categorically different calculations. One calculation concerns the chances of reducing Johnny's learning and the likelihood that his singing is significantly affecting his immediate neighbours. The alternative type of calculation relates not to the probability of various outcomes but to the value which the teacher attaches to these outcomes. Suppose that the teacher considers it highly likely that, if he is admonished, Johnny will be antagonised and will learn less, also that those around him are suffering. He may choose to do nothing because he is keen to get Johnny doing some work at last, and he normally gets a good deal of work out of Johnny's neighbours. The high value placed on Johnny's (marginal) learning relative to that of his neighbours has a critical influence on the decision, and the teacher is prepared to accept the fairly probable price of some loss of their learning.

Had the relative valuation put on the learning of Johnny's neighbours and of Johnny been reversed, the teacher's choice might well have been for action—even if his estimate of likely consequences for all concerned had been unchanged. Sequel valuation is no less critical than probability calculation in this representation of the choice process.

However numerous the options in a choice set, the value which the teacher places upon the most preferred option next to the chosen option is the price or cost of that choice. This valuation can be regarded as the product of probability and value. For a given choice, the comparative valuation of options is speculative and ephemeral, even if it is the product of long-held and strongly felt preferences. Such valuations perish on the instant of decision. Choice, in Shackle's terminology, is a 'self-destructive experiment'. Once choice is made, the discarded options are ruled out of existence. There can be no return to see whether probabilities attached to rival options would have been realised. The classroom, too, is a Heraclitean flux.

Classroom decisions of teachers or learners can be characterised in terms of concepts which economists use to explain consumption or investment behaviour. The unrefined model of teacher choice used here draws freely on both analyses of decision-making. It would be possible to go over well-trodden ground and analyse the decision problem with great rigour, at least in terms of manipulation of symbols. But that kind of rigour is often achieved at the expense of relevance, because the rigorously manipulated symbols are inadequately identified with real entities or they are badly defined. So this model is not greatly elaborated, and the focus is kept on its principal components and characteristics.

A simple economic model can be used to analyse one incident, such as the decision over Johnny's singing, or an entire pattern of decision-making. The basic logic of choice, in terms of opportunity cost and the marginal principle, can be applied to both kinds of classroom decision-maker, learner and teacher. Ultimately, analysis has to focus on the interactive reality of their decision-making. In this paper, simply in order to facilitate analysis and exposition, their decision-making is considered separately, and largely in terms of the teacher.

It does not matter whether the teacher's decision is so hasty as to be almost a reflex, a minor modification of some routine, or the product of a long-considered plan. The decision may be based on only the most cursory search for information and scant evaluation of alternatives. It may be preactive, or interactive, curricular, disciplinary or instructional. All these are species of the same genus. Because economics addresses itself to a fundamental condition of human experience, the scarcity of means with which to achieve ends, it can be developed into a generalised study of choice behaviour. The basic model of choice employed here is no more than one variant of economic model of choice. But it is nevertheless a general model, which tries to explain any of the heterogeneous activities normally collected under the umbrella of 'teaching', as long as there is some element of scarcity and choice in these activities. Choice is what it seeks to explain.

The first major concept in this model is the concept of opportunity cost. In Buchanan's formulation this is the choice-influencing cost of any action, i.e. the expected benefits from the most preferred rival course of action, the benefits renounced at the moment of choice (Buchanan, 1969). Choice costs are rejected net benefits, i.e. advantages net of disadvantages. The second major concept is the idea of equilibrium at the margin. Decision-makers can be represented as spending time, or any other scarce resource, in a distribution between rival expenditures which tends to equalise the ratio between the cost and the benefit of every marginal commitment of resources. If there is no interruption, this equalising adjustment of expenditures will bring about a situation in which no further shift of the pattern of commitments can increase benefits. This is a state of equilibrium, to be upset only if the decision-maker's disposable stock of scarce resources changes or if there is a change in his perception of benefits to be expected from competing employments for his resources, and therefore in the cost of his commitments. The link between opportunity cost and equilibrium at the expenditure margin is the decision-maker's estimate of the cost of any extra commitment in terms of benefit from an alternative use of those resources.

Of course, this model has to be considerably developed if it is to have much leverage on reality. It is one thing to state an economic rationale of choice evaluation in general terms. Streams of future benefits and of future costs, adjusted for uncertainties, are discounted by a rate reflecting the private rate of time preference. They are then compared and the option with the most favourable cost-benefit ratio or the greatest net worth is selected. But the general statement so familiar in neoclassical economics refers really to a deterministic model. The process of teacher decision-making is marked by a significant element of voluntarism. It is a process in which the individual *imagines* rival courses of action, guesses the associated advantages and disadvantages, takes some account of their likely incidence over time and the satisfactions and dissatisfactions likely to accrue, adjusts his estimates according to his attitude to risk-taking—and chooses.

The process of valuing the options which are perceived to compose the choice set is complicated by numerous factors but especially by the fact that expected benefits accrue over time. The value of a prospective outcome is not a straightforward product of its probability and its value. Most imagined sequels will have gains and losses attached, and our valuation is adjusted in the light of their timing. Put another way, the valuation of these outcomes is sensitive not only to their size and certainty but also to the time shape of the net benefit stream. We prefer benefits now, rather than later. The degree of this preference can be expressed as a time preference rate. A private time preference rate is in effect a subjective rate at which the teacher discounts an anticipated stream of benefits. It is usual to express the value of a stream of future benefits in terms of its present value in order to make the benefit valuation comparable with the present sacrifice necessary to acquire it. The higher the individual teacher values a benefit now compared with a year later, the lower will be the present value to him of that future benefit. By putting together the process of equalising the return on all commitments of resources at the spending margin and the process of adjusting prospective benefits from options for their time values, the valuative process combines comparative valuation at a moment in time, horizontally, and over future time, vertically.

Moreover, the decision-maker does not employ only one time preference rate. He operates in a number of choice sets, some of which he chooses to regard as non-competing. This fact considerably modifies the tendency to equalise returns on resources right along the expenditure margin. It is probably more realistic to conceive of teachers equalising at the margin in a number of different choice sectors (each comprising a group of choice sets), with time preference rates varying sector to sector. The teacher may exhibit a very low rate in one sector and a much higher one in another. This variation is accounted for by a difference in his view of the activity or behaviour which is the focus of each sector.

For instance, decisions concerning the learning of a basic skill like counting or reading may be accorded a low time preference rate. The teacher is almost indifferent between achieving this learning now and at a future date, as long as it happens. He puts little premium on a quick return. He is prepared to invest his time and skills and wait patiently for achievement. The options in this choice set may be different strategies for assisting such learning, implying different times to achieve mastery. Differences in time to mastery are not, in themselves, likely to affect very much the relative evaluation of strategies, and therefore the choice. By contrast, decisions about discipline may be accorded a much higher time preference rate. An option promising quick results is then greatly favoured compared with one yielding slower results. The present value of its prospective benefits will tend to be a considerably larger fraction of the sum of the unadjusted values accruing over time than will be the case with the slow return option.

One characteristic of teaching decisions is the variability of the period over which benefits can be expected. In the case of learners the prospective benefit stream may even stretch away over decades. The time value of prospective benefits can be a very important factor in the valuative process, and choice becomes quite sensitive to the rate at which the chooser discounts, i.e. the rate he uses to compute the present worth of future benefits. Clearly, one way of influencing teacher or learner choices is to change the time preference rate which is being applied in any particular sector of choice. Such rates would seem to be a function of personality characteristics, and especially of preferences and of attitudes to uncertainty and risk-taking. The subject would bear more thorough investigation.

However, valuation shift is only one of at least three major sources of change in a teacher's distribution of time, skill and effort between competing employments. A change in estimated probabilities is a second source, and a third is change in the composition of one or more choice sets, whether this is an 'objective' change or a change in the teacher's perception of possible actions and their sequels. Change the choice set, or the estimates of probability and value which rank the options within that set, and the decision is likely to change, not merely in that set, but probably in other sets too.

This is true because the interdependence of teacher decisions is a further critical feature. Most decisions are interwoven in a pattern of preceding and consequential decisions, not free-standing. One decision is part of a perpetual on-going process of marginal adjustments. Very little is needed in order to trigger a ripple of choice modification, certainly nothing so fundamental as a marked preference shift and therefore a major change in the valuation of outcomes.

The classroom choice environment can be represented as a mixture of an *n*-person game and a game against nature. Sometimes the teacher shares control over outcomes with other players, learners in the first instance, parents and other teachers at one remove. Sometimes he cannot affect the environment by his moves. In the *n*-person game different responses from other players may alter teacher choices. In the game against nature, he may revise his estimate of the 'state of nature' of his pupils or of the probability of learning occurring. In either case the change may not only affect his choice of action within one choice set but trigger adjustments in other choice sets. If, for instance, the teacher chooses to devote more time to one particular activity, he must, other things being equal, decrease his commitment of time in other choice sets. The teacher, managing a finite stock of scarce resources, operates in many choice sets and his activities often constitute the principal medium through which these sets are connected, through which the ripple moves. The teacher devotes more time to A, and now a little less to B, C and D, adjusting towards the behavioural equilibrium where ratios of anticipated marginal resource costs to marginal benefits are equal—in so far as continuous adjustment is feasible (i.e. choices are not 'lumpy') and the interdependent sets all fall within one sector of choice.

This process of marginal adjustment is also a critical ingredient of the valuative procedure. When a teacher considers a particular option, he does not value the prospective benefits in isolation, merely in terms of his preference for the imagined outcomes and his attitude to the envisaged time path. Other preferences for other outcomes in other choice sets are brought into the valuative matrix. The teacher does not have a hierarchy of goals or actions in the sense that he will not strive for Z until he is satiated with X and Y. Any option which would require some commitment of scarce resources represents one or more possible goals. The goal or goals implicit in one option are not autonomous. It is heteronomy which characterises teacher choice objectives. They are linked together, more or less dependent upon one another, though not necessarily in a pyramidal structure. The teacher pursues simultaneously some of X, some of Y, and some of Z. The teacher may be willing to sacrifice some of X or Y for some more of Z, but whether he does so depends on what is technically described as his subjective marginal substitution ratio between X, Y and Z. Substitution via increments and decrements of X, Y and Z will continue until the teacher reaches a preferred state. This state is the distribution of his resources of time, effort and attention where he is indifferent about an exchange of a decrement of one resource commitment and an increment of another, and so on through all feasible pairs of marginal changes in his use of resources.

It may be worth underlining the implication that, in this model of the choice process, there is no inherent value attaching to any given action or use of resources. The value of the marginal action or commitment of resources is the only value which is accessible to investigation at all, because it is the only value which enters into actual decision-making. What the teacher weighs in the balance is not all Johnny's learning and all that of his neighbours, but a little more by Johnny against the possibility of a little less by them. Actual decisions in the classroom are not usually concerned with total change, e.g. with deciding whether to spend any time at all on exposition or any time at all in teacher instructions concerning individual project work. Most classroom choices are concerned with the problem of deciding whether to spend slightly longer on one activity and slightly less on another: they are concerned with relatively small tactical adjustments along the margin. The key to the valuative operation is the amount of time or the action which the teacher, personally and subjectively, considers to be a substitute for another use of time or action elsewhere amongst the whole range of his options.

In the past the analysis of this behaviour, of valuation and choice, has frequently been cast in terms of utility-maximisation. But it may be misleading to describe the teacher as a utility-maximiser, because people tend to think then of some pre-defined and objectively ascertainable quantum of satisfaction and, worse still, that this inheres in particular activities and experiences. Actually, the economist nowadays tends to think of utility differently, as an indicator for ranking options according to a person's preferences. Choice behaviour can then be conceived as the chooser's search amongst the available options for that pattern of choices, and that distribution of his resources, which accords most nearly with his preferences.

How can choice behaviour, so conceived, be investigated? On this model a teacher's choice could scarcely be more inaccessible to retrospective investigation. After the decision all kinds of unforeseen factors produce outcomes different from the choice-influencing projections and valuations of the decision-maker. Opting for one course of action irrevocably displaces the next best option. As Buchanan argues, the actual consequences of a decision are not the data of choice and may indeed be a misleading guide to the understanding of that decision. The choice-influencing cost, the anticipated benefits from the rejected option in an either/or choice, remain forever unrealised and inaccessible. At the moment of choice they are merely a prospect in the imagination of the chooser. How can someone other than the chooser, or even the chooser himself at a later time, study the decision and discover the choice-influencing cost?

Clearly, the only mode of investigation is by sympathetic infiltration of the decision-maker's thought, by imaginative reconstruction of the choice set as perceived by the chooser, a procedure very close to historical method as it was conceived by Collingwood. Strictly, the act of choice destroys the data of choice. What's past is dead and gone. All that can be done is to construct a simulacrum, a fictional account resembling the data of choice in some particulars. The test of this simulation, this working diagram of a past choice, is not so much its historical verisimilitude as the extent to which it works in the present, helping us to understand, explain and predict the world of classroom decision-making.

The methods of investigation may draw on various research traditions as long as they help to inform the imagination of the investigator. Taping, commentaries, interrogation, time budgeting can be used alongside the traditional craft of the historian or the experimental psychologist's ability to explore the teacher as an intuitive statistician. The kind of model which has been outlined is suggestive of research topics rather than research techniques. Choice sets and the valuative operations of decision-makers must be the prime targets.

To investigate choice sets is to investigate the properties of choosers as well as the properties of the choice environment. What matters for choice is the chooser's perception of the environment. The choice set is his creation. In the past, teacher personality research seems sometimes to have been marred by concentration on the relationship between teacher variables and educational outcomes, without paying sufficient attention to the environment from which particular behaviours or personality facets were ripped, e.g. the teacher-pupil interaction and the culture of the classrooms. Characteristics and values operate *in loco*, not *in vacuo*. The conventional psychometric approach was always in danger of paying too little attention to the unique subjectivity of individual decision-making and the uniqueness of contextual circumstances, missing the essence of choice in a maze of factors and dimensions. The prime research target is teacher perceptions of the number and character of options composing the choice set, as opposed to the options which exist in the perceptions of other people. A secondary target for investigation is teacher reactions to alterations in these (perceived) choice sets, especially the speed and mode of adjustment to the revised environment of choice.

Following H. A. Simon, what 'approximating' and 'short-cut' devices do teachers use in their valuative operations? Simply because of the high costs of acquiring information, and our limited computing capacity, the rationality of 'bounded rationality', of not trying to achieve complete rationality, has long been accepted. In order to cope with his limited capacities for acquiring and handling information the teacher, like anybody else, constructs a simplified model of the choice situation. Understanding and changing these procedures for coping with his limitations would be likely to alter the teacher's choices. Simon's insistence on the importance of 'satisficing' was based on the observation that in actual decision-making people often seemed to abandon evaluation as soon as they reached the first reasonably satisfactory option. Attention then focuses on the teacher's procedures for (a) searching out options, (b) evaluating them and (c) choosing between them.

By way of illustration, two specific aspects of the chooser's valuative operations may be considered. One aspect is the way in which teachers deal with uncertainty when assessing possible outcomes. Obtaining separate estimates for the probability and the value attributed to an imagined outcome is not easy. But the discovery of systematic biases in teacher estimates of the probability of different outcomes would be significant. The unique and unpredictable characteristics of each choice would not disappear; but this is no reason to ignore those features of human response to the choice environment which are available to investigation in terms of probabilities. The obstacle is the need to shift the investigation from gaming experiments to the far more complex classroom setting (see Shavelson, 1976, pp. 388–91).

A second aspect concerns the way in which teachers cope with multi-faceted valuation, for example of Johnny's prospective learning, that of his immediate neighbours and the whole-class deterrent effect. Consideration of this persistent problem soon leads to the thorny question of the structure of and changes in teacher preferences. Here neoclassical economics is particularly unhelpful because economists have tended to avoid the problem by assuming consistency of taste and preference with the help of a generous *ceteris paribus* clause. Preferences are then fundamental but unexplained data of choice. If they do change, it is in response to variables external to the model. This analytical convenience has enabled bourgeois economists to concentrate on relating choice to changes in price or income rather than preferences changes in price or income being somewhat easier to handle. But in a model of teacher choice, preferences and preference changes can hardly be excluded in this way. Possibly as one heuristic, by analogy with standard neo-Marxist reasoning (see Gintis, 1974), teacher preferences could be regarded as developing in response to variables endogenous to the model: the opportunity costs of perceived options, availabilities of time and goods, the social conventions of classroom and school, all conditioning the learner's as well as the teacher's use of resources. This would be difficult. But at least the model would not be ignoring the problem of socially unacceptable distributions of individual preferences, as neoclassical economics is inclined to do. The distributions are seen to be vital to the understanding of choice. They help to explain the pattern of resource commitment amongst rival choices by tracing the setting of implicit prices on options to that process of comparative valuation of options which (for a given state of information) fixes the opportunity costs of choice.

To develop a model of the kind which is sketched in this paper, through social scientific research, is extremely difficult as long as social science tries to model itself on the natural sciences. The model emphasises the particularity of each choice. To stress the subjectivity of choice, within a particular context of time and place, inhibits the production of general propositions. But it is the attention of the model to the unique circumstances of each choice which may help it to account for differences in teacher choices, and that would be worth a little methodological deviationism.

Such a model does not assume that the teacher actually employs so rational a calculus, not even a 'bounded rationality'. It merely lays over observed choice behaviour a transparency upon which is etched a pattern of choice behaviour implied by the model. Shavelson has shown how the statistical models of decision theory can be used as heuristic for examining teachers' decision-making. This very different model is, on the face of it, at least as suitable for analysing classroom choices. Negatively, its value depends on its ability to spread doubt and caution by undermining confidence in some of the other models. Positively, its value depends on its capacity to influence research programmes and teacher-training strategies. Explanation is attempted in terms of a microeconomic model to see whether the resulting account improves in any way on rival accounts and is suggestive of new research emphases, likely targets and ways of testing the implications of the theory for consistency with observed behaviour.

Perhaps the most critical distinguishing feature of this kind of model is that it does not share the fundamental determinism of the conventional choice models of neoclassical economics and of statistical decision theory. Shackle and Buchanan, in particular, have emphasised the tendency in economic models of rational choice towards a model of man as an automaton. Traditional economic man and the decision theorists' maximiser of subjective expected utility are rationalists who are not really choosers at all. Both are programmed to select predictably in response to stimuli from the environment of choice. For them no real alternative exists, so no real choice is possible. At first sight the conventional economic model may seem to deal with preference and choice. But, as Keirstead (1972) points out, choice is more or less eliminated by means of simplifying or excluding assumptions which cut away 'the distinguishing human attributes of individuality and imagination' (p. 162).

By contrast this model emphasises the uniqueness and voluntary character of choice. However fleeting and habit-ridden the teacher's estimate of the unknown future, the decision about Johnny's singing changes the future and the same teacher will never envisage the same future. The teacher is not 'an engine that moves in predestinate grooves'. Non-divisibility and non-seriability are characteristics of many of his classroom decisions. Such choices are not amenable even to the actuarial approach through probability. For convenience, the uncertainty variable used up to this point has been the traditional one of probability. But it may well be that Shackle's critique of the notion of probability in similar circumstances requires a different kind of uncertainty variable, either his 'potential surprise' or some other (1961, p. 60).

The philosophical difference is the most important distinction between this kind of model and its well-known economic and statistical rivals. In its present form, and even more so if it were to be developed along lines derived from Shackle's work, it rejects cause and effect analysis in the form so familiar in the physical sciences. Shackle holds that the economist 'often pretends to discuss choice', meaning thereby 'the determinate response of men with given desires to their assumedly fully-known circumstances'. His anti-determinist stance is as appropriate to the crude model of this paper as it is to his own sophisticated conception of human choice. He espouses

a view of human affairs which some of you will dismiss as an extreme of subjectivism entirely abhorrent to the scientific outlook. Science searches for cause and effect. Cause and effect are indispensible to my argument, but only subject to the exemption of thought itself. Let the statistician interpret me as meaning that thought is random, let the poet understand me as saying that thought can be inspired (Shackle, 1976, p. 22).

Chapter 7

Towards a political economy of decision-making in the classroom

Paul Bellaby

In this paper, I wish to explore the possibility of analysing at least some secondary school classrooms in the terms of Marxist political economy. This is not the first essay of its kind.[1] However, it has two claims to some novelty. First, it seeks to ground generalisations about the links between schooling and capitalist society in a detailed analysis of classroom regimes, extracting the 'macro' from the 'micro', and leaving much of the micro intact at its own level. To work in reverse, thus subsuming micro-processes under broad structural generalisations which lack clear concrete reference, is, it seems to me, a characteristic weakness of Marxist analysis of education.[2] Second, the paper focuses upon decision-making by teachers, and seeks to show why school classrooms are as they are, and possibilities for alternative action.

There is, however, an important preliminary exercise. The two weekend symposia that gave rise to the present collection of papers revealed not only the expected divergence of perspectives between disciplines and within disciplines more or less faithfully reflected here, but also much uncertainty as to what 'decision-making' might mean. This is a problem which must be addressed before concrete analysis can begin.[3]

'Objectivist' versus 'subjectivist' concepts of decision-making

Decisions are nothing if not choices. We cannot choose unless alternatives are open to us, and we are aware of them.

The phrase 'decision-making' implies these and more besides. The other, highly contentious element is 'rationality'. In its most restricted, and therefore most rigorous sense, a decision is 'rational' when the

93

outcome of that decision meets the actor's goal and does so at least cost. Here rationality is defined objectively. The outcome intended by the actor can only follow his decision if the structure of the system to which his thinking is directed permits it. The most careful and pro-longed cogitation will fail to start your car if it leads you to turn on the windscreen wipers by pressing the wrong button. The same applies when the system that is the object of decision-making is social rather than mechanical.

There is, of course, a radical alternative to this objective approach to rationality in decision-making. It is to ask *how* decisions are made. Now rationality becomes a property of a subjective course of action, if in-deed the term is retained at all. Within this frame of reference it be-comes relevant to ask whether the actor knows all that is involved in his decision. If, and only if, the actor has *perfect* foreknowledge of the consequences of taking each of the alternatives to hand, his action can be 'rational' in the objectivist *and* this subjectivist sense simultaneously.

In practice, the actor seldom has perfect foreknowledge. Without it, there is a greater or lesser element of risk in each alternative facing him. Attempts to understand the ways in which actors cope with risk (or uncertainty) reveal a divergence among those who take the subjectivist approach. On the one hand is the argument that it is the task of a science of decision-making to explain and/or predict particular decisions under given conditions. This task can be fulfilled if it is assumed that actors have probability distributions in mind, representing their assess-ment of the uncertainty within each alternative. This view is rejected, on the other hand, by the argument that the human sciences cannot predict, and can explain only by 'understanding' action *in the actor's own terms*. It is easy to demonstrate that everyday actors do not build models incorporating probability distributions when they make deci-sions. One reason is that they often act under pressure of time.

The latter position, which we may call 'humanist', must either reject the term 'rationality' or accept *all* action as in some sense 'rational' in the actor's own terms (which may of course be those of his culture or subculture). From this point of view, the rhetoric of 'decision-making' is irrelevant, and may mislead the analyst into a scientistic account of human action. There is not space to argue against this humanist version of social science and psychology, but the reader must accept that it is ruled out in what follows.[4]

Instead I propose to develop the *objectivist* approach to decision-making in specific ways, and with decision-making in the classroom at the forefront of my mind. My central focus is what I shall call the 'dilemma'.

The dilemma poses further difficulties for a subjectivist *science* of decision-making. It is obviously easier to handle the way an actor makes a decision if all he must choose is the means appropriate to and efficient for a single goal. In practice, however, whether he wills them or someone else does, the actor often faces two or more goals, in greater or lesser conflict with each other. The course of action he chooses either discounts some goal(s) or seeks a compromise between two or more. The specific difficulty this poses for a science of how individuals make decisions is that actors cannot always achieve complete success (or 'maximise') in two or more different directions at once. This is more fundamental than the problem posed by uncertainty where one goal is followed, because so long as the most probable way to success can be found, an actor can be construed as seeking to maximise attainment of his goal. However, where there are several conflicting goals, the actor may have to be satisfied with something considerably less than 'maximising' in each direction: in Simon's terms, he must 'satisfice'.[5]

This pessimistic conclusion originates in the subjectivist premises of the argument. If decision-making is theorised in objective terms, a very different set of possibilities for a science of decision-making, and indeed for social action in general, will emerge.

In the objectivist view, rationality is the conjunction between an actor's intention and the structure of the system—mechanical, social or otherwise—upon which he seeks to act: in short a decision is rational if it pays off. Let us suppose now that in social systems, unlike the mechanical, there are *contradictory* processes. If so, from an individual viewpoint, it is not possible to have a rational intention: nothing one does can pay off in the final analysis, for in following one's immediate interests, one may be undermining one's position in the long term. The only rational action is that which removes the contradictions.

Now we can conceive of social institutions and ideologies as collective solutions for underlying contradictions in the societies from which they arise: from collective bargaining for the contradiction between labour and capital, to belief in an afterlife for the contradiction between life and death. Once such solutions have emerged, individuals have a framework within which there are orderly consequences to actions, and so in which they may behave rationally. However, these collective solutions arise out of the contradictions, and persist precisely because the contradictions remain. We cannot call them 'rational', even though we can find the *logic* of their origins and persistence. From the standpoint of society, rationality remains what is was for individuals 'prior to' the emergence of institutions and ideology, namely the removal of its underlying contradictions.[6]

Of course this 'objectivist' analysis of decision-making presents its own problems. The most crucial is how any action can be taken which is rational from the standpoint of society and *ipso facto* non-rational for individuals. There appear to be two answers to this, though the first is of doubtful consistency. The doubtful one is to appeal through 'criticism' of existing social institutions and ideology to a general audience, or perhaps more specifically to fellow intellectuals, revealing to them the fundamental irrationality of social arrangements. This method was followed to some degree by most members of the Frankfurt School and survives in the influential work of Habermas.[7] The inconsistency in it is that the critique demonstrates only the basis for further criticism, not a rational praxis—a strategy for changing society. A more satisfactory answer is that attempted by Marx which was to point to the class(es) upon whom the contradictions of society were focused, whose collective interests were themselves most in contradiction with social institutions and ideology and aligned with destruction of these, and of course elimination of the contradictions themselves. In acting alongside this class, the critic of society might shape the praxis which would change it.[8]

Having thus begun to sketch the profound connections between a concern with 'decision-making' and the analysis of society offered by classical and modern Marxist political economy, I can turn to the specifics of *classroom* decision-making.

Classroom regimes in three schools[9]

The three schools I shall discuss were in the same new town. None started as a comprehensive, but all had been 'comprehensives' (at least in intake) for five years when they were studied. They were purpose built as bilateral schools, each predominantly 'modern', but each with a selective stream which was either 'grammar' or 'technical'. Castle Town was for some years the only school in the town with a grammar stream. Hinsley Mill was opened as the complementary technical/modern school to Castle Town. It served an area of the town and the part of the surrounding countryside that, while not principally middle class, yet had more middle class families than the area served by Cross Street. Cross Street teachers saw their school as a Cinderella. They were inclined to exaggerate its lack of 'high ability' intake.

Hinsley Mill school had built a reputation in the town by competing with Castle Town—the 'grammar school'—on nearly equal terms, acquiring even open awards at Oxbridge. The school's tactics for catching up with Castle Town included an extremely flexible streaming procedure, a sort of League Table, in which teams could be demoted or promoted even in mid season. In both Castle Town and Hinsley Mill students were streamed at entry on the basis of VRQ scores; but the likelihood of being moved from your original stream was about 1 in 3 at Hinsley Mill compared with 1 in 5 at Castle Town. Castle Town school also kept its top stream relatively discrete from others. After the first year or so it was left with its then membership, and these students were expressed to O-level GCE in four years instead of the usual five for the second and part of the third stream who were entered for the same examination. This difference between Hinsley Mill and Castle Town is the initial basis for assigning the schools to Young's achievement streaming and ability streaming types respectively.[10] Coupled with their different streaming practices were different approaches to discipline. Hinsley Mill was by far the more 'well-ordered' out of class, an impression one can document and which was supported by the education officer and the HMIs.

Cross Street school resembled Hinsley Mill in its streaming practices. It arrived at them by a similar invidious comparison between its own status and that of other schools in the town. The essence of achievement streaming is the desire of staff to exploit the limited talent they feel is available in their school, by inducing *competition* and maintaining critical pressure upon students who seem likely to succeed. However, the head of Cross Street (and the vertical clique associated with him) rejected repressive discipline on principle. He could not prevent it in the classroom, but he inhibited the formation of so effective a collective regime of repression as existed both in and out of class at Hinsley Mill, actively encouraged by the head.

What follows is a detailed but formal analysis of patterns of interaction between teachers and third-year pupils in class in the three comprehensive schools. I concentrated on the same two streams in each school—the top and the fifth of seven streams in each school—and followed them from lesson to lesson for a week. One has to look for something specific, since lessons are too complex for one person to record in their entirety. I focused on verbal exchanges between teachers and pupils, chiefly 'across the classroom', because I could not hear what pupils said to each other or teachers said to pupils over their shoulders.[11] This meant that my observations of 'formal' lessons were often more 'complete' than those of lessons of art, handicrafts and games. Of these formal or classroom lessons, six groups concerned subjects that both streams in the three schools shared. I have singled out English, history, mathematics and geography for special attention, leaving religious instruction and music on one side, since some forms had only one period for these. I have done a qualitative analysis of the lessons I observed, but there is not the space to present it in this paper.[12] The aim of my analysis here is to show whether teachers consistently handled the two streams in different ways and got different responses from them. It is also to see if the schools varied.

The tables analyse the patterns taken by these lessons. Only the regular teachers are included, for now and then students or 'caretaker' teachers stepped in for the regular teacher, and usually handled the form rather differently. The tables are in four parts, Tables 7.1 to 7.4. In Tables 7.1 and 7.2 each regular teacher's lessons are shown. The three left hand columns add up to 100 per cent in most cases, and fail to do so only where there were remarks that could not be classified.

TABLE 7.1. Analysis of verbal exchanges between teachers and pupils in a series of lessons involving four subjects that the first and fifth streams both studied : (a) English and history.

Subject, Stream, School			Form of Exchange						Ratios			No. codes (lessons)
		Teacher Directive	Encouraging	Pupils unslctd	Total %	to: Indls	Class	Rebukes	Dir./Enc.	Reb./Enc.	Indl/Class	
English	1st	Cr St	66.1	10.2	23.7	100.0%	39.0	37.3	27.1	6.48	2.66	1.05	59 (2)
		Cs Tn	34.5	51.0	14.4	99.9%	22.2	63.3	8.9	0.68	0.17	0.35	90 (4)
		Hy Ml	75.0	18.0	6.8	99.8%	54.6	38.4	36.2	4.17	2.01	1.42	115 (4)
	5th	Cr St	56.6	23.3	20.2	100.1%	34.8	45.1	34.1	2.43	1.46	0.77	129 (5)
		Cs Tn	59.6	32.6	7.8	100.0%	53.2	39.0	10.7	1.83	0.33	1.36	141 (5)
		Hy Ml	70.2	15.8	14.0	100.0%	28.1	57.9	24.6	4.44	1.56	0.49	57 (3)
History	1st	Cr St	71.9	17.5	10.5	99.9%	15.8	73.7	15.8	4.12	0.90	0.21	57 (2)
		Cs Tn	52.6	31.6	15.8	100.0%	18.4	65.8	15.8	1.66	0.50	0.28	38 (2)
		Hy Ml	69.4	22.2	8.3	99.9%	41.7	50.0	33.3	3.13	1.50	0.83	36 (2)
	5th	Cr St	60.7	13.1	26.3	100.1%	32.2	41.7	42.9	4.63	3.27	0.77	84 (3)
		Cs Tn	(63.4)	(16.9)	16.8	97.1%[a]	40.8	42.6	12.7	3.75	0.75	0.96	71 (2)
		Hy Ml	88.9	0.0	11.2	100.1%	33.4	55.5	38.9	b	b	0.60	36 (1)

[a] In these cases a small number of questions from teachers were unclassed.
[b] The values of the ratios are here 'infinity', because of no 'Encouraging' codes.

TABLE 7.2 Analysis of verbal exchange between teachers and pupils: (b) maths and geography

Subject, Stream, School		Teacher Directive	Encouraging	Pupils unslctd	Total %	to: Indls	Class	Rebukes	Ratios Dir./Enc.	Reb./Enc.	Indl/Class	No. codes (lessons)
Maths	1st	Cr St	76.2	6.5	17.3	100.0%	18.4	64.3	17.2	11.72	2.65	0.29	93 (3)
		Cs Tn	46.1	35.2	18.8	100.1%	12.6	68.7	16.4	1.31	0.47	0.18	125 (4)
		Hy Ml	61.7	20.2	18.1	100.0%	25.5	56.4	31.9	3.05	1.58	0.45	94 (3)[c]
	5th	Cr St	55.9	37.5	6.5	99.9%	48.4	45.0	9.8	1.49	0.26	1.08	184 (5)
		Cs Tn	77.3	18.2	4.6	100.1%	50.0	45.5	40.9	4.25	2.25	1.10	22 (1)
		Hy Ml	72.6	2.5	25.0	100.1%	18.4	56.7	15.9	29.04	6.36	0.32	120 (4)
Geography	1st	Cr St	(25.0)	(17.9)	28.6	71.5%[a]	7.1	64.3	8.9	1.40	0.50	0.11	56 (2)
		Cs Tn	66.7	15.2	18.2	100.1%	6.1	75.7	9.1	4.39	0.60	0.08	33 (1)
		Hy Ml	(70.5)	(8.2)	18.0	96.7%[a]	21.3	60.7	18.0	8.60	2.20	0.35	61 (2)
	5th	Cr St	73.0	4.5	22.5	100.0%	19.1	58.4	22.5	16.22	5.00	0.33	89 (3)
		Cs Tn	76.5	1.5	22.1	100.1%	10.3	66.2	19.1	51.00	12.73	0.16	68 (3)
		Hy Ml	73.0	0.0	27.0	100.0%	37.8	35.1	37.8	b	b	1.08	37 (3)

[a] In these cases a small number of questions from teachers were unclassed.
[b] The values of these ratios are here 'infinity', because of no 'Encouraging' codes.
[c] These three lessons at Hinsley Mill were in 'sets', but the sets coded were predominantly top stream pupils.

Two columns show exchanges where the teacher took the initiative. The other presents the pupils' initiatives, which normally involved a question or request to the teacher. Of course pupils often initiated an exchange with the teacher unwittingly, by doing something the teacher disapproved of; but these are not included in the 'pupils unsolicited' category, for here the initiative belongs with the teacher. 'Directive' versus 'encouraging' is a relative distinction. The teacher 'encourages' by making an instruction permissive rather than mandatory ('Will someone open the windows?' rather than 'Smith, open the windows will you'); by following a 'Socratic' line of enquiry in which the pupil helps solve the problem, rather than expecting 'right' or 'wrong' answers on matters of fact; and by praising someone for good work or effort rather than criticising when he fails or is badly behaved. In the middle columns of Tables 7.1 and 7.2 are the proportions of the teachers' initiatives which were directed at individuals and at the class; and the percentage of all his remarks that were rebukes of one kind or another, to individuals or the class as a whole. Finally, in the right hand set of columns are some summary measures of the teachers' handling of their lessons: the ratio of directive to encouraging remarks; of rebukes to encouragement; and of remarks addressed to individuals and to the class. Table 7.3 aggregates the four academic subjects the forms shared in common, giving the same measures. It is convenient to start with a discussion of this overall picture.

Several things emerge from Table 7.3. There are overall differences between schools, and there are variations between streams in each school. Let us take the top stream first. If Cross Street and Hinsley Mill practise 'achievement' streaming as I have suggested, we can also expect teachers there to put more pressure on their most talented pupils than do staff at Castle Town. This should come out in the form of more rebukes and less encouragement. Teachers should be more directive than in the less pressured school. The table bears this out. Hinsley Mill seems to have the highest rate of rebukes, whether we look at in in terms of the percentage of teachers' remarks which censure the class or some individual, or at the ratio of rebukes to encouragement. This may be one reason why fewer exchanges in its lessons are initiated by pupils. Several teachers there marvelled at how quiet and modest the form was. Table 7.3 suggests that Hinsley Mill teachers are more likely to address themselves to individuals in the form. If we rank each of the top stream's subject teachers by the various ratios, we find a slight positive correlation between 'Indl/Cls' and 'Reb/Enc' (Kendall's $\tau = +0.20$) and a better positive correlation between Dir/Enc and Reb/Enc ($\tau = +0.51$). In other words it seems that being directive goes along with being critical, and if a teacher is critical of the top stream it is frequently the case that he picks on individuals when he addresses the form. Castle Town teachers rank lowest on Reb/Enc and Indl/Cls, while Hinsley

Mill teachers rank highest. In Cross Street there is a one-to-one correspondence between being critical and 'picking on' individuals. This and the picture for Hinsley Mill add weight to the view that these schools put more pressure on their top streams in day-to-day encounters than Castle Town. In only geography is Castle Town more directive and critical of pupils than another school—here Cross Street has a slight edge.

TABLE 7.3   Analysis of verbal exchanges between teachers and pupils: lessons aggregated and broken down only by school and stream

		Stream and School					
		First stream			Fifth stream		
Form of exchange		Cr St	Cs Tn	Hy Ml	Cr St	Cs Tn	Hy Ml
Directive		62.3	45.8	69.3	60.1	62.3	74.4
Encouraging		12.1	37.1	16.3	23.5	24.2	4.8
Pupils unsolicited		19.6	17.1	13.7	16.5	12.9	20.8
Total %		94.0[a]	100.0	99.3[a]	100.1	99.4[a]	100.0
Teacher to:	Indls	19.3	15.4	37.9	36.6	39.1	25.2
	Class	61.1	67.5	48.4	46.9	47.7	54.0
Rebukes to:	Indls	12.8	7.7	17.7	15.0	7.6	15.6
	Class	4.5	5.2	13.4	9.3	7.6	8.8
	All reb.	17.4	12.9	31.1	24.3	15.2	24.4
Ratios	Dir/enc	5.15	1.23	4.25	2.56	2.57	15.50
	Reb/enc	1.44	0.35	1.91	1.03	0.63	4.75
	Indl/cls	0.32	0.23	0.78	0.78	0.82	0.47
Total number codes		265	286	306	486	302	250
Total lessons		(9)	(11)	(11)	(16)	(11)	(11)

[a] In these cases a small number of questions from teachers were unclassed.

Table 7.4 gives an approximate breakdown of lesson time into different types of task. For the first stream, the outstanding feature is that Cross Street pupils spent so much time doing exercises by themselves, and taking part in what amounted to verbal quizzes around the class. Surprisingly, Hinsley Mill's time is no more used up in such competitive activities than Castle Town's. Indeed, a large portion was given over to 'group work'. This was due to the English teacher who said she wanted to keep the head's influence at bay. She saw it as a mission to 'bring out' the first stream by giving them drama work, getting them to give their own lectures to each other and the like. It seems she may be the exception that proves the rule. We may also note that Castle Town pupils were more often engaged in open dialogue in class by teachers.

TABLE 7.4   Amount of lesson time spent in various activities while these four subjects were taught, broken down by school and stream

| | Stream and School | | | | | |
| | First stream | | | Fifth stream | | |
Type of activity	Cr St	Cs Tn	Hy Ml	Cr St	Cs Tn	Hy Ml
Class as a whole						
Listen to T	3.0	35.0	30.6	20.0	12.1	6.1
Involved in set						
verbal tasks	21.0	7.9	4.8	6.4	34.4	2.5
Involved in 'open'						
dialogue	10.7	24.5	10.5	41.3	14.5	12.6
Class working						
in groups	8.0	0.0	29.9	0.0	0.0	9.1
Indl work in class						
Copying	0.0	1.5	4.6	9.5	1.1	34.3
Reading	15.4	2.6	1.4	0.0	1.4	2.5
Exercises,						
note-making etc.	42.0	28.5	18.3	22.8	36.6	32.8
Total %	100.1	100.0	100.1	100.0	100.1	99.9
Minutes	338	457	438	514	366	396
(Lessons)	(9)	(11)	(11)	(16)	(11)	(11)

We should now turn to the fifth stream. At Hinsley Mill and Castle Town the fifth is more directed, less encouraged and more rebuked than the top stream, as Table 7.3 shows. Table 7.4 reveals that teachers there are more likely to give the fifth exercises to work on individually than the top stream; at Hinsley Mill they appear to do a great deal of copying of notes, maps and diagrams, while at Castle Town, they are much more often orally quizzed in lessons than the top stream. All the measures that are also given for the individual subjects (Tables 7.1 and 7.2) show a high degree of consistency from subject to subject. Teachers at Hinsley Mill and Castle Town are sterner with the fifth than the top stream. However, by and large the pattern is reversed at Cross Street. This may have more to do with many Cross Street teachers' extreme difficulties in controlling the fifth stream than these statistics could indicate. In fact the rate of rebukes per period is higher for the fifth than the top stream. Cross Street teachers' punitive behaviour to the fifth seems less of a strategy for *maintaining* control, than a rearguard action to stem disorder, by shouting the class down.

The result of this peculiarity about the Cross Street figures for the fifth stream is that the difference we expected between the permissiveness of Castle Town and the directiveness of Cross Street emerges in only one respect—Cross Street's high proportion of rebukes. Hinsley Mill teachers are plainly much more directive, less encouraging and more censorious towards the fifth stream than Castle Town's. These results are perfectly consistent from subject to subject.

In spite of the relationship we found for the top stream, Hinsley Mill teachers are *less* not more likely to address themselves to individuals in the class. If we rank each teacher by his ratio scores as we did for the top streams, we find a yet stronger, indeed near perfect correlation between Dir/Enc and Reb/Enc—being bossy towards the fifth stream is hectoring them as well ($r = +0.97$). But instead of a positive correlation between talking to individuals and being directive and critical, we find a *negative* relationship. τ is -0.26 between Reb/Enc and Indl/Class, and this *rises* to -0.36 when rebukes are taken out of the tally of remarks addressed to individuals and class. In other words, it would seem that when teachers make remarks to individuals rather than the class in the fifth stream it is more often because they are encouraging in their general treatment of the form than because they are critical. This is the reverse of the situation with the top streams.

Once again this suggests that different regimes are adopted with top and bottom streams. 'Formal' teachers put pressure on individuals in the top stream and regiment the class impersonally when taking the fifth stream. 'Informal' teachers personalise their treatment of the fifth, but, taking off the pressure on the top, let individuals merge into the mass. The key to the difference between streams is that the top is expected to be highly motivated and competitive; the fifth is expected to be the reverse.

Turning back to Tables 7.1 and 7.2 where the different subject lessons in the three schools are shown individually, we should note that there is sufficient consistency from subject to subject within a school to suggest that there is pattern that overrides such contingencies as the teachers' personality, the timing of the lessons and its physical setting, even though those undoubtedly *are* important. Differences between the schools could still be attributed to the period during the Spring term when each was observed. However, no form was observed in the early or late weeks of the terms, and observations were staggered by school and form in an effort to randomise the remaining influence of time during term. All this suggests that these tables show regular differences between schools that are to be found in several lessons for each form.

In summary, we can draw three conclusions from this micro-analysis. First, there are plainly differences between schools, and differences within schools in the treatment of streams, that override the expected idiosyncrasies of individual teachers. This strongly suggests that there is institutionalisation in the streaming system and from school to school of the everyday decisions that teachers take in handling classes. That these institutions may be informal rather than formal is clear in the divergence of classroom regimes at Cross Street from the progressive, positive approach to social control favoured by the head and embodied in a number of policy statements and formal practices.

Second, there appears to be a link between decisions teachers take every day in class and at least two out-of-class collective practices. One is the keeping of order between lessons, during breaks and lunch-hour and in assemblies, which distinguishes Hinsley Mill from the other schools. The other is the frequent promotion and demotion of pupils between streams which characterises Cross Street as well as Hinsley Mill, and sets both apart from Castle Town. The latter keys in with the different ways in which the schools treat the top stream. More pressure is brought to bear on individual pupils in Hinsley Mill and Cross Street: in short the atmosphere is more competitive. Hinsley Mill with its sterner and more consistent policy of discipline outside lessons seems to furnish the counterpart of this in treatment of the fifth stream: there this form is regimented. Quite the contrary at Castle Town, the top stream is treated *en masse*, while teachers pay more attention to individuals in the fifth, generally in an encouraging vein. At Cross Street, teachers are forced by the disorder they find into shouting down the fifth stream.

If a school, like Hinsley Mill and Cross Street through their policy of promotions and demotions and pressure on individuals in the top stream, seeks to 'motivate' its pupils, it must change their out-of-school identities while they are in school. In short, there must be considerable tension between the world of school and the world outside.[13] One way of achieving this, if not the only way, is by regimenting everyone in the classroom and outside it. On the basis of this regimentation, 'promising' individuals can be given a more privileged status (or promotions) and made sensitive to personal criticism by teachers. Those who are *not* promising are merely regimented. This is the position at Hinsley Mill. Cross Street is a less successful school academically. Here both pressures on promising individuals and containment of the remainder seems to fall on the shoulders of the class teachers, without forming a coherent and non-contradictory school policy.

Castle Town teachers appear to take the motivation of their top stream pupils for granted. Indeed they are singled out almost from entry to the school, given a distinctively academic syllabus and expressed uniformly to O-level GCE in four years. So much confidence is felt in their ability to progress with guidance but without pressure, that Castle Town's experienced and qualified staff are distributed evenly over all streams, high and low, and in several instances, new staff are given the top stream. Exactly the contrary policy is followed by heads of department at Hinsley Mill and Cross Street, most of whom teach the top stream themselves, leaving the fifth stream to more junior teachers, quite a number of whom are part-time staff. In complementary fashion, Castle Town takes a *laissez-faire* policy on discipline, and—though in some cases with reluctance—staff tend to underline this in their lessons. The fifth stream is not regimented, and except for the odd lesson is not shouted down either: rather teachers often address individual pupils in personal and 'encouraging' terms.

The third conclusion we can draw is that resistance to the regimentation and punitive regimes imposed by teachers, specifically at Hinsley Mill and Cross Street, comes from the fifth more than from the top streams. To amplify this would require details of pupils' attitudes to authority and their self-reports of 'misbehaviour'. I have not space to give these, but the reader can find the details in print elsewhere.[14] Now the class of origin of pupils in stream five is far more often manual than that of pupils in stream one. This undoubtedly contributes to the fact that these pupils are in the fifth stream. Beyond that we should note that stream itself is a more direct and parsimonious explanation of not only attitudes to authority and reported misbehaviour, but also of orientations to the future and the part that school might play in them. Thus fifth streamers at all three schools say they expect to get manual jobs (by and large if male) and routine clerical work or jobs as shop assistants (if female), and that they will leave school as soon as legally possible. At Cross Street and Hinsley Mill these 'Leavers' are almost uniformly more disaffected and deviant than those in the top stream. At Castle Town, the differences are in no way so pronounced, except that pupils in the lower streams absent themselves far more often than the 'Ambitious' pupils in the top stream. The top stream pupils in all three schools say they expect to get professional, technical or sometimes managerial jobs, even when they do not have a particular career in mind, and that they will stay at school probably to enter the sixth form. Friendships tend to form within streams, and even more directly in relation to pupils' plans for the future. They do not reflect class of origin with anything like that consistency. Thus we can argue that resistance to 'oppression' at school (in Cross Street and Hinsley Mill) comes from those whose *future expected* class is manual or lower non-manual; while broad acceptance comes from those whose future expected class is upper non-manual. This assigns the class base of attitudes to school more accurately than the class into which pupils were born, but does not make resistance and acceptance any less a class phenomenon.[15]

Towards a macro analysis of classroom regimes

For the sake of clear exposition, I must now stand off from these data and discuss the elements of a political economy of mass education under capitalism that should throw further light on much of what is happening in the top and fifth stream third year classes of these three comprehensive schools.

According to the structuralist-marxism expounded by Althusser, at least before *Essays in Self-Criticism*,[16] schooling functions within capitalism to reproduce labour power and to reproduce the social relations of production. In reproducing labour power, the school resembles the capital goods industry. It replaces the stock of labour power consumed by the passage of succeeding generations through the labour process. In reproducing the social relations of production, the school socialises the pupil into the roles he is likely to play at work, having selected him for this role or that according to personality or social characteristics, and also secures his commitment to the production system as a whole. We may call the first the school's *economic* function, and the second the school's *ideological* function. According to this argument the school fulfils both its functions by *ideology*, rather than by repression. Its relation to capitalism *per se* identifies it as an apparatus of the capitalist state—an ideological state apparatus.

I want to criticise this argument on two levels. First, it tends to overstress the structural integration of the system, at the expense of sufficient attention to the contradictions within it from which change may arise. Second, the 'state' *qua* government apparatus is reduced to the role of mediator between capital and the school; its relative autonomy from capital is not acknowledged and the specific effects of state intervention in schooling are not singled out.

We may start to unravel the contradictions of capitalism with which schooling is implicated by pointing to what Mao has called the 'principal contradiction' of capitalism: between the developing forces of production and the dominant relations of production.[17] Schooling can contribute to the *reproduction* of these social relations, but it must presumably do more than 'reproduce' labour power. Indeed it must transform the distribution of skills in the labour force and the content of particular skills. It must do this even if it only reacts to changes in the labour process brought about by capital accumulation; should it in any way *promote* economic growth, then 'transformation' is a yet more suitable word than 'reproduction'. In this distinction between the reproduction of social relations and the transformation of labour power, we can recognise the antithesis between two perspectives in the sociology of education. The first views education as the transmission of culture. The second sees it as the selection of the gifted, their training and their allocation to occupations. The first sees the process as integrative; the second sees it as a process of differentiation. I am simply suggesting that both perspectives are necessary, because they each draw attention to educational processes, but processes that are in contradiction.[18] Their contradiction is a 'refraction' at this level of the principal contradiction within capitalism.

The contradiction between these two processes is the first, usually submerged, point I wish to make. The second point is that neither process is in the nature of schooling itself: indeed schooling takes shape under constraints specific to those societies of which it is a part, and the intervention of public bureaucracy is one such specific constraint in modern capitalism, which makes the reproduction of relations of production and the transformation of labour power efficient pressures on our schools.

In modern capitalism the school is constituted by the principles of rational-legal authority embedded in bureaucracy. It is formally open to all classes, both sexes, all creeds and all races and on equal terms to all. It is true, of course, that class, sex and race inequalities are manifested in the personal careers of pupils. It is true also that pupils emerge from school unequal. Yet some safeguards against inequality of *opportunity* to classes, sexes and races are given by compulsory attendance, as by open entry or else formal criteria of selection for progress up the educational ladder. Furthermore, equality of opportunity is an expectation attached to schooling by the intervention of the state. It is a sufficiently pervasive expectation to promote broad acceptance of education as a means of personal social mobility, or even collective mobility on the part of 'professions', and to render 'discrimination' and 'disadvantage' alike key terms in criticism of the school system.

State intervention militates against, though it does not prevent, the reproduction in school of the divisions among people in the locality served by the school. It is true that central control of the curriculum and organisation of teaching is unusual rather than the rule among capitalist countries. In England school teachers, or perhaps more precisely their heads, have considerable formal autonomy. But professionalism among teachers plays a similar part to central control, in so far as it leads to extensive standardisation of the 'core curriculum', some fundamental similarities in school organisation and even family resemblances among teaching methods, at least within each of the main sectors of education—primary, secondary, further and higher. Standardisation in schooling makes it difficult for parents and local notables to influence the content of the curriculum and how children are taught.

The underlying tendency here is to offset the uneven development of localities within each national economy, and indeed, worldwide, to offset the underdevelopment of *most* national economies relative to the 'advanced' countries. Education spreads outward from the metropolis. The sons of peasants are taught not the traditional methods of cultivation, but often those perfected in the metropolitan countries; if they are members of an advanced country, like France, they are trained in the means to leave the land for industry. In a similar fashion, contradictions not only of town and country, but also of dominant and

107

minority racial or ethnic groups, of boys and girls and of local petty bourgeoisie and local workers, are, in appearance and to a degree in truth, negated.

This negation is in the name of equality of opportunity, but its functions are for capital-in-general and in the longer term. First the pool of employable labour is expanded. Second, the rudiments of a division of labour within capitalist employment is established by sorting pupils into different types of school, different tracks or different streams: this division of labour is hierarchical, that is it recognises degrees of super- and sub-ordination.

From one point of view, the successful fulfilment of these functions is equivalent to integrating children with the *dominant* relations of production. However, it should be noted that even this 'reproduction' may be set at odds with local pressures on the school. It is not equivalent to reproducing in the school distinctions of race, sex, rural and urban or even class, in its peculiarly local forms. In practice the disjunction between the divisions fed into the school and those produced by it at the end will depend on the circumstances in which the school is found: within England it will be greater in a small town in a rural area, in a decaying industrial town, and in a run-down inner city area, than in new suburbs or new towns.

The successful outcome from the standpoint of the reproduction of relations of production is the acceptance by pupils of the principle of wage-employment, acceptance of a division at the least between mental and manual labour, and the allocation of the right personalities with the right attitudes to the various strata in school that prefigure the division of labour.

The transformation of labour power is the other process I have identified in capitalist education. This process differentiates between individuals, not in the sense of allocating them to social roles within an embryonic division of labour, but by training them in skills, and—more important—motivating them to acquire such skills for eventual personal gain. The field open for employment is seen as an 'opportunity structure'. Individuals are set on their careers by inducing competition among them in the classroom (and probably also at home) when they are young. According to Bronfenbrenner's comparative study of the USSR and USA, this is strikingly distinctive of classrooms in the West.[19] In separating those with promise and willingness to work from others, whether by streaming, tracking or simply different work-cards in a mixed ability class, schools may engender what we may call a 'consciousness of *future* class', and provide the structural bases for antagonism between groups of pupils and between rejected pupils and teachers. All these consequences flow from the attempted transformation of labour power by the school, its *economic* function. They are inimical to its ideological function.

The political economy of decision-making by teachers in Castle Town, Cross Street, and Hinsley Mill schools

The three parts of this paper—the development of an 'objectivist' approach to decision-making, the micro-analysis of classroom regimes in three schools, and the macro-analysis of education under the state in modern capitalism—can now be drawn together. I shall summarise the links I am trying to make in four propositions, all of which can be supported with evidence from the schools study, though in varying depth.

Proposition One

In all three schools there is commitment to 'equality of opportunity': this corresponds to the rational-legal constitution of schooling under the state in modern capitalism.

Proposition Two

The schools offer different ways of realising 'equality of opportunity': ability streaming, as at Castle Town, and achievement streaming, which is most consistently exemplified at Hinsley Mill. These are institution-alised solutions to a dilemma posed for the secondary school by its two, contradictory functions of reproducing social relations of production and transforming labour power. Ability streaming is adapted to the ideological function, achievement streaming to the economic, each to some extent to the neglect of the other function.

Proposition Three

Within achievement streaming, there arise antagonisms between tea-chers and 'rejected' pupils: the alignment among pupils corresponds to consciousness of *future* class, rather than to class of origin or sex (there were no Blacks in the schools).

Proposition Four

Within ability streaming, while these antagonisms are absent (or, more correctly, at Castle Town, less marked), little motivation to succeed is induced by the school, most stems from class of origin or sex.

None of the schools resolves the underlying dilemma. The response of pupils to their classroom regimes make 'failure' evident to some teachers. Castle Town appears to promote harmony: acceptance of the authority of teachers by almost all pupils, and willingness to be separated by ability. And yet, in the words of one dissatisfied teacher, 'Castle Town is a youth club where some try to teach during the day.' Hinsley Mill generates competition and motivates its promising pupils, but at the expense of tensions between teachers and pupils, especially between the lower stream pupils and the teachers, none the less real though they are repressed. In recognition of this members of the English department see it as their mission to make pupils less inhibited about speaking in class, more prepared to co-operate in group learning.

Cross Street is of special interest because the dilemma expresses itself in the inconsistency between the head's policy and the practices of most of his staff, as well as in the responses of pupils to the classroom regime. The head's objective is to promote harmony in his school, through pastoral care for individual pupils, the encouragement of co-operative activities among pupils, and the development of a sense of responsibility to other pupils for misbehaviour. The instruments of his policy are a 'tutor group', based on the streamed form that shares most of its lessons together, led by a teacher who stays with the group until leaving age, and meeting regularly for registration and tutor group periods; together with a system of 'points' to reward good conduct and effort in school work, regardless of ability, which cumulate for the tutor group and form part of school competition, not between individuals, but between the groups. The head resists repressive discipline, whether by teachers or prefects, and whether inside or outside the classroom. His staff, however, try to induce competition between individuals who are promising, and to repress the rejected pupils. Their control is critical or punitive, not by rewards. Indeed, against the head's will, they have even succeeded in adding 'negative' points to his system of rewards. Needless to say the lower streams, especially in the third and fourth years, earn a disproportionate share of negative points, quite often enough to obliterate the positive points that teachers are under some duress to record each week for members of their form. This manifestation of the dilemma in conflicts with the head has two consequences: the first, a high level of staff turnover; and the second, the cultivation by the head of a 'vertical clique'[20] of young, and often new staff who sympathise with his policy (though they do not necessarily practise it) and, like him, wish to extend its principles, as they believe quite logically, to the introduction of mixed ability teaching.

Now, there is a number of 'contingencies' which are not covered by the macro-theory I have developed, but still contributed to the adoption of these differing solutions by the three schools. There is, first of all, a common ideological background to both ability and achievement streaming. Both 'solutions' assume that *sponsorship* of the most able by teachers, and in groups, like streams, kept together for their education after separation at a relatively early age, is the appropriate strategy. This was by no means untypical of English schools of the time, the late 1960s, which were in the early stages of reorganisation. Today the assumption is challenged, but is not supplanted.[21] Then again, we must recognise that the schools evolved their particular types of sponsorship because of *local* circumstances. Castle Town had been the town's 'grammar school', with a weighting towards graduate staff; the other schools wanted to emulate Castle Town's record of academic success, and believed, not always correctly, that their intake was less promising than Castle Town's. For its part, Castle Town was trying to adjust to pressures from the education office and many teachers to recognise that it was not attracting so many of the cream as before, and that it must evolve ways of handling those of lower ability (basically, more discipline and more pressure). Hinsley Mill had made the most successful adjustment to comprehensivisation: it had eliminated barriers to promotion and demotion between the 'selective' and the 'non-selective' sides of the bilateral arrangement, long before being declared comprehensive, and it had turned what seemed a sow's ear of pupils of less than grammar ability into a silk purse of academic honours. The head was awarded the CBE. Cross Street, riven by internal conflict, vacillated in following the example of Hinsley Mill, and more recently has turned towards mixed ability teaching, advertising itself as a 'progressive' school: perhaps, the claim to being progressive is a viable alternative to Hinsley Mill's image in attracting new staff. These are all local circumstances, though they may again be fairly typical, especially of the early stages of reorganisation.

Yet it may be that there is a link between comprehensive reorganisation as state policy and the desire to promote the transformation of labour power: this is consistent not only with the Labour Government's then commitment to the 'white hot technological revolution', but also with much semi-official justification of the reorganisation of secondary education.[22] If this is so, what happened locally in this case may not only be quite typical of England at the time (late 1960s) but also reveal the operation of the mechanisms postulated in the earlier analysis at the level of 'policy-making'.

Alternatives

The solutions evolved by the schools to the dilemma I have identified go far to absolve *individuals* of the responsibility to clear away the contradictions, for they permit teachers to act rationally in their own classrooms. Each solution is so consistent on its own terms and so conditions the actions of teachers and pupils alike that the outcomes of everyday decisions are predictable. Indeed the teacher who seeks to be 'informal' in teaching a class in Hinsley Mill cannot expect pupils to respond in a 'responsible' fashion: he will find that pupils 'take advantage' of the relaxation in discipline. Such teachers are likely to adapt their style to that of the school and the stream they teach, or leave the school.[23]

However, the contradictions are not in fact resolved by the schools' proffered solutions. There is on the grander view every scope for *alternative* action which is rational in its objectives, rather than rational only in the means individuals select for objectives that are predetermined by the school.

The most obvious alternative is to reproduce within the school the social divisions that exist in the local community, by reinforcing, or even creating cultures that correspond to class, race or sex. Collins has suggested that American education is more satisfactorily accounted for as the reproduction of 'elite' culture than as the transformation of labour power (i.e. by the 'technical function' theory as he calls it).[24] In England, this argument seems to fit readily with the case of independent schools, and for perhaps most who have attacked the grammar schools, it has a counterpart there too. Both types of school are accused of 'elitism'. Of course the restriction of entry to both types of school *has* had the effect that middle and upper class children are disproportionately represented. Furthermore, it is plain that attempts to harness the growth and changing content of education to the demands of the economy for skilled manpower and even more so, social mobility to IQ and years of schooling achieve less than satisfactory statistical support.[25] But it is quite another matter to find support for the counter-thesis proposed by Collins, and implied in the attacks on the independent and grammar schools I have mentioned. The reformed public schools of the nineteenth century and the County grammar schools of the twentieth century did *not* simply reproduce 'elite culture'. The pupils of independent schools were resocialised by seclusion from the outside world, and were detached from their ties to *local* status groups and made into what Musgrove has aptly called a 'migratory elite'.[26] Lacey's observations in Hightown Grammar on the decline between the wars of the finishing school for the local petty bourgeoise, and the rise of a professionalising institution devoted to producing a migrant *new* middle class, is a parallel to what happened in the independent sector in Victorian times.[27] In this context, truly 'elitist' education, devoted to the rentrenchment of the high and petty bourgeoisie through creating for them a 'culture' is indeed an alternative to the long-term trends in education.

A less ironic use of the term 'alternative' is in relation to so-called 'working class education'.[28] It is less ironic, but logically equivalent to the one I have just discussed. Here the explicit objective is to reproduce working class culture—to focus upon the experiences and interests of the children of manual parents, and to assign them value in the school, rather than dismiss them. The strategy is based on the assumption that schools do reproduce elite (or middle class) culture, and only allow children who are of middle class origin or who adopt middle class values to succeed. Much of my argument may be regarded as a criticism of this assumption: in place of 'middle class' domination of education, I have put that of the state under modern capitalism. Working class education is in opposition, but not only or even primarily to middle class domination of the schools, rather to the functions of the school for capital-in-general in the long term. Its opposition is 'romantic' or 'utopian', for it is pitted against forces far stronger: it seeks to retrench a culture that is being eroded, and it cannot resolve the central contradiction between the development of the forces of production and the existing social relations of production, for both are opposed to the reproduction of divisions by class, sex and race within the school.

There is another, yet more limited alternative available within the constraints. This is to modify the prevailing terms on which access to 'elites' is negotiated. I have in mind here the shift which is indicated by comprehensive schooling, by the fudging of 'failure' at O-level and by pressure to introduce the 16+ exam, from a sponsored mobility ideology and corresponding practice of streaming, to a contest mobility ideology and corresponding practice of cooling out the over-ambitious.[29] Both ideologies legitimate existing inequalities. In England sponsored mobility ideology was a bridge between status by ascription and status by achievement: in other words it permitted the acceptance of the idea of meritocracy by a society that has never quite freed itself from the grip of landowning and finance aristocracy. In America, and increasingly in England, the route to the imagined meritocracy is depicted as a contest in which all start equal. In England, higher education is likely to find itself under pressure to adopt so-called 'open' entry, and is already attacked in political and Ministerial circles for 'elitism'. Such an opening of formal access to higher education may not increase the access of the disadvantaged,[30] and will not remove the unequal relations of production into which those emerging from education will be inserted. The ideology of contest mobility is in no way free of contradiction: the principal aspect of the contradiction it carries is rebellion among failures and the cooling out of those who overreach.[31]

A more viable alternative may be found in the conflict of the oppressed leaver—the lower stream drop out—and the teacher. The alternative is afforded by students. 'Indiscipline' is a long-standing phenomenon in compulsory schooling. In recent years it may have become more closely associated with the decisions that pupils take at 13/14 about their future position in the labour market, and how far, if at all, schooling can improve their chances of new-middle-class employment. As progress at school and differential access to the labour market have become more closely associated, if not factually then in the eyes of participants, so these decisions have become more fateful. A decision against further schooling is often a decision for employment or marriage as soon as possible. Its attraction is heightened by the rite of passage it effects from childhood to adult status. Once made the decision renders continuance at school irrelevant, and attempts to engage the student in official school activity, whether in the classroom or extracurricular, are interpreted as 'oppression'. Oppression of the student through the agency of the teacher is of the essence of achievement streaming as I have presented it. For leavers this essential relation is not viewed for what it is, i.e. in terms of control of the student in the interests of transformation of labour power, but as oppression none the less, a sense of oppression *by the teacher*, which generates not revolutionary consciousness, but what Camus calls 'resentiment'.[32] If this consciousness were given direction by radical teachers or by the Schools Action Union it might generate a positive alternative. As it is, it leads most teachers to attempts at repression of the kind found in Hinsley Mill, and even more so, Cross Street schools. Further, *resentiment* is self-limiting, because it draws energy from the tension between being at school involuntarily as a 'child' and escaping into the outer world of 'adult' responsibilities and freedoms. Once that escape is effected by leaving school, *resentiment* is glossed retrospectively as 'childishness' or 'irresponsibility' and in some cases rejection by the school is viewed as failure by the individual to take advantage of his opportunities. That gloss may have a permanent effect in inducing workers to view the penalties of employment as a burden to be tolerated 'like a man' and to view managers and professionals to whom they are subordinate as people of true ability and merit.

Pupils who rebel against oppression at school actually experience, if at a remove, the contradictions between reproduction of relations of production and the transformation of labour power. They do so because they find themselves rejected by schools whose focus is the transformation of labour power and which pursue that path by regimenting the pupil body and inducing competition among promising pupils. Such schools fail to gain pupils' acceptance of relations of production. If these pupils are to contribute to overcoming a contradiction, which has its roots in capitalist society, not in the school, then some teachers and/or organisations of pupils must give their rebellion a sense of purpose and value. Individual counselling tends to achieve the opposite effect. The only conceivable means is to promote understanding of the society in which the pupils find themselves, and in particular of the relation of what is happening to them in school to the dynamics of capitalism. Such understanding derives both from social theory and analysis and from practice—the practice of collective criticism of the exercise of authority in the school is a first step.

Of course, if a whole school were to adopt this stance, the basis for struggle by pupils would be removed: if no one is rejected and oppressed, the contradictions are not experienced. The paradox for teachers is that it is only individuals within schools who can, by considerable sacrifice of their own interests, promote progress to a more rational goal for education. Otherwise the impetus must come from organisations formed outside the schools which seek to infiltrate classrooms. In any event the argument points to the conclusion that institutional reform of schooling within the framework of the state under modern capitalism is a strategy likely to be of limited success. Radical change in education must be sought through struggle in the classroom. Its theory must be grounded in an understanding of decision-making in the classroom, not merely in generalisations about social structure.

Notes

1 Among others are L. Althusser, 'Ideology and Ideological State Apparatuses' in his *Lenin and Philosophy*, London: New Left Books, 1971; P. Bourdieu and J. Passeron, *Reproduction in Education, Society and Culture*, London: Sage, 1977; S. Bowles and H. Gintis, *Schooling in Capitalist America*, London: Routledge & Kegan Paul, 1976. See also the collection by R. Dale, G. Esland and M. Macdonald, *Schooling and Capitalism*, Routledge & Kegan Paul, 1976.

2 I am not excepting my own earlier work, e.g. *The Sociology of Comprehensive Schooling*, London: Methuen, 1977.

3 For a clear discussion see A. Heath, *Rational Choice and Social Exchange*, Cambridge University Press, 1976.

4 Critiques I find useful are: Ted Benton, *The Philosophical Foundations of the Three Sociologies*, London: Routledge & Kegan Paul, 1977, and Edo Pivcevic, 'Is a phenomenological sociology possible?', *Sociology, 6* (3) Sept. 1972, pp. 335–49.

5 H. Simon, *Administrative Behaviour*, New York: Free Press, 3rd edition, 1976, pp. xxviii–xxxi. Simon's concept of 'satisficing' includes meeting the dilemma but is less specific. He seeks to substitute for 'economic order' a model of 'bounded rationality', 'administrative man'. In my view little is gained and much rigour is lost by this attempt at 'representing' man more faithfully in theory.

6 See the argument that objective rationality has been supplanted by subjective rationality—values by technical means—in the aftermath of the Enlightenment, advanced by Max Horkheimer, *Eclipse of Reason*, Oxford University Press, 1947; M. Horkheimer and T. Adorno, *The Dialectic of Enlightenment*, London: Allen Lane, 1973.

7 See in particular J. Habermas, *Knowledge and Human Interests*, London: Heinemann, 1972 and *Legitimation Crisis*, London: Heinemann, 1976.

8 It has to be said that, quite apart from the questions of freedom and necessity raised within so-called 'orthodox', i.e. post Second International and Stalinist Marxism by this remark about praxis, the relation between Marxist analysis of class relations and revolutionary praxis has been called in question of late. See A. Cutler, B. Hindess, P. Hirst and A. Hussain, *Marx's Capital and Capitalism Today*, Routledge & Kegan Paul, 1978, vol. 2, Conclusion, and P. Hirst, 'Economic classes and politics', paper presented at Communist Party Sociology Group conference on 'Class and Class Structure', November 1976.

My position in response to orthodox Marxism is that the so-called 'laws of development' are at best tendential, not necessary, and that organised political action is thus no less justified by theory than it is by historical experience. In response to Hirst *et al.* I would argue that the principal contradiction which determines strategy is given by broad Marxist analysis; while the tactical question of alliance with other classes and parties is, as Mao has argued, to be determined in practice by the unfolding political situation.

9 There is a more detailed discussion of the three schools in Bellaby, *op. cit.*, chapter 4; also in my unpublished doctoral thesis, 'Attitudinal measurements of the effect of systems of social control in different secondary schools', University of Cambridge, 1975, chapter 3.

10 D. Young, 'Comprehensive schools—the danger of counter-revolution', *Comprehensive Education, V* (1967), p. 6.

11 These exchanges are largely ritualised. It is true that such rituals may conceal from the observer the (private) bases on which teachers and pupils make their individual decisions. However, the practical limitations of classroom observation fit the theoretical approach of this paper quite well. I am focusing on the social as opposed to the individual aspect of decision-making. The ritual of verbal exchanges between teachers and pupils is a major part of the social frame that constitutes individual decision-making and determines its outcomes. Moreover, in so far as these exchanges are ritualised, they are less likely to be radically affected by the presence of an observer in the classroom than are subjective states.

12 See Bellaby, unpublished thesis, pp. 107–18.

13 The argument is adapted from E. Goffman, *Asylums*, Harmondsworth: Penguin, 1968, 'The inmate world'.

14 P. Bellaby, 'The distribution of deviance among 13/14 year old students', in J. Eggleston (ed.), *Contemporary Research in the Sociology of Education*, London: Methuen, 1974.

15 Cf. J. Ford, *Social Class and the Comprehensive School*, London: Routledge & Kegan Paul, 1969.

16 Compare Althusser, *op. cit.*, and in *Essays in Self-Criticism*, London: New Left Books, 1976.

17 Mao-tse-Tung, *On Contradiction*, Peking, Foreign Language Press: 1963.

18 The apparent theoretical alternatives are argued, for example, by I. Davies and E. Hopper respectively in their contributions to E. Hopper

(ed.), *Readings in the Theory of Education Systems*, London: Heinemann, 1971.

19 U. Bronfenbrenner, *Two Worlds of Childhood*, New York: Russell Sage, 1970.

20 The concepts are adapted from M. Dalton, *Men who Manage*, Chichester: Wiley, 1959, pp. 57–60.

21 See C. Benn and B. Simon, *Halfway There*, Harmondsworth: Penguin, 2nd edition, 1972. Also my *Sociology of Comprehensive Schooling*, especially chapters 1 and 5.

22 See Benn and Simon, *op. cit.*, pp. 35–6. A parallel in western Europe is given by R. Poignant, *Education and Development in Western Europe, the United States and the USSR*, New York: Teachers' College Press, 1969.

23 Of course the same will apply to 'traditional' teachers in a 'progressive' school. For tensions that can arise in those circumstances see L. Berg, *Risinghill, Death of a Comprehensive School*, Harmondsworth: Penguin, 1968.

24 R. Collins, 'Functional and Conflict Theories of Educational Stratification', *American Sociological Review, 36* (1971), pp. 1002–19.

25 For a clear discussion of the complexities of this area see W. Tyler, *The Sociology of Educational Inequality*, London: Methuen, 1977.

26 F. Musgrove, *The Migratory Elite*, London: Heinemann, 1963.

27 C. Lacey, *Hightown Grammar*, Manchester University Press, 1976, chapter 2.

28 See the collection edited by N. Keddie, *Tinker, Tailor*, Harmondsworth: Penguin, 1973.

29 See my *Sociology of Comprehensive Schooling*, chapter 5.

30 A. Little and J. Westergaard, 'The Trend of Class Differentials in Educational Opportunity in England and Wales', *British Journal of Sociology, 15*, p. 301, show how limited was the change in class differentials over the fifty years to 1964, especially in access to universities in spite of outstanding expansion at secondary and higher levels.

31 A. Stinchcombe, *Rebellion in a High School*, New York: Quadrangle Books, 1964. Burton Clark, 'The "cooling out" function in higher education', in A. Halsey *et al.* (eds), *Education, Economy and Society*, New York: Free Press, 1961. A. Cicourel and J.I. Kitsuse, *The Educational Decision-Makers*, Bobbs-Merrill, 1963.

32 A. Camus, *The Rebel*, Harmondsworth: Penguin, 1960. See also P. Willis, *Learning to Labour*, Colchester: Saxon House, 1977.

Chapter 8

Control in the comprehensive system

Colin Hunter

To understand the process of decision-making—whether at individual, group, organisational or societal levels—there are at least two essential questions which need to be considered:

Who influences the outcomes?
How is the outcome legitimated and accepted by others involved in the situation?

There are contained within these questions assumptions which are connected with the two major concepts of Power and Ideology which coexist in an intimate relationship. These concepts need to be explored so that elements of the decision-making process and the question of control in schools can be highlighted. In this paper some examples are drawn from a case study conducted by the author in a large comprehensive school.

Weber (1947) describes power as 'The probability that one actor within a social relationship will be in a position to carry out his own will despite resistance, regardless of the basis on which this probability rests'.

It could be inferred that, within this outline definition, there must be a conflict of interests or values between two or more persons or groups; that one person or group actually bows to others' wishes; and that one party must be able to invoke sanctions against the other for non-compliance, thereby making the cost of compliance less than the cost of experiencing these sanctions. That is, the act of complying, no matter how reluctantly, is usually based on a rational decision.

Dahl (1958) has suggested that the overt decision-making processes are in fact synonymous with power processes and that concrete decisions by individuals, organisations, communities or society can be examined and researched to locate and explain who has power. Elsewhere, Bachrach and Baratz (1962) argue that there is another dimension of power which is not adequately covered in this approach. They identify an aspect of power which is exercised by a person or group who confine the scope and area of decision-making to relatively 'safe' issues which do not threaten their superior position.

In describing these two faces of power (p. 947), they state:

> In each, A participates in decisions and thereby adversely affects B. But there are important differences between the two: in the one case A openly participates; in the other, he participates only in the sense that he works to sustain those values and rules of procedure that help him keep certain issues out of the public domain.

What Bachrach and Baratz do not account for in their article is that the most effective use of the second type of power is based not on the active participation of the powerful 'manipulating the agenda', but on the passive acceptance of the premises of decisions by those who are being dominated or influenced by others—that is, the accepted parameters within which change can take place are sedimented and taken for granted by the participants, and this acts in favour of those who hold power because it excludes a wide range of alternatives which could challenge or question the status quo.[1]

This acceptance of unconscious or unquestioning assumptions of people at routine or habitual levels in the ordering of everyday affairs makes the third face of power anonymous and discreet, but it is nevertheless effective and pervasive in its influence—usually in substantiating and upholding those already with dominant positions. These parameters, taken for granted because of their institutionalised characteristics, are often structural in nature and have a constraining effect on individuals in their milieux. It is this third aspect of power which facilitates the bridging of the so-called dichotomy of the problems of order and control and which underlines Marx's point that men make their own world, but not in conditions of their own choosing. Meaning and identity through interaction take place within limits which are structural in nature.

It is this point which Sharp and Green (1975) emphasised in their research in a 'progressive' primary school. Their approach was described by Apple (1977) as,

> A critical social interpretation that looks at the negotiation of identities and meanings in specific institutions like schools as taking place within a context that often determines the parameters of what is negotiable or meaningful. This context does not merely reside at the level of consciousness; it is the nexus of economic and political institutions, a nexus which defines what schools should be about, that determines these parameters.

It is necessary, therefore, for schools to be viewed in their social context, within structural constraints, as well as to be viewed as examples of organisations which are maintained by individual interactions and perceptions. A school has certain aims which are the outcome of decisions made outside and imposed upon it and of autonomous decisions made within the school—both aspects are significant and require consideration.

There appears, however, to be a lack of literature in the sociology of the school which uses this approach. Organisational studies of schools have concentrated on such aspects as selection or streaming or the effect of the personality of the Head on the running of the school. Often excluded are the intra-school structural aspects such as the communication system, effects of school size, the formal distribution of authority, formal and informal sanctions, and teacher participation and extra-school structural matters such as comprehensivation, the growing insistence on teacher accountability, and other socio-political demands overtly and covertly placed on the school system. Basically, the question of control as it affects schools has been largely ignored (until relatively recently).

Increasingly, however, the question of control in comprehensive schooling has become more central largely due to two developments:[2]

1 An attempt by outside school political and economic pressures to increase the accountability of teachers.
2 An attempt by teachers to increase their participation in the running of schools.

Both of these developments concern a potential redistribution of power and involve a conflict of ideologies. Ideologies here are regarded as having the following characteristics: they are based on beliefs and values which may, or may not, have rational support; they simplify highly complex social and situational processes in terms of what ought to be; and they do so to sanction a particular course of action.

Education is an area fertile to the growth and development of ideologies. Many of the issues involve value disputes with relevant 'objective' theoretical knowledge being in short supply, particularly concering the feasibility of goals and outcomes of decisions. Positions are therefore taken which are basically ideological in that they seek to persuade rather than rationally to explore and evaluate.[3]

So, for example, Anthony Crosland could claim,

> Our belief in comprehensive education was a product of fundamental value judgments about equity and social division. Research cannot tell you whether you should go comprehensive or not—that's a basic value judgment. (Kogan, 1971, p. 190)

There has been clear evidence of a change in emphasis of ideologies in the contemporary political scene, where decisions concerning education are made at some distance from the school processes they affect. It is argued that education in the mid-'seventies is in a crisis which is partly economic, partly administrative, political and ideological in nature, and a consequence of the failure of previous educational policies.

In the early 1960s there had been a significant conjunction of the aspirations of politicians, the findings of social researchers, the theories of educationalists and adequate concomitant economic means. It was felt that qualitative changes could be made towards the making of a more egalitarian society and a more efficient technological economy, through quantitative growth in educational resources. There were therefore high expectations for the returns on the increasing investment in school facilities, training of teachers, comprehensive education, raising of the school leaving age, curricular innovation (teacher directed), compensatory and expansion of higher and further education.

As Finn *et al*. (1977, p. 81) suggest, this was a period when education was regarded as a 'good' thing, 'that the teachers could do the "job" with the right materials, [and] that intelligence was amenable to policy initiatives'.

The evidence emerging in the 1970s was that the qualitative change had not in fact occurred and that institutional arrangements, universal access to education, and compensatory programmes in themselves were not sufficient in attaining social justice and good economic returns.

The more pessimistic approach of social commentators such as Jencks gives credence to the more severe political attitude towards education which now exists. He argues that schools and schooling are not significant variables in societal change.

> Our research suggests that the character of a school's output
> depends largely on a single input, namely the characteristics of the
> entering children. Everything else—the school budget, its policies,
> the characteristics of the teachers—is either secondary or com-
> pletely irrelevant. (1975, p. 255)

Others, such as Bowles and Gintis (1976) and Willis (1977), regard the educational system as an integral element in the reproduction of the prevailing class structure of society.

> Schools foster legitimate inequality through the ostensible merito-
> cratic manner by which they reward and promote students, and
> allocate them to distinct positions in the occupational hierarchy.
> (Bowles and Gintis, 1976, p. 11)

The neo-hereditarian arguments of Jensen, Eysenck and Herstein—in which they re-assert the importance of genetic factors in educational performance—are indicative of the changing climate in educational theory, as is the re-emergence to prominence of the 'Black Paper' activists. The 'new' sociologists of education are not optimistically prescriptive in policy terms as sociologists were in the 1960s (such as Halsey, Douglas, Vaizey), but emphasise the relativism of knowledge and question the legitimacy of assumptions (see, for example, Young, 1971).

The political contribution to the increasing breakdown of the 1960s educational consensus is being undertaken on two fronts, the economic cuts and the call for accountability of those involved in schooling. Both were highlighted in the 'Great Debate', and both developments crucially affect the running of individual schools.

Heads and teachers are still coping with the consequences of the high expectations placed on them in the last decade with institutional, curricular, examination and selection reforms. They are doing so, however, with resources which are defined by current, and very different, ideological political decisions, in a changed economic climate. This has created a number of practical difficulties in the running of schools so that short-term strategies for coping become increasingly necessary.

At the same time, the aims of the school are coming under closer scrutiny from non-teacher sources of which the Bullock Report, Callaghan's Ruskin Speech, DES Yellow Book, Auld Report (*re* William Tyndale School) and recent HMI National Reports are examples.

The consequences of this in some respects cause uncertainty, low morale, and not a little frustration in heads and teachers and add to the pressures experienced in working in schools. These points were highlighted in a case study undertaken in a large comprehensive school (1,200 pupils) in a Yorkshire town. It was formed by the merging of a secondary modern school and grammar school in 1969 on an enlarged campus at the latter school. The focus of attention was upon the staff rather than the students, and the research methods included participant observation (for 16 months) and unstructured and structured interviews. The school, while in some respects unique, shared many of the problems and issues of other comprehensive schools at this time.

The head highlighted what he thought many of these problems were in a Speech Day address:

Society expects too much! Think what it has done to education in the last decade or two. Expanded it enormously; diluted its staff; expected it to keep up the same basics whilst catering for a mass of new or expanded syllabuses. . . .

Oh, for a more consistent political leadership! Oh, for a Left which did not rush its comprehensive fences with such doctrinaire enthusiasm, and which gave to its new schools resources needed if an improvement in standards is to accompany a simultaneous advance towards social equality. Oh, for a Right which wittered less about standards, for its dislike of Comprehensives, and which truly accepted the pattern of education which for good or ill is now the dominant one in Britain. Oh for a Centre which didn't tend to disintegrate into a bumbledom of busy-bodies bleating for parent power, pupil power, rights of the child, abolition of the cane, and so on.

The leaders of the majority party become day to day administrators instead of policy makers—bureaucrats in fact; or Lord High Executioners axing one employee here, retiring one there, transferring one somewhere else. We are now living on overwork and charity. . . .

This school, typical of many, has had to undergo successive concussions of amalgamating two separate schools into one; turning comprehensive, enduring the noisy construction of these buildings round its academic calm, facing local government reorganisation, and absorbing examination reforms which occur in almost every year that passes. And now the economic cuts!

This is an interesting passage from an embattled head publicly defending the school and attacking the sources of constraint with an ideological rhetoric that, in presenting a prescriptive, simplified picture of the complex workings of the school, seeks to persuade rather than describe.

'We aim', he says, 'to turn our pupils into critical adults who will be responsible citizens and flexible workers in a fast changing world', in the school which he describes as, 'a tranquil oasis of civilised and noble virtue'.

There is much evidence to suggest that this latter description is not a representative picture of the normal day to day experience of the great majority of pupils and teachers in the school. It is, though, acceptable fare for the relevant audience of Speech Day, including local education officials, governors and parents. It is also an example of an ideology which seeks to present a corporate sense of unity of purpose rather than to reflect actuality. It identifies the enemy, praises the 'war-effort', and concludes that despite the problems the battle is going well to the credit of 'the school' and its occupants.

'I can assure you that [the school] has nothing at all to fear from the "Great Debate" '—evidence includes examination results above the national average and links with local industry.

'You can guess who do the overwork' (the teachers), 'the charity is that of the parents and well-wishers. . . . Thank God, for an excellent community here to rely on, our pupils themselves' or '95 per cent of them anyway, who are a grand lot'.

As a public relations exercise, the speech constitutes an erudite and persuasive performance. It does, however, highlight an element in the difficulties encountered in the organisation of schools. The head experiences the external political and economical constraints in a different way from the teachers: The head relates the outside influences to internal administration at a general, overall level; the teachers experience them at a personal, individual level. The head thinks in terms of general rules and uniform events; teachers think in terms of concrete situations, unique individuals and extenuating circumstances. The head uses universalistic criteria as a basis for decision-making; the teachers' situation often calls for consideration of particulars.

So, to take a common place example, one can understand the mild resentment of a practical subject teacher whose class was waiting at the door to leave two minutes before the final afternoon bell after putting away a great deal of equipment and material. The head entered, pointedly looked at his watch, and commented on the 'early' finish. His view was influenced by the general rule that as much teaching time as possible should be utilised. The teacher's view was dominated by the specific situational variables such as the relationship with the pupils involved, the activity undertaken by them and the time of day.

This point of diverse perspectives is crucial in understanding the internal decision-making process in a school, and particularly the nature and extent of the participation that teachers have been demanding in the running of schools in the last few years. In the participative procedures the two, often conflicting, perspectives are brought together, but organisational problems and issues are usually considered by heads (and senior staff) at the universalistic level, while the interests of the staff are often focused on the particularistic level. It is suggested here that the head is able to control the extent and effectiveness of teacher participation and to legitimise his control through the mechanisms of power described above—the use of sanctions, communication system, ideology of consensus, manipulation of the agenda, and the existence of taken-for-granted parameters—but in a way more acceptable to the democratic and power sharing values prevalent today.

The head in the case study, for example, justifies the taking of decisions himself (though strongly advocating 'participation' by all teachers) argument that only he sees the whole picture from his special vantage point, which is not influenced by sectional interests. The explanation for accepting some remedies of a staff working party, rejecting others, and introducing quite separate remedies in some cases, was made by the head to a full staff meeting in these terms:

> I liken my part to that of the Prime Minister. I hope that doesn't seem too grand. They [the working party] report back to me, and I have got measure changes in the light of the whole. This has to be done in that they don't necessarily see the whole field. Then I, and my senior staff who advise me, look at the recommendations. With the best will in the world we are unable to take up some of the points.

Given this, the machinery for participation is complex and all-embracing. There are eight types of meetings (other than the staff meeting) with an opportunity for every member of staff to attend and give his views. There is much evidence to suggest that the different perspectives held by head and staff and the power distribution make such an exercise largely irrelevant to many staff.

For example, after a staff meeting an elderly assistant teacher remarked on a discussion regarding the use of classrooms as teacher bases:

'It was a waste of time last night. The head stopped it [i.e. he ruled the discussion out of order] and what happened after was a waste of time. We didn't get our say. The important point didn't come up about having to carry all your material to classes. I cricked my back when I slipped on the stairs with an armful of the stuff. What happens is we don't carry the materials, and the kids don't get any geometry.'

At the same meeting, concerning another topic, a head of department commented,

'It's like banging your head against a brick wall. They never take any notice.'

At another meeting, a junior member of staff thought that there was,

'a lot of frustration there under the surface, but it didn't come out. *S* was getting at the system you know.'

The point that the challenge to the system had to be inferred and was not explicit reflects a prevailing characteristic in that the staff were often markedly reticent about expressing in open meeting the opinions they talked about in the semi-privacy of small groups in the staff room, and particularly if the head was present. Apathy, timidity and caution were some of the reasons presented, the latter reason some claimed through experience.

'It does you more harm than good to speak your mind.'
'The hierarchy take it out of you.'

Such comments often accompanied staff room anecdotes about the use of direct sanctions by the head and the 'dominant coalition' of deputy heads—and sometimes the head of schools. Admittedly, the head did possess overt sanctions such as control of resources, access to promotion, job references and even direct admonition. It was difficult empirically to substantiate use of such sanctions, and if used, they were used sparingly and discreetly. More to the point, many of the staff believed they would be used—but even more importantly, the need for such sanctions was minimised by the selective use of the sanction of appointment.

As the deputy headmistress explained:

'We do an awful lot in considering the appointments of staff. We want people who fit in with this type of arrangement. There are one or two who don't toe the line. They are sparks in a sense, and this is necessary.

I could see a situation where a large number of people like this might bring havoc in my opinion. Those who would demand that the school be democratic, with votes, and so on. This would cause disruption. . . . On the whole, in general, the system is accepted.'

This acceptance cannot be understood purely in terms of the overt dimension of power. The control of the flow of information in the school is an example of the second face of power (see Bachrach and Baratz, 1962).

In analysing the number of contributions to staff meetings, it was quite clear that it was the head and two deputies who controlled the proceedings, in that the ratio of their contributions was 13 to 4 (from twenty heads of department): to 1 (from forty-two other members of staff). If the volume of contributions were to be added, the disparity in the ratio would be much greater.

Even this crude indicator shows the extent to which staff meetings were used to disseminate information downwards from the head to the staff rather than being used as an open consultative process. This direction of information flow was supplemented by memos, notices and information sheets (over 200 of which were collected by the writer in one academic year).

The flow of information upwards to the head was efficient and often filtered via the most senior staff, the head being relatively isolated from individual members of staff because of the other demands of his job. The deputy headmistress saw the function of keeping the head informed as being of great importance:

'If there are any moans or grumbles, I usually try and find out some more in the staff room. . . . It goes through the senior staff to the head. . . . All senior staff are aware of the duty of being in the common room to hear first-hand comments. One of the first bits of advice that was given to me by the old headmaster was that it was an important part of the job to be there in the staff-room.'

The horizontal flow of information within the school among the staff, on the other hand, was haphazard, unorganised, discreet and unofficial, depending largely on friendship and departmental groups. The situations in which a horizontal flow of information could be used for corporate decisions to be made are defused in that the head gives the meetings no executive powers and the agendas are not specific enough to encourage expectations of decisions being made.

For example, the head made these introductory remarks in opening discussion at a 'senior staff meeting' which was considering the curriculum organisation of the school's first year:

'I call this gathering of regional heads the cabinet. You do not meet
as frequently as the most senior staff of deputies and sometimes
the head of schools—they are the inner cabinet. This is an informal
get-together to swap ideas with me listening in, and you listening
to one another. . . . Let's give it three quarters of an hour, shall we?'

This type of arrangement maximises the flow of information, but minimises the pressure for instant decisions resulting from these exercises in 'participation'. This procedure tends to generate a sense of frustration in many of the staff involved in that no indication is given as to which of the views, if any, are noteworthy or significant. The head is able to keep his options open, but on the other hand expects others to express information or opinion instantly. As a senior staff member commented:

'He expects immediate answers and evaluations from you when he
asks for them, and if you don't give them there and then your
chance may have been lost.'[4]

The constraints which affected the working parties—crucial instruments in demonstrating the reality of 'participation'—were of a different kind, but did lessen the parties' effectiveness as tools for fundamental re-appraisals of policy.

Terms of reference given by the head to the 12–16 curriculum working party were:

to look into the modifications necessary to our curriculum, in the
12–16 range, in the light of the changing demands placed upon us
by a rapidly evolving international society; to consider the relevance of existing subjects, and the need to introduce new subjects
or combine subjects.

This appears as a wide and open brief, but there were many hidden constraints which effectively narrowed the decision-making potential so that a broad endorsement of the status quo was a logical outcome. These constraints included the fact that the chairman of the working party was the deputy headmistress, who laboriously constructed the complicated timetable throughout the summer term—a responsible chore anxiously undertaken. Any new ideas regarding curriculum innovation or changes in the organisation of subjects and classes came under her critical scrutiny with respect to their feasibility in terms of time-tabling. She is confident of the support of the head in upholding her definition of timetabling problems:

We try and compromise if possible, and try to meet them [other staff] as far as possible. If I get to the situation where I cannot do what they want—it would depend on my trouble with the time-table—I would stick out, and the head would probably back me.

Her defined needs of timetabling therefore dominated much of the discussion of the working party. A second constraint was the composition of the committee chosen by the head. There was a predominance of senior staff (four heads of department; a head of school; deputy headmistress) with three assistant teachers. Another weighting was that there were five of the senior staff who were former grammar school staff, and even after a number of years of comprehensive schooling this fact tended to be of significance. Group discussions which have the aim of achieving consensus can easily become oppressive to divergent opinions, and this was the experience of one of the juniors, a former secondary modern school teacher who tried to introduce points which would have involved fundamentally re-appraising the school's curriculum.

A third constraint on the working party was the time available. After two preliminary meetings towards the end of the autumn term, written evidence was sifted from heads of departments. The committee were then given the two months of January and February to discuss and report so that recommendations could be available for the head to announce decisions regarding the next year's timetable at the March staff meeting. For the terms of reference to be considered seriously, there needed to be a much longer period for discussion on what ostensibly was a radical appraisal of curriculum needs.

It is, therefore, not surprising that the recommendations were not contentious and indeed, in parts, they were complacent. They were, however, administratively more convenient as far as timetabling was concerned, involving slight shifts of procedure and emphases and limiting students' choice of subjects. The one curriculum innovation was a section involving two periods per week for two thirds of students in the fourth and fifth years. The complete recommendations and conclusions of the working party were:

(a) The range of subjects offered at all levels is good, and the curriculum relevant to this present age.

(b) With the possible exception of one of the second foreign languages, there is no desire to eject or to introduce any subjects, nor is there a desire to combine subjects (the reverse is the case of Social Studies). Traditional subjects are changing within themselves both in content and approach, to meet the changing needs of today.

(c) The second and third form curriculum should be more uniform if a banded system is to operate, and the second language not introduced until the third year, and then as an option.

(d) Whatever system is used in Main School, the present range of subjects should stay, though a reduction in choice would be preferred.
(e) In the C groups, Social Studies should become History and Geography, and there should be some changes in Leisure Activities.
(f) A two-year general course is proposed for all Main School G and GC groups—at least two periods per week.

This result vindicates Perrow's (1972, p. 292) analysis of the results of increased sharing in organisational decision-making:

> The prospects for participative management are dim; they are reduced to minor innovations within a complex network of established premises for action. The organisation is not static, by any means, but change is incremental, partial, hit or miss, and channelled in the well-worn grooves of established adaptions.

The extensive consultation in the school concerned, it could be argued, is almost a process which has as an end in itself to simulate a democratic decision-making process, to foster the involvement and commitment of the participants, and to legitimate the resultant decisions. It also acts as a channel to keep the head informed, thereby facilitating his control and substantiating his claim that he is the only one in a position to have an overview of the whole scene.

These indirect forms of control used by the head are more compatible with democratic values of human freedom and individual integrity than the more overtly autocratic behaviour traditionally associated with school heads in the past. They are, at the same time, more effective means of control in that they reduce resistance through calls to collective responsibility—the price required for involvement in participation.

The head made just this point in a letter to the local newspaper defending *his* decision not to publish pupils' exam results:

> School policy is not the mere whim of a headmaster, but rather
> the product of a continuing dialogue between governors, staff,
> local authority, the DES (and other national institutions), parents,
> pupils, and so on. There are always dissenters, even in the governing
> body, but once policy has emerged and been tested, it becomes
> rather like cabinet responsibility. That is to say, it is supported by
> all those in authority—supported critically if you like, but supported
> loyally until new circumstances demand new policies.

Woodward (in Musgrove, 1971, p. 79) says of another situation that elaborate systems of internal communication and of representation have not given workers power, 'rather do they constitute a means of reinforcing the power of management over the managed.'

Crozier (in Musgrove, 1971, p. 86) agrees and adds, 'If one accepts participation, one is bound to co-operate, i.e. to bear one's co-participants' pressure whether they are one's equals or superiors.'

In the school studied, despite the existence of democratic organisational procedures, it was evident that the policy formulation was largely conducted by the head, with a small number of senior staff having some influence. The underlying reason why teacher participation had so nebulous an effect was that its definition, accepted by all concerned, was that of *consultation* rather than a *sharing in the making of decisions*. This is one of the taken-for-granted assumptions that constitute the parameters of the third 'face' of power mentioned above—the existence of which reinforces the control, in this situation, of the head.

The existence of these parameters becomes apparent only when they are breached or challenged and the power that usually lies dormant is activated to maintain the status quo.[5] There is a limit to the effectiveness of this procedure in that overt use of power exposes its limitations. It is therefore in the interests of the powerful that the parameters remain hidden by remaining at an accepted, routinised level. The head was acknowledging this fact when he emphasised his reliance on consensus. In interviews he commented: 'Politics is the art of the possible—it's the same with headmastering' and 'I have one simple rule—one can only rule with consent'.

This attitude was mirrored in a remark to a member of staff concerning the problems of another head, 'I would never get myself into a position in which my orders were unenforceable'.

There was, however, one occasion when the taken-for-granted parameters in the school were breached, and the usually latent power resources were activated. The incident involved the majority of staff, unilaterally deciding at a hastily convened common room meeting (with senior staff and head absent) that they would not teach two pupils who had vandalised a staff member's car during the previous week-end. This constituted a reversal of the usual relationship in that the staff were dictating to the head on matters of school policy.

The next day the staff were summoned to a staff meeting in which the head spoke forty-five minutes justifying his actions (or lack of them) after the damaged car was discovered. While acting consistently with regard to his doctrine of the art of the possible, he reluctantly conceded that he agreed that the pupils should be expelled; but in doing so he made it plain that such future action by staff would not be tolerated. The meeting ended thus:

Head. 'I think I can say (pause); I think I can say that I am behind the staff regarding expulsion. However, you went about it in the wrong way.'
Staff Member. 'How else could we have done it?'

Head (immediately). 'Not like Hailwood Car Factory Workers. . .
However, I do have one last word to say. Don't ever hold a pistol to
my head again. My job is difficult enough with the public. It would
be more difficult without a unified staff behind me. Some people
say I'm obstinate. You will find that I am obstinate to the point of
single-mindedness. Don't ever hold a pistol to my head again.'

The significant outcome of this meeting was that the head's stand
was not challenged by the staff. It was evident that his reaction re-
stored the taken-for-granted parameters as to the distribution of power
and the relative juxtaposition of teachers' professional autonomy and
other bureaucratic requirements. The staff as a whole may have maturely
found an equilibrium maintaining 'a balance between the conditions
conducive to creativity, and those conducive to control' (see Purvis,
1973, p. 44).

More pessimistically, it could be argued that the school organisation
is in fact an oligarchy which masks its real identity in democratic procedures and rhetoric. Teachers join the ranks of other institutional
professionals who, Salaman suggests, on the whole conform to their
organisationally determined tasks, objectives, and procedures; they
are free to act autonomously as long as their decisions are appropriate
and conform to the organisation's notions of rationality.

Perrow (1972) is even more biting in his remarks:

The professional—the prima donna of organisation theory, is really
the ultimate eunuch—capable of doing everything well in that harem
except that which he should not do, and in this case that is to mess
around with the goals of an organisation, or the assumptions that
determine to what ends he will use his professional skills.

The head, however, is not invested with the concomitant power that
would befit a dominant position as an accepted 'democratic dictator'
in schools. Rather, it seems as if he is continually trying to create room
for manoeuvre within severely delineated limits imposed from outside
the school. The process of policy-making, over which he presides,
appears to be reduced to minor adaptions within a complex framework
of taken-for-granted assumptions or premises for action.

This framework is altered not by participants within the school, but
by forces (often political and economical) which have their locus outside of the school. The effects of rapid externally imposed change are
often reflected in the lack of informal consensus within schools—hence,
the need for official rhetoric to create a sense of unity of purpose,
which may not reflect the actual situation. For teachers, this rhetoric
is often of little help or relevance in their particular school experience
in that it is often based on general rules and explanations, giving
mechanistic answers to organistic problems.

Thus, we have teachers who are isolated from the policy-making process of a school and who concentrate on coping strategies to deal with day to day contingencies, while the head, in a restricted milieu, attempts to come to terms with outside factors over which he has little control—the school being bounded by legislative, administrative, political, ideological and economic structural constraints.

But these structural constraints are not co-ordinated in their influence. They are often in opposition so that the school is often confronted by contradictory pressures. The present role of the Education Secretary illustrates this dilemma. The Minister, at her political level, tries to balance the potentially conflicting forces of imposed economic restraint with the pressure, mostly from her political opponents and industrialists, for increased 'standards' in schools.

This balancing act has affected schools in that resources and manpower are becoming increasingly limited and teacher competency is questioned in terms of greater public accountability and possible contraction of teacher autonomy. At the same time, the schools and teachers are asked to do more in the 'national interest', which is defined almost completely in economic terms.

This gives some indication of the societal process which Raymond Williams[6] has described: 'materialism and idealism play a see-saw game in our culture; each thriving on the weakness of the other'. After the idealist 1960s and early 1970s we are lurching into the more materialistic mid and late 1970s; and schools and teachers are experiencing this shift at structural, organisational and individual levels.

It is conceivable that future developments in schooling could be characterised by the results of the alternate domination of opposing emphases. Such a drift would involve policy being based not on the strength of arguments but on the strength of commitments, not on quality of arguments but on the quantity of support.

Alternatively, control may evolve into the hands of a commanding narrow elite. Or there may be a move towards democratisation in terms such that those vitally affected by any decision may have an effective voice in that decision, so that decisions relate in a meaningful way to those who experience the consequences.[7]

One of the main variables influencing future development will be the extent of the understanding that people (in this case teachers, heads, administrators etc.) have of their situation and their place in the societal perspective.

C. Wright Mills (1970) describes this in terms of the coming together of private troubles and public issues. This involves the individual and his milieux being located within the social structures they form. As he puts it:

When we understand social structures and structural changes as they bear upon more intimate scenes and experiences, we are able to understand the causes of individual conduct and feelings of which men in specific milieux are themselves unaware.

The decision-making process (here pertaining to schools) has been described as being complex and almost opaque, involving many levels of interaction and the concepts of power and ideology. Awareness of this process is crucial, for only increased knowledge and understanding of what IS can pave the way for a more reasoned and shared definition of what OUGHT to be.

Notes

1 C. Wright Mills (1970) makes this point at a societal level: 'Much power today is successfully employed without the sanction of the reason or the conscience of the obedient. Justification of rules no longer seem so necessary to exercise their power. At least for many of the greatest decisions of our time. . . mass persuasion has not been "necessary", the fact is simply accomplished. . . the frequent absence of engaging legitimation, and the prevalence of mass apathy are surely two of the central political facts about Western society today' (p. 50).
2 More teacher participation has been sought not only by the more radical groups such as Rank and File. The following NUT Executive Resolution of 1973 was strongly endorsed by the Conference: 'The Union shall commit itself fully to the immediate objective of establishing mandatory consultations in all schools. After this has been achieved, and its effects assessed, there should be consideration of the desirability of legal and other changes aimed at the further devolution of responsibility within schools.'
3 For further discussion on this topic see Naish, Hartnett and Finlayson (1976).
4 As Warwick (1974, p. 73) has commented, 'It is in the interest of management to ensure as much predictability as it can in its own workforce, by hierarchical structuring, spreading organisational ideologies and manipulating the flow of information, or regulating access to it.'
5 An example of this aspect at societal level is given in the recent William Tyndale school case (see Gretton and Jackson, 1976).
6 Raymond Williams, review in *Guardian*, 9 March 1972, of B.F. Skinner, *Beyond Freedom and Dignity*, quoted in A. Dawe, 'The Role of Experience in the Construction of Social Theory', *Sociological Review, 21*, no. 1, February 1973, pp. 51–2.
7 This approach is being attempted in a school situation at Countesthorpe College, Leicestershire (see Watts, 1977).

Chapter 9

Strategies, decisions and control: interaction in a middle school classroom

Andy Hargreaves

It has been said of the 'new' sociology of education that: 'As yet. . . the excitement accompanying the identification of a neglected problem has not so far been followed by much empirical research.'[1] However, the growing bubble of classroom interaction studies would seem to constitute at least a mild rebuttal of such a claim. The promises (and threats) generated by the emergent 'interpretive' paradigm in the sociology of education are not *entirely* unfulfilled.

Within the British context of classroom research, a criticism can nevertheless be made that the dominant emphasis thus far has been upon formal, traditional secondary school teaching (e.g. Barnes, Britton and Rosen, 1969; Keddie, 1971; Hammersley, 1974, 1976 and 1977a; Woods, 1975 and 1977; Delamont, 1976; D. Hargreaves *et al.*, 1975). A good reason why this should be the case is that the public, explicitly available forms of discourse which make up such forms of teaching are relatively simple to record, transcribe and analyse when contrasted with more individually oriented forms of teaching. The problems posed by a seemingly archaic style of teacher-pupil interaction in the secondary school also present themselves more readily for analysis than do the more subtle teaching styles of the informal progressive primary school. The critic might argue that although such studies have a pioneering quality about them, their concern is with an area of education which is now rather passé. It may indeed be felt that informally organised progressive schools and classrooms would provide a more appropriate object of research at a time when, it has been suggested, the developing tradition of British 'open' education is gaining in strength via the expansion of middle schools (Lynch, 1975).

And yet, the Plowden rhetoric must not be consumed too readily. There are grounds for scepticism regarding the democratisation of learning, which is often seen to flow from the archetypal pedagogical style of the primary school. I have elaborated these grounds in another paper (A. Hargreaves, 1977a) and shall not reiterate them here. However, further doubt is raised by the fact that traditional modes of teaching of the secondary school type often persist within primary and middle schools (Jenks, 1973; Sinclair and Coulthard, 1975; Bennett, 1976; Harrod, 1977). Although some primary and middle school classrooms may be organised almost entirely on 'traditional' lines, there will be occasions in most such schools when the teacher addresses, organises and disciplines the class as a whole. This would appear to be the case in even the most progressively organised institutions.[2]

The substantive focus of this paper is on one such occasion in an inner-city middle school. I shall argue that the specific techniques used by the teacher to organise the school class in instances of this type can be embraced within a more widely defined coping strategy where the teacher is engaged in actions which can be described as policing. In contrast to the general features of the management of pupil behaviour within such a coping strategy, I shall also document the ways in which teachers handle one particular deviant pupil, Charlie, in an attempt to avoid direct confrontation with him in the classroom. The two coping strategies of *policing* and *confrontation-avoidance* will be analysed in terms of the degree of their mutual compatibility. I shall argue, in fact, that basic incongruity between these two coping strategies results in unintended consequences which affect both the 'efficient' management of classroom life by teachers, and the process of identity-formation on the part of the deviant (Charlie).

More generally, such a substantive analysis, I suggest, provides a focal point for considering the relationship between power and decision-making in the educational process. Here, situationally specific decisions will be viewed as *negotiative strategies*. These are considered qualitatively different from the more generalised definitions of teaching behaviour embraced by the concept *coping strategy*.[3] Steven Lukes's (1974) typology of three approaches to the analysis of power and decision-making is highly suggestive here in the extent to which it might enable a recognition of both the uses *and the limits* of strategic interactional analyses of classroom decision-making processes.

Organising the school class: the role of policing

The seminal work on the organisation of the school class is that written by Parsons (1959). This article set the tone for later contributions (Musgrave, 1968; Shipman, 1968) by treating the school class as an organised system of elements. Theoretically, the school class is regarded as *organised*. Its systematic character is presented to the reader as a *fait accompli*. This is the case whether that system is seen to be in equilibrium and based upon consensus values with a relatively harmonious interlocking network of roles, or whether it is viewed essentially as one of pluralist conflict, as in later contributions.

In contrast to the stress placed upon the *organised* character of institutions, those researchers who may loosely be included within that wide range of perspectives encapsulated by interactionism emphasise instead the *organising* practices of an institution's members. Systemic harmony (or conflict) is not regarded as pre-given but is seen as at least partly contingent upon what an institution's members achieve through interaction. The social order is seen at least partly as an interpersonally negotiable phenomenon. Lessons are 'made' to happen (Payne, 1976), pupil participation requires organising (Hammersley, 1974), and pupil attention has to be mobilised (Hammersley, 1976). Similarly, disciplinary techniques such as showing a pupil up (Woods, 1975) occur not through the automatic employment of a set of available and technically learnable social skills but, rather, are seen as contingent for their effectiveness upon the recognition of their intention by pupils and upon the strategic negotiation of their meaning and legitimacy between teachers and pupils.

Second-level decisions

My concern here is with one particular way in which the school class can be and often is organised. Although my dominant emphasis is upon the interactional work which must be accomplished in order to achieve such organisation, it should not be assumed that the classroom order is entirely a product of negotiations within and between the ranks. I shall have some cautionary comments to make on this point towards the end of the paper. The specific type of occasion I explore is one where the teacher employs a coping strategy which I shall call policing. This entails the management in bodily terms of a large crowd of pupils by a single teacher or, in this instance, two teachers. The management of pupil control over their own bodies is, in this coping strategy, also accompanied by the close monitoring of pupil talk.

The data analysed here were collected as part of a small project carried out in an inner-city middle school in a social priority area.[4] The group of children concerned are thirty 9- to 10-year-olds in the first year of that school. Their open-plan classroom is situated in a wooden terrapin building adjacent to the main lower school block. For much of the day, the children work within an integrated-day system which was initially imposed by the headmaster against many of the staff's wishes. After stimulus periods, pupils work on one of three alternative areas of the curriculum. The work is often heavily programmed in the form of work cards (especially in the 'linear' subjects) and checks are systematic and rigorous. These occur through step-by-step evaluation of pupil work, where the teacher ticks off individual work cards when assignments have been satisfactorily completed. This is a necessary condition that must be fulfilled before the pupil is. allowed to move on to work in any other area of the curriculum. Spot checks are also carried out daily to ensure that pupils are seated in the right place for the task on which they are engaged. This checking involves the momentary (and momentous) suspension of classroom activity so that checks can be conducted in a formal, public manner.

The general pattern of classroom life is therefore one of individually based learning where strong control is nevertheless exerted through the heavily programmed character of pupil learning and through a rigorous, systematic procedure of evaluation. This general pattern is complemented by a set of occasions when the class is addressed as a whole. These include 'stimulus' periods, story time and, as in the example offered here, drama lessons. The public, repeatable and testable character of teacher-pupil interaction and the rules it embodies in such situations, contrast sharply with the more private individuated forms of interaction which constitute the general pattern of classroom life.

The particular lesson under scrutiny is a drama lesson, predominantly taught by one member of staff, though assisted by another. Under normal circumstances, drama is held in the school hall (which is allocated to classes at specific times for this purpose), but on this particular day, the hall is being used for a concert rehearsal by another year group. As a result, if drama is to be held at all, then it must take place within the classroom area and the architectural restrictions, both real and defined, which that imposes upon the possibilities for drama activity.

In the circumstances, the teachers are initially presented with two second-level decisions that need to be made. By second-level decisions, I mean those decisions which are made and resolved before a lesson actually begins. These decisions possess defining features and frame the parameters within which classroom activity is to take place.[5] Given the very real constraints which a terrapin building and the clutter of classroom furniture place upon the teaching of drama, it would be quite justifiable to substitute another learning activity more suited to the surroundings. Such flexibility in arrangements would not be inconsistent with the general philosophy of integrated teaching. Yet, in opting to continue with drama despite the difficult circumstances, the teachers seem hardly to have made a conscious decision at all. Discussion between them centred around what kind of drama should take place rather than whether indeed it should occur. When I asked if they had considered alternative activities, one teacher stated that 'the pupils expect it [drama] at this time' and asserted also that 'they like to know where they are'. These remarks are quite probably empirical statements of fact. It is a mundane point that if events have occurred

137

routinely at the same time on the same day, then it is reasonable to expect affairs to continue in this way. But expectation might additionally mean desire. In this sense, to expect drama to be the next lesson is to look forward to it. Where, from the pupils' point of view, subjects are hierarchically organised in terms of their desirability, i.e. their approximation to play rather than 'real work', then to remove a 'desirable' subject not only violates a pupil's sense of order but also amounts to the imposition of a sanction. The maintenance of such 'soft options' even in conditions of adversity is therefore reasonable from the teacher's point of view not only on 'humanitarian' grounds but also in terms of the maintenance of social order, for 'truce' situations between teacher and pupil are partly predicated on the assumption that desirable and undesirable subjects are traded off against one another in the preservation of a precarious equilibrium (Woods, 1977).

The third assumption contained within the teachers' justifications is that not only do pupils actually *have* an appreciation of orderly relations, but that they also *need* a sense of social order. The ambiguity of the statement 'They like to know where they are' captures and intertwines both these possibilities. The justifications, as they are offered, break down the demarcation line between structurally produced expectations and an imputed set of moral imperatives couched in terms of pupils' needs. The view that the pupil *should* know where he is can here be equated with the injunction of Plowden that the deprived *need* 'affection, stability and order'.[6]

The other second-level decision involves the choice of a *particular* drama activity. After brief discussion the teachers opted to do mime 'because it's less chaotic than anything else'. Despite all the cognitive benefits which might accrue to pupils from their participation in mime, the teachers' decision here is clearly related to its potential for social control. For this very reason, mime is something of an 'old chestnut' for teachers and is employed in many classrooms where drama activity cannot take place in a spacious hall or studio. This is by no means universally the case, however, for I have occasionally witnessed exciting incidents of spoken drama in the restricted space of school classrooms which were, unlike the lesson under review, also near other classes.

The choice of mime as the most suitable drama activity cannot, therefore, be related solely to the constraints imposed by the physical confines of the classroom, although these matters are not insignificant. Mime also offers greater potential for the surveillance of pupil behaviour than other forms of drama. By the suppression of legitimate talk (that which is seen as necessarily related to cognitive learning), illegitimate talk (perceived as unrelated to learning) is identified more easily. So deviant activity can be quashed at its inception. Even if legitimate talk is integral to lesson activity (e.g. planning a group mime), conditions can be invoked (e.g. whispering) which allow surveillance.[7]

Consequently, mime is selected not only because of a set of physical constraints but also because of its surveillance potential under the felt threat of impending anomie. As Becker (1952) has pointed out, the experience of such a threat and the problems of teaching and behavioural control intensify when the clientele predominantly comprises children whose parents are lower class. For this reason, I suggest that in social priority area schools, the primary orientation of classroom teaching will be towards the moral dimensions of school life rather than towards the cognitive ones, though legitimation may derive from the latter.

Parsons (1959) noted how the moral and the cognitive aspects of the organisation of the school class are conflated within the elementary school.[8] It must also be noted, however, that the nature of that conflation will vary with the social class background of pupils. Given the ideological assumption that such children *need* structured learning and stability,[9] and that disorganisation of a personal or systematic kind will otherwise prevail, then the moral dimension will be in the ascendent. Decisions will therefore be made primarily on moral (behavioural) grounds. This applies at all levels. General curriculum programmes such as ROSLA curricula may be implemented (though not necessarily legitimated) on such assumptions. Specific curricular decisions such as the choice of 'mime' might also flow from such assumptions. General pedagogical coping strategies similarly may be largely based on this kind of moral premise. In this school, where the 'integrated day' had been imposed upon the staff, this was translated into a heavily programmed form of individual instruction embodying a regular, routinised system of evaluation which served to structure pupil learning more rigorously than was implied in the intentions of the original scheme. Policing can also be viewed as one such morally based coping strategy.

This is not to say that the cognitive dimension is irrelevant in the teaching of lower working class pupils, only that the moral aspect takes primacy. In this sense, social control becomes inseparable from curriculum planning, preferred styles of teaching and classroom organisation. It can often come to constitute the definition of teaching.[10] For this reason, I wish to regard the use of 'mime' as a means of social control. Its selection by teachers provides the grounds upon which specific decisions within the lesson can be made and negotiated. At the same time it closes off alternative possibilities for action.

Coping strategies have a predefinitional quality about them. In so far as they involve second-level decisions and assumptions about the selection of 'appropriate' curricular items (e.g. mime as a means of social control) and about pedagogical styles (e.g. policing), all subsequent action is framed within these predefined parameters. Nevertheless, the second-level decisions and assumptions which make up coping strategies must still be accomplished through the practice of teacher-pupil interaction. The practical techniques of control and instruction employed by teachers and the negotiations which arise between teachers and pupils are the necessary means by which coping strategies are affirmed or modified. Each coping strategy implies its own degree of latitude in first-level decision-making. Policing, I suggest, implies a narrow range of possible negotiation in classroom practice. The boundaries of power, autonomy and decision-making are explicitly demarcated through the utilisation of techniques which make up this pedagogical style. It is to a detailing of such techniques that I now turn.

First-level decisions

Philip Jackson (1968) has emphasised that 'crowds' are one of the most pervasive features of classroom life. Although his concern was with the effect this had on the decoding of the hidden curriculum by pupils, this phenomenon is also crucially relevant to the techniques of classroom management which teachers employ. In this sense the teacher acts as policewoman in so far as she engages in 'crowd control'. Crowd control entails first-level decisions about exclusion (who is allowed to be part of the crowd), the movement of the crowd as a whole, and the movement of individuals within the crowd. The orderly organisation and spatial distribution of pupils is the essence of good policing.

The first specific decision concerns who is to be included in the crowd:

T2   Donald, are you in this?
D   No, Miss.
T2   Will you move toward the wall, then. (lines 173-8)

Pupils may be excluded purely for the preservation of classroom harmony. This kind of decision has its parallels in the placing of disruptive children outside the classroom, in the setting up of special isolation units and in the practices of suspension and expulsion. But the practice takes on another dimension when desirable activities are involved. Any crowd may in toto be denied access to the desirable activity. An analogous situation here is the disciplinary stipulation that soccer clubs play several crucial games away from their home supporters when the latter have been held accountable for disruptive behaviour. The threat of action involving the imposition of unpleasant alternatives may be used in classrooms as a means of establishing pupil conformity:

T1   You do it without making a lot of noise (raised voice), otherwise we won't bother. We'll just come and sit down here and you'll get your reading books. (57-60)

The threat of expulsion is linked in this pedagogical style to the statement of a rule, e.g. 'making a lot of noise'. The combination of the threat of exclusion and the articulation of a rule may also be applied to individual pupils. The first example here refers to the rule of 'being sensible'.

T1   Right now, you've got to be really sensible because if Mrs H sees anybody being silly or I see anybody you will come and you will sit down. You won't take part in it again this afternoon. (71-4)

The link between the threatened sanction, the rule, and behaviour which violates that rule may require more inference on the part of the pupil, though in the public situation characteristic of this coping strategy the data from which inferences can be drawn are readily available. For example,

T1   What we're going to do this afternoon is something that only very, very sensible people can do. You'd better put your foot down, Terry Carter. People who behave like Terry Carter can't do it. (6-10)

Inappropriate positioning of the body can here be linked to a breaking of the rule, 'being sensible'.

In acting as policewoman, apart from decisions regarding exclusion and expulsion, the teacher also makes decisions regarding the movement and positioning of the crowd *en masse*. As a consequence of the successful enactment of these decisions, pupils, through their occupation of a particular position within the classroom and through their common adoption of a certain position (e.g. sitting), are more open to surveillance. Such crowd control techniques may be articulated prescriptively or proscriptively, and may refer either to the occupation of a particular space or to the way in which that space is occupied. For example, all children may be required to occupy a particular part of the classroom:

T1   The people over there; can you move over here so that whoever's doing it can (Pause) be in front of you. (95-7)

The need to maintain easy surveillance also necessitates the proscription of certain areas which become 'out of bounds':

T1   You can go anywhere in my area, in the little corner or anywhere in Mrs H's area where we can see you. (30-2)

Pupils are more easily surveyed and controlled when they adopt certain bodily positions rather than others. That pupils are seated, for example, while the teacher stands, places the latter in a 'superior' position both physically and symbolically. Sitting may be prescribed,

T1   Right, sit down on your bottoms, all of you. (101)

or movement may be proscribed:

> T1   Don't you dare move. You're liable to get your heads chopped off. (106-7)

The occupation of space and its manner of occupation may be combined. The last example illustrates this in the form of a proscription. An alternative one shows how such an injunction may be expressed in the form of a prescription,

> T1   Right, all of you, sit on the carpet. C'mon (Pause) Go sit on the carpet. (1-2)

Policing may also involve the separation into and the handling of sub-groups. Although such decisions *may* take the form of *segregation* for social control purposes, in this extract the formation of groups would seem to be integral to the teaching of mime.

> T1   I want you to get into little groups of four. (11-12)

Such movement within the mass increases the possibility of disorder and is therefore accompanied by the explicit statement of rules according to which this separation into groups is to be accomplished, i.e.

> T1   . . . without fussing (Pause) without talking and shouting or whatever. . . . (10-11)

Even such stringent safeguards do not ensure that the teacher's requirements will be fulfilled automatically. Simple mathematical difficulties may entail some negotiation about the formation of the groups.

> P   There's only two of us—me and Colin   ⎫
> T1   Well you can still do. . . .   ⎬ complex interchange
> P   We've got two   ⎭
> T1   There's two of you. Right, well you four join together then.
> P   Miss, there's only three of us.
> T1   Well go (inaudible) then. It doesn't matter. (75-81)

Apart from the interestingly exceptional case of Charlie, who will be discussed later, the latitude allowed for negotiation here is extremely restricted. Consequently, the negotiative decisions tend to rotate around minor points of classroom order and procedure.

The third major form of crowd control involves the close monitoring of individual pupils with respect to their position within the crowd and to their gestures and general demeanour. Pupils may be ordered to change positions in the classroom:

> T1   Right Pam, c'mon over here. (23)

More typically, strict control is exercised over posture:

> T1   You'd better put your foot down, Terry Carter. (8)

The teacher here acts less like a policewoman and more like a puppeteer in the extent to which she governs the most detailed movements of pupils in her charge. Otherwise idle hands are, through such techniques of puppeteering, allotted a specific function and their mischievous potential is thereby removed. The success of such techniques is marked by the degree to which they become employed routinely and ritualistically. The placing of hands upon heads as a means of preventing or suspending all deviant activity is one such commonly used device (lines 18-27).

Policing implies most of the above techniques, though for others, the metaphor of puppeteering would seem more appropriate. The utility of policing as an adequate metaphor is lost, however, when consideration is given to the particular techniques which the teacher employs in the control of pupil talk. In the extent to which she facilitates, delimits, terminates or reformulates such talk, the teacher, in fact, is more akin to a barrister.

References to pupil talk are almost always proscriptive in form. The major exception is when the pupil is invited to make contributions through the system of participation which the teacher organises. Invocation of the 'no talking' rule can vary from explicit statement to paralinguistic indication.[11] The following are explicit statements,

> T1 Now then, without fussing (Pause), without talking and shouting or whatever, I want you to get into little groups of four. I said without talking, so sit down again. (10-13)

or:

> T1 Your group. C'mon in this space. Now then, you will have to be *really* quiet. (112-13)

Rather than a statement of the rule which is being broken, a noise like 'Sssshhh!' which is conventionally associated with the suppression of noisy rule-breaking behaviour, might be uttered instead (e.g. lines 52 and 115).

As another alternative, the teacher may merely state the behaviour in which the pupil is indulging, leaving the latter to infer that, by its very remarkability, such behaviour constitutes the infraction of a rule. For example,

> T2 You are talking. (124)

The teacher may also criticise pupil behaviour in a more diffuse manner, where the pupil must infer that 'talking' is the specific behaviour that has to end.

> T1 Are you listening? You're being very bad mannered, Barry. (60-1)

The grounds for such inference would still appear to be explicitly available in the teacher's speech, however. Given the fact that within the coping strategy of policing those grounds comprise strict rules about talking and the use of the body, the fixed attention of the teacher through the use of 'the look' (55–6, 62) on any particular pupil will be sufficient to indicate to him both his characterisation as deviant and also the grounds of his deviance.

Under the experienced conditions of impending anomie, stringent control over pupil talk and bodily movement becomes a central feature of teacher behaviour. It is not surprising, therefore, that infractions often involve a combination of talk *and* bodily movement (e.g. lines 56–9, 81–2).

Possibly the most interesting and disturbing feature of the coping strategy of policing is the extent to which the moral features of class-room life take priority over the cognitive. In this sense, forms of teaching (at the second level of decision-making) and particular nego-tiative strategies[12] (at the first level) which are organised primarily around principles of social control come to be, at the very least, in-distinguishable from forms of teaching which are cognitively based. The strong element of this thesis would state that in schools comprising mainly lower working class pupils, teaching decisions at both levels are taken on largely moral grounds and the cognitive dimension becomes merely a weak legitimation of the former. Under these circumstances, social control passes for teaching.

I have already pointed out how the choice of mime (at the second level) as a curricular item contains marked advantages for social con-trol in so far as it enables an efficient separation of legitimate from illegitimate talk. To some extent, the principles lying behind the choice of a curricular item re-emerge at the first level of decision-making in the classroom.

(1)   T1   Now then, we'll give you about five minutes in which to get. . . your mime ready. You do it without making a lot of noise (raised voice), otherwise we won't bother. We'll just come and sit down here and you'll get your reading books. . . . And then when you've done it. . . you're all going to show us in your groups in turns and we're going to see if we can guess what you've been doing. So you've got to be very quiet because if you stand over there and shout 'Oh, let's do this, let's all be milkmen'—everybody'll know before you even start. So you get together and you whisper very quietly and then. . .you work it out and you go practise it—very quietly. (55–69)

(2)   T1   Right, very quietly, in your groups. (81–2)

(3)   T2   Stop! Everybody stop! What's a mime? Nora?

N   It's when you don't speak.
T2   There is no speaking *at all*. So it's no good saying 'Well,
     I'll come and so and so to you and you do such and such
     to me'. There's got to be no talking at all. So really we
     shouldn't hear any sound from you at all. (86–93)

Within these extracts, the teachers, through their employment of strategic decisions, specify more closely the meaning and definition of 'mime' for their pupils. In the first extract, the cognitive and the moral reasons for maintaining quietness in producing a mime are closely bound together. When this close specification of the curricular item, mime, fails to restrict pupil speech to 'acceptable' noise levels, then a further, rather specious set of conditions is invoked. In the third extract the teacher draws a tenuous connection between the silence required in order to perform a mime and the required behaviour in planning such a mime. It is difficult to see how effective planning within a group could in fact be achieved without the use of pupil talk to elaborate meanings and intentions.

The reasons both for choosing mime and for the particular way in which this curricular item is transformed into a pedagogical strategy are, I should argue, primarily moral in character. There is, of course, an interpretive problem in assessing the status of cognitive factors as either implementing reasons or legitimating justifications. My reason for opting for the latter alternative is the way in which the teachers, in an ad hoc manner, *extend* the relevance of the 'no talking' rule to all behaviour beyond the mime itself. Through this procedure the cognitive justification becomes extremely attenuated. Yet, it is the very binding together of (albeit attenuated) cognitive justifications and moral reasons within the teachers' talk which not only presents the observer with interpretive difficulties but also marks the process by which social control passes for valid teaching.

To expose the moral basis of policing is not to make an indictment of teachers' attitudes and behaviour. It should not be thought that teachers are unenlightened repressors of pupil spontaneity. Similarly, the problem is greater than one of 'real' learning being obstructed by the social functions of language. Teachers themselves, it must be remembered, work in an environment of abundant social constraints. These constraints may be so severe in a school of social priority area status that teaching necessarily becomes organised around survival (Woods, 1977). The coping strategy of policing is under these circumstances a reasonable, constructively articulated adaptation to the demands imposed by a school which caters predominantly for lower working class pupils. Given the felt threat of impending anomie presented by such demands of the school and through their difficulty in responding to subtly articulated and individually oriented modes of

145

social control more typical of the 'progressive' primary school and the 'new middle class' professional family, then such 'repressive' coping strategies will emerge with almost ineluctable certainty. This is so because they 'work'. Their practical effectiveness ensures their perpetuation. In consequence, teacher survival is maintained and the social order of the school is reproduced.

To sum up, the coping strategy of policing comprises three elements: The first is rigorous and systematic control over pupil talk and bodily movement. The second is an explicit articulation of the rule system and a public display of the hierarchical relationship which obtains between teacher and pupil. This is manifested in the detailed first-level negotiative strategies included under the first·element but is also exemplified by other features of classroom life. These include the frequent use of imperatives; the repeated use of attention maintaining devices and signals which indicate a switch in the phase of the lesson and hence the rules which are appropriate to that phase (D. Hargreaves *et al.*, 1975), e.g. 'Right'; and finally the use of non-voluntarist modes of speech, e.g.,

T1   *You're going to* get together and *you're going to* think of
       something to mime. (32–3; see also lines 61–9)

The third element arises because of the problems presented by lower working class children in a school environment. Coping strategies of policing and second-level decisions about the curriculum, in addition to specific negotiative strategies at the first-level of decision-making, are all based primarily on the necessity to maintain social control. Where cognitive justifications are invoked in order to legitimate such strategic decisions, control may well pass for teaching.[13] Survival strategies can, according to Woods (1977), 'appear as teaching, their survival value having a higher premium than their educational value'.[14]

Confrontation avoidance: an alternative coping strategy

The elaboration of an exhaustive list of negotiative strategies which comprise any particular coping strategy is by no means sufficient for developing an understanding of strategic decision-making and classroom control. At one level, I would not claim that the list I have drawn up is in any way exhaustive.[15] But more than this, strategies should not be regarded as just a set of gamey techniques. Erving Goffman has pointed out that strategic decisions have *fateful* consequences. In defining strategic interaction, Goffman[16] states:

> Two or more parties must find themselves in a well structured situation of mutual impingement where each party must make a move and where every possible move carries *fateful* implications for all of the parties.

The fateful character of interaction might refer only to its mere consequentiality in so far as any act delimits the realm of possibility for subsequent acts. Yet fateful consequences might also occur with respect to the constitution of the self. In the true spirit of symbolic interactionism, Goffman[17] points out how notions of 'self' and 'other' are integral components of any model of strategic interaction:

> Courses of action or moves will then be made in the light of one's thoughts about the other's thoughts about oneself. An exchange of moves made on the basis of this kind of orientation to self and others can be called strategic interaction.

In Goffman's case, however, this flirtation with *symbolic* interactionism is only an instrumental one in so far as the essential reflexity of the self is seen to be one of the necessary mechanisms which renders a strategic model of interaction possible. Any substantive consequences for the self which flow from such a process are not considered by Goffman here, although he has implied them elsewhere.[18] The *effects* of strategic interaction upon the constitution of the self and the concept of self are not discussed by him. This is an important omission, for where such effects are negative, strategic interaction might be seen to possess not only *fateful* but also possibly *fatal* consequences. It is to such *fatal* consequences for one particular pupil that I now turn.

My concern is with a coping strategy which I term 'confrontation avoidance',[19] and the consequences which this has for the identity and self of the pupil. Particular strategies of confrontation avoidance can be found in earlier work on the sociology of the classroom. Werthman (1971) describes how some teachers attempted to 'bribe' gang members of whom they were afraid with high grades. Wegmann (1976) has illustrated how pupil challenges to teacher authority may be redefined by the teacher as literal contributions to democratic rational discourse, so that some semblance of order can be sustained within the classroom. In the classroom with which I am concerned here, the salient feature of confrontation avoidance is either a refusal to act upon pupil challenges or a minimisation of response to such challenges. In the maintenance of this low profile orientation, it should be remembered that any refusal to act does not constitute the absence of action because

> no action at all. . . can have fully serious clear-cut consequences and hence constitute a move 'in effect'.[20]

Second-level decisions

The child who is the object of such (in)attention is Charlie, a 10-year-old West Indian boy. Charlie carries a nefarious past in tow because he was expelled from his previous school after committing acts of violence (throwing furniture) against the headmistress.[21] The possibility that such action might recur is an understandably frightening prospect for teachers and presents them with the acute problem of how this potentially explosive and volatile individual is to be handled. The chosen coping strategy is the avoidance of confrontation with Charlie wherever possible. Within the individualised learning process of the integrated day system, this seems to reap *some* rewards from the teachers' point of view. The general policy is summed up by the head of the year group:

> We're not too bothered if Charlie doesn't do much work providing he's reasonably quiet.

To the amusement of the teachers, Charlie could often be seen wandering about the classroom looking out of the window, drawing, singing to himself or talking to other children. Through broadening the latitude of acceptable behaviour beyond conventional bounds little of Charlie's behaviour became sanctionable and peace often prevailed.

The second-level coping strategy of confrontation-avoidance was sometimes realised in more subtle ways:

> If we want Charlie to do something, we don't tell him. We don't say 'Charlie, get in the queue'. We say 'C'mon Charlie, which end of the queue do you want to go to, front or back'. He thinks he's got a choice.

The essence of the strategy here is the close specification of the framework within which Charlie is to make decisions. That framework comprises a *finite* set of alternative possible decisions from which Charlie is able to choose rather than a set of conformist or *oppositional* decisions involving compliance or non-compliance which would be opened up by the use of direct commands and orders.

The intention contained within these second-level decisions which make up the coping strategy of confrontation avoidance is to frame the parameters of interaction such that Charlie will be made organisationally proper. The teachers here can be seen to be 'making a proper Charlie' of him. This is a deliberate use of irony on my part, for the implementation of such a coping strategy may have fatal consequences for Charlie's self and identity, even though it may defuse his explosive potential.

There are strong connections between involvement in social interaction, the presentation, implementation and mutual recognition of identities and the development or sustenance of the self. Now, although the coping strategy of policing and other explicit, formal, public modes of classroom interaction involve a depersonalisation of the pupil (i.e. he is manifestly treated as one of a type rather than as a unique individual), nevertheless the explicit, public character of such forms of interaction makes available the hierarchical nature of the relationship which obtains between teacher and pupil and hence establishes the communication and imposition of an identity upon the pupil by the teacher. Such identities are not necessarily accepted by the pupil. They need not be incorporated into the definition of his self. Indeed, Goffman has pointed out that through the employment of secondary adjustments 'the individual stands apart from the role and the self that were taken for granted for him by the institution'.[22]

The totalitarian quality of classroom life characteristic of policing entails the exertion of teacher control over the most detailed of pupil actions and it closely circumscribes the latter's autonomy. Yet it also facilitates the recognition of *an* identity, and the preservation of the self through a distancing off from such institutionally imposed identities. In individualised patterns of classroom interaction, these possibilities are reduced. The avoidance of confrontation, where it comes to constitute the avoidance of interaction, can lead to the removal of communicable identities and hence can invite dissolution of the self. Such is the case with Charlie. Since the self is constituted reflexively through interaction with others, where such interaction is seriously diminished, then the absence of communicated identities might well lead to the self perceiving itself as a non-entity. Had individualised interaction been the only form of classroom discourse, then it would have been reasonable to have hypothesised the dissolution of the self in Charlie's case.

There are two factors which obviate such a process, however. First, Charlie, like other actors, is more than merely a passive recipient of an imposed social order and possesses the ability to respond constructively to pressures which he experiences. Secondly, the presence of some formal, explicit, public classroom contexts (e.g. policing) provides a platform upon which Charlie can present and assert witnessable definitions of his own existence and worth.

First-level decisions

Charlie, then, has an interest in presenting a definition of his self—in asserting an identity, possibly *any* identity. This interest is not only normal to social interaction, but is, I would suggest, particularly acute for West Indian boys, given the active expressivity of their culture (Driver, 1976). Charlie's need to establish an identity coupled with the teachers' wish to avoid confrontation result in 'interesting' negotiative processes at the first level of decision-making.

Early in the lesson one of the teachers sets about organising the class into groups of four to construct and perform their mimes. The teacher counts slowly up to five to allow time for this to be completed.

149

T   Four (class is now quiet—three-second pause) Five.
Ch   We haven't got four.
T1   Right. Everybody's ready. Now then, what you're going to
        do with your group. . . . (26–30)

A true, 'legitimate' statement uttered by Charlie (there were only three
in his group) is here ignored by the teacher. Charlie seeks attention by
stating that his group does not come up to organisational requirements.
The teacher responds by not responding, i.e. she does not engage in any
(spoken) interaction with Charlie. That this would seem to be a reaction to Charlie-making-the-statement, rather than to the statement
itself, is confirmed when another pupil in Charlie's threesome reiterates
the problem.

P   Miss, there's only three of us.
T1   Well go (inaudible) then. It doesn't matter. . . (80–1)

Because the transcription is inaudible at one point, it is not perfectly
clear whether or not the teacher's response constitutes a rejection of
the legitimacy of the pupil's observation. The important point, however, is that this pupil receives recognition whereas Charlie did not.

Charlie's second contribution to the proceedings constitutes the first
instance of rule transgression on his part. Martyn Hammersley (1974)
has noted how, in formally organised classrooms, pupils are often invited and required to participate in lessons when the teacher signals
that this is appropriate. The complex procedure of participation is rule
governed partly for the maintenance of orderly social relations within
the class. Charlie succeeds skilfully in breaking one important and
fundamental rule of participation—not speaking out of turn. In this
instance, the teacher is inviting suggestions for a mime:

P   Tidying up
T1   Tidying up ∧
P   Clearing up
T1   Clearing up ∧
P   Being the milkman
T1   Yes ∧
P   Going to school
T1   Going to school. ∨ It can be anything you can think of.
Ch   Swimming.
T1   Sssshhhh-er-If we see anybody being silly, you'll come and sit
        down here and you won't take part in the lesson. . . .(43–53)

The requirement for continued participation is here indicated by upward intonation in the teacher's voice.[23] The downward intonation in
line 50 signals the termination of legitimate suggestions. This signal is
reinforced by the closing statement, 'It can be anything you can think

of'. It is at this point that Charlie again asserts his existence by inserting a suggestion at an inappropriate point, one reserved for teacher talk. In effect, Charlie temporarily takes the teacher's talk away from her. Although the teacher's next utterance 'Sssshhhh' appears to be a response to Charlie, in fact it was directed more to the class as a whole, many of whom were now shuffling and muttering considerably. Again, therefore, Charlie's 'contribution' is ostensibly ignored through another non-response on the teacher's part. To reiterate an earlier point, this non-response is not inconsequential, for it constitutes an action of *intended* avoidance. The likelihood follows that Charlie will make additional moves in order to have an identity recognised and witnessed. Yet the teacher too is intent on avoiding overt conflict with Charlie. The negotiative strategies hence proceed and escalate. Consider the next extract, where the pupils are attempting to guess what has just been mimed. Several suggestions have already been offered:

T	Charlie?
Ch	Eating sweets and taking 'em off 'em. . . .putting 'em up at wall.
M	We're not eating sweets.
P	Eating bubbly gum.
M	(Shakes head)
Ch	Eatin' sausage roll.
P's	(slight giggles)
T2	We've already said they're eating sweets. (141-9)

Charlie first offers what would appear to be an authentic suggestion of what is being mimed. This guess is incorrect. After another incorrect pupil attempt to guess the mime, Charlie puts forward a more comic suggestion. It is somewhat equivocal whether or not this suggestion constitutes an intentionally deviant act. Though our own common sense would tell us that a guess is incorrect because it wrongly identifies the action (eating) rather than the object (sweets), such a distinction is not drawn within the mimic's reply, 'We're not eating sweets', nor anywhere else in the transcript so far. It is therefore *possible* that Charlie's second guess ('Eatin' sausage roll') is an honest contribution, although the smile which accompanied his remark might indicate the opposite. If there is any initial doubt, however, the pupils' giggles in response to his suggestion retrospectively confer upon it a deviant status. This is the first time that Charlie's remarks produce an effect (giggling) upon the rest of the class. Interestingly, it is also the first time that his remarks merit a spoken response on the part of the teacher.[24] It is therefore at least plausible that the intervention of the teacher is connected to the potential threat of the wider breakdown of classroom order which Charlie's remark creates.

In view of the teacher's intention to avoid confrontation, the substance of her response is especially interesting. It is, in fact, a lie. The teacher's non-controversial response imputes an alternative intention to Charlie's utterance. In re-defining the remark as a reasonable contribution rather than an intended challenge, direct confrontation is avoided (Wegmann, 1976). Charlie's contribution is treated as incorrect rather than inappropriate. As a result, Charlie's intentions are not besmirched by the teacher. However, I am not suggesting that the felt necessity to avoid direct confrontation has led the teacher to construct a calculated lie. Rather, the urgency of strategically avoiding confrontation would seem to engender a particular structuring of perceptions which might then lead to the inadvertent statement of 'false' reasons on the part of the teacher.

In producing a response from the teacher and hence a witnessable recognition of his existence, Charlie has had an initial glimpse of 'success'. The 'silly foods' theme, from Charlie's point of view, is worth developing.

P Being naughty.
M No.
T2 You'll never guess.
Ch Got fish and chips.
T1 Charlie! (150-4)

Charlie's contributions are amusing in so far as they constitute a redefinition of the game (What's my mime?) as one of guessing increasingly absurd objects as opposed to actions. In so doing he undermines the teachers' conventional definition of mime and thereby constitutes a threat to classroom order. The teachers are confronted with an escalating series of challenges from Charlie which present them with increasingly difficult decisions whereby the necessity to maintain classroom order must be traded off against a wish to avoid direct confrontation when dealing with Charlie. This dilemma is exploited with great skill and success by Charlie in his development of the 'silly foods' theme. At this point the trade-off results in the teacher paying attention to Charlie and, through her tone, indicating to him that he is being deviant. By 'naming' Charlie, his deviance is pointed out but the exact nature of Charlie's deviant act is not explicitly stated. When a teacher only *names* the miscreant, then the nature of his deviance must be *inferred* by all who hear this naming (D. Hargreaves *et al.*, 1975). The act, and the identity that attaches to the act, are not in this instance spelt out.

Charlie has thus far transformed the response of the teacher to him from one where she avoids interaction altogether to one where, by being named, Charlie's deviant behaviour and deviant character are implied. Charlie takes the process one step further and achieves startling results after the next mime (delivering milk) has been performed.

T1   Right, well don't look at me, ask them.
M   Charlie?
Ch   You're having a bag of chips.
M   No.
T1   Right, we're not going to ask Charlie in future 'cos he's being silly. (197–202)

The highly lucrative 'silly foods' theme is here extended to its ultimate conclusion—its insertion into a situation where the actions involved in the mime could not, even by the most imaginative speculation, be regarded as embodying any kind of eating. The absurdity of Charlie's contribution and the alternative definition of classroom events which he thereby puts forward pose a more serious threat to orderly classroom relations. The teacher abandons the delicate process of trading off alternatives and opts instead for more direct confrontation. Charlie is named as a deviant, his deviant acts are explicitly stated and notice is given of his future exclusion and the grounds for this exclusion.

Charlie, it could be argued, has proved victorious. Using an ingenious set of negotiative strategies, he has succeeded in having an identity recognised and publicly proclaimed. For a brief moment, through having to make a first-level decision which resulted in a confrontation with Charlie, the teacher has been momentarily prised out of the framework circumscribed by the coping strategy of confrontation avoidance. Yet any success on Charlie's part is a Pyrrhic victory. It is true that the negotiative strategies he employed and the counter-strategies which these induced may well have averted the wreckage and loss of the self, but fatal consequences have followed in the hardening of a deviant career.[25]

The classroom negotiations in which Charlie has been involved can be seen as one small phase in the much broader process of deviancy amplification. Such a process involves a hardening of the deviant's identity[26] and the committing of further deviant acts largely as a result of the way in which social control agencies define and treat him. In this process of secondary deviation (Lemert, 1951), the deviant (Charlie) develops defence mechanisms in order to cope with the problems created by the reaction of the control agents to him as a deviant.

To sum up, through his expulsion from a previous school and through the reports accompanying that expulsion, Charlie is defined as a deviant. On the basis of this definition, teachers adopt a coping strategy of confrontation avoidance in an attempt to frame the parameters within which subsequent interaction can occur. As these second-level decisions are translated into first-level decisions which initially involve the general evasion of interaction with Charlie, problems are created for him. These problems concern the threats posed to the maintenance of the self through the difficulty of having an identity recognised and witnessed by others. Charlie, therefore, at the second level of decision-making adopts the coping strategy of identity recognition. This coping strategy is translated into first-level decisions which are enacted as negotiative strategies. These involve the presentation of alternative definitions of classroom events and the breaking of organisational (interactional) rules. As these strategies escalate in severity, the teachers are increasingly constrained into recognising Charlie's new deviance and into explicitly stating the precise nature of his deviance. Through this process, Charlie's deviant identity is confirmed, hardened and perpetuated. In the establishment of ominous future careers, strategic interaction and the decisions which it incorporates can indeed have both fateful and fatal consequences.

From the above evidence, two specific conclusions can be drawn, although these clearly require substantiation in further research. First, the coping strategies of policing and of confrontation-avoidance are mutually incompatible. The former, indeed, provides the grounds for the negation of the latter. Charlie would have found much greater difficulty in asserting his identity and provoking confrontation in a less explicit and less public interactional context. Second, the unintended consequence of the employment of these strategies in combination is that the very deviance which teachers are seeking to eliminate or control is exacerbated. The management of classroom life no longer remains efficient and where this situation continues, the strategy of expulsion will be turned to as the last resort. This ultimately happened in Charlie's case and marked another definitive stage in the development of his deviant career.

The obvious question which will now present itself to the reader is: If the coping strategies of policing and confrontation-avoidance are mutually incompatible, is it not *technically* possible to replace one of them with a superior alternative? It is to such 'technical' matters, and the fact that they cannot be adequately solved (or framed) at the interactionist level alone, that I turn in the final section.

Strategies, decisions and social power

Interactionist accounts provide necessary but not sufficient explanations of power and decision-making in schools and classrooms. If structural and ideological considerations are eschewed, it might naively be thought that where teacher strategies and decisions prove inefficient and counter-productive, then the remedy is to suggest and experiment with different techniques. In this way, the academic researcher supplants the common-sense rationality of the teacher with his own 'scientifically based' means-end rationality. However, the exposure of inefficiency and the suggestion of alternative remedial proposals begs

the question of what efficiency is for. As the new technocrat of pedagogy, the researcher, in adopting such an approach, fails to appreciate
the constraining and defining features of the societal context and to
consider the presently absent structural alternatives which might offer
very different criteria of efficiency (Fay, 1975). Habermas (1971)[27]
has commented perceptively on this crucial issue:

> Within the framework of research operations that expand our
> power of technical control we can make no cogent statements
> about 'value systems', that is, about social needs and objective
> states of consciousness, about the directions of emancipation and
> regression.

There are, of course, immense difficulties in forging the necessary
connections between structural and interactionist levels of explanation.
It is partly for this reason that discussion on this topic has thus far been
largely programmatic and exhortatory in character (Bernbaum, 1977;
Karabel and Halsey, 1976). Research within the sociology of education
has been conducted at *either* the interactionist *or* the structural level.
The schism is neatly symbolised in the Open University's production of
two parallel course texts for the 'Schooling and Society' course. The
reader on 'Schooling and Capitalism' (Dale, Esland and Macdonald,
1976) contains articles which are 'assembled to show how the capitalist
mode of production influences one social institution, schooling', whereas the reader on 'The Process of Schooling' (Hammersley and Woods,
1976), despite the repeated cautionary remarks of its authors, nevertheless comprises papers which are broadly articulated at the interactionist level of explanation. The main substance of *this* paper has
also, of course, been generally interactionist in tone.

In this final section, although I cannot propose any sweeping solutions to such difficulties, my aim is to provide a skeletal outline of a
model which might allow a more meaningful interrelation between
structural and interactionist considerations to be achieved. Initial
connections will be suggested between first- and second-level decisions,
negotiative and coping strategies, and decision-making and social power.

The model I propose is based upon Steven Lukes's formulation of
three dimensions of power, though there are some points where Lukes's
model is not *directly* applicable to the classroom context.[28] Lukes outlines three dimensions of power in which, as one moves from the first
to the third dimension, processes of decision-making become less observable and accessible and more difficult to demonstrate empirically.

For Lukes, the *one-dimensional view of power* is typified by Dahl's
book, *Who Governs,* on community power structures and decision-
making processes. In this view, those who have power are those who get
their decisions accepted. Through empirical observation of the process
of conflict which comes to produce any concrete decision, who has

power can be inferred from noting who succeeds in getting others to do something which they otherwise would not have done. Conflict, negotiation and decision-making are hence concrete, observable processes which reveal the exercise of power in any given situation.

The parallel here would be the classroom context of observable interaction between teachers and pupils. The techniques of policing and the strategic interaction in which the teachers and Charlie engaged would here be seen as revealing the exercise of power on any specific occasion. Such an interpretation would accord with some perspectives within classroom interaction research which assume that the structures of power and control are directly inferrable from observed interaction between teachers and pupils. Within such a view, Charlie might be seen to have relatively *more* power than the rest of the pupils in his class in so far as he engages more actively in processes of teacher-pupil negotiation. The one-dimensional view of power would therefore comprise almost solely analyses of first-level decisions and negotiative strategies and would lend itself to *technical* proposals for reform, by way of, say, equipping teachers with the requisite social skills to 'handle' difficult pupils.

The *two-dimensional view of power* involves an examination of the processes of both decision-making and non-decision-making. Non-decisions are those crucial issues which through skilful manipulation never appear on the agenda of discussion and therefore do not arise and are not manifested as *observable* conflict. Such non-decisions therefore have considerable defining power in so far as they result in the

> Suppression or thwarting of a latent or manifest challenge to the values or interests of the decision-maker.[29]

Lukes is eager to point out that

> so called non-decisions which confine the scope of decision-making are themselves observable decisions.[30]

In an educational context, the two-dimensional view of power can be seen as embracing second-level decisions and coping strategies. The choice of mime as a means of social control is an instance of such a process within the area of the curriculum. Policing and confrontation-avoidance are examples of coping strategies which are selected and implemented at this second level. Although such strategies and decisions demarcate the boundaries within which specific successive encounters will be situated, they are themselves available in teacher accounts, informal staff discussions, staff meetings etc.

The two-dimensional view clearly adds considerable weight to any analysis of classroom processes. It instructs us to recognise that in the study of teacher-pupil talk, although we may feel strongly that we are 'where the action is', the crucial definitive actions may nevertheless be occurring elsewhere. For example, survival strategies can be more subtly dissected into those appropriate to the second level (coping strategies) and those techniques and devices appropriate to the first level (negotiative strategies). There are two main difficulties with the two-dimensional view, however. First, in an educational context, there is the problem of infinite regress. If second-level decisions are those taken elsewhere (other than the classroom), then there would seem to be no necessary reason why analyses must remain in the staffroom alone. The activities of examining boards, LEA policy makers, the Schools Council and the Assessment of Performance Unit are but a few examples of locales where decisions are taken which are consequential in enabling and enclosing possibilities for classroom teaching and learning. Second, the central concern of the two-dimensional view with observable processes of decision-making obviates any consideration of the nature and source of the dominant assumptions which underpin definitions of valid curricula and conceptions of teaching and learning.

A fundamental concern with sociopolitical and ideological constraints upon decision-making has led to Lukes's elaboration of a *three-dimension view of power*. Now, to talk of constraints must involve some discussion of *experienced* constraints (although, interestingly, this is an aspect of the decision-making process which Lukes ignores). Such a discussion not only calls for a situationist analysis of the influence of factors such as class sizes on decisions and strategies, but also necessitates an explanation which would show how features of the social and political structure are institutionally mediated, experienced and coped with by teachers. For example, the relationship among an objective class structure, the teacher's typifications of different social classes and the problems which these groups are seen to present to her teaching, discipline and cultural standards of propriety has been teased out by Becker (1952). Similarly, in the lesson which has been analysed in this paper, the teachers' coping strategies of policing and confrontation avoidance can be seen as creatively articulated responses to the problems presented by lower working class pupils, both behaviourally and academically. First- and second-level decisions can therefore be seen as constructed responses to institutionally mediated constraints, which frame the range of possible practices which teachers and pupils may subsequently engage in.

Concrete experienced constraints of both a situationist and a derived structural kind are crucial features which are absent from Lukes's model. On the other hand, in his three-dimensional view of power, Lukes succeeds in showing that power may be present in the absence of overt conflict. Where decisions are not taken, or felt necessary, the very existence of consensus may be the result of

the supreme and most insidious exercise of power (which is) to prevent people to whatever degree, from having grievances by shaping their perceptions, cognitions and preferences in such a way that they accept their role in the existing order of things, either because they see or imagine no alternative to it, or because they see it as natural and unchangeable. . . .[31]

The engineering of social consensus may come to mean the definition of the very boundaries of common sense within a society. Where a dominant class controls not only the economic and political institutions of a society but also the ideological ones (e.g. mass media and education), then, according to the Italian Marxist Antonio Gramsci (1971), it also has the power to define accepted ways of life and thought and the very 'parameters of legitimate discussion and debate over alternative beliefs, values and world views' (Sallach, 1974). This process of ideological dominance Gramsci referred to as hegemony.[32]

An attempt to identify hegemonic parameters in particular ideological institutions has been made by David Sallach (1974). In considering the educational system, Sallach points out that curriculum content insulates children from political conflict and from oppositional values. In this sense, through the characterisation of sex roles, racial minority groups etc. in texts and in teachers' talk, the political socialisation of the child is normative in character.

The assumption behind Sallach's work, however, is that ideological hegemony is expressed only through the content of learning. That forms of domination may themselves be routine, taken-for-granted ideological components of the educational, social and political process is a question not raised by Sallach. This brings us full circle to the empirical material in this paper: underlying the coping and negotiative strategies which teachers employ are a set of ideologically dominant, yet taken-for-granted assumptions about the 'needs' of working class children, about who shall ultimately control the acquisition of knowledge and about who shall be the arbiters of pupil behaviour. The dominance of the teacher may be so taken for granted and seem so natural to the reader that he may think it absurd even to raise the point as one worthy of debate. Yet the question is not so much one of pupil control versus adult control, of youth power, or of the de-schooler's romantic celebration of the self-regulated child. The question is a deeper and ultimately an historical one. The substitution of State control of the educational process and the appointment of its own agents to do this work for attempts by the working class to control the education and, hence, consciousness-formation of its own members in the form of secular Sunday schools etc. was, historically, a highly contentious issue. In time, the form of education provided by a State, which essentially serves the interests of the dominant class, therefore becomes the dominant but also, eventually, the legitimate and taken-for-granted form, such that its evolution may even be viewed retrospectively as a process of liberalisation. Since the State also monopolises the schooling process experienced by other class groupings, its influence therefore appears both universal and neutral (masking the differential effect of various modes of domination in schools, classes, streams and sets which cater largely for children from different social classes). As a result, forms of domination which derive, historically, from problems of class come to manifest themselves as problems of generation such that their over-throwal appears utopian or absurd.

Apart from the insights provided by historical analysis, the proof of ideological dominance also lies in those rare occasions when practices change, assumptions are undermined and tacit shared understandings are momentarily torn asunder. Garfinkel (1967) has shown how such natural or engineered disruptive incidents may lay bare the tacit understandings and common sense knowledge upon which everyday social life is founded. This also applies to the substantive elements of common sense thought. The events at William Tyndale, where priorities were allocated to working class pupils rather than to a 'successful' sponsored pupil elite, exemplify such a process:

> All teachers have a chance of where to lay the emphasis in classes, which group will get the time and attention. The vast majority opt for the privileged children. But Tyndale had its priorities and the managers recognised its danger.[33]

In the middle school classroom considered in this paper, teachers operated within a framework of unchallenged assumptions. That working class children needed stability and order and were to be behaviourally regulated rather than academically pushed was one such basic assumption. That the teacher selects, organises and evaluates the knowledge to be acquired and displayed by children is a further un-questioned assumption. The dominant position of the teacher is itself a crucial component of such ideologically dominant forms of thought.

Coping strategies therefore can be seen as alternative techniques of domination, manipulation and persuasion within a framework pre-dicated on the tacitly accepted understanding of the teacher's domi-nance—her control of the knowledge production and acquisition pro-cess. As a set of managerial and pedagogical techniques, coping strate-gies (despite their creatively articulated character), negotiative strategies and the first- and second-level decisions which accompany them are not organised within any conception of the social whole. They are a response to constraints but do not provide the means for overthrowing them. Through the practical knowledge enshrined in teacher 'experience' they persist as techniques of domination, yet the roots of that domi-nation remain unquestioned and unchanged. When strategies and de-cisions are merely technically available alternatives within an un-articulated and unquestioned educational and social whole, then they

will inevitably become fragmented, incompatible and contradictory—
this is the origin of the incompatibility between policing and confrontation-avoidance.[34]

Significant educational change will therefore not result from an overhaul or replacement of strategies and decisions when these are considered as techniques in isolation from any constraining or enabling
social and educational structure. The forms and the content of domination can be transcended only through the consideration of alternative
structural possibilities and (by significantly changing the relationship
between educational theory and teaching practice) through the re-
constitution of teacher 'experience'. The pragmatic adaptive function
of 'experience' might then be transformed into a critical libertarian one.
Reconstituting teacher experience entails not only engaging in critique
with teachers. Important though this is, there is also an urgent necessity
to transform the institutional conditions within which teachers work:
to reduce class sizes, improve material facilities and democratise staff
relationships so that at least some effort is made to provide the institutional conditions under which collective critique would become both
meaningful and possible. If we fail to attend to these material pre-
conditions for meaningful critique, there is a trap waiting which has
ensnared many a sociologist lured by the bait of 'critical theory'. This
trap is the belief that the sociologist can engage in meaningful dialogue
with other members of the social world through a process of undistorted
communication made possible by the elimination of any asymmetric
elements in the discourse group/institution/society. Through the
critique of common sense which critical theory provides, it is said, the
veil of everyday thought will be lifted to reveal an 'objective' view of
the present along with a vision of the future. This may provide the
sociologist with a mission. In his role as theoriser, he may even feel a
little smug. However, the world is not transformed through thought
alone. The teacher's common sense conceptions, though essentially
conservative in their implications, persist because of their very ability
to enable the teacher to survive in the face of overwhelming constraints.
These constraints, in so far as they delimit the teacher's actions and
thoughts along with her opportunity *and energy* to think otherwise,
provide their own guarantee for their continued existence. The easing
of such constraints is thus an essential part of any programme to re-
constitute teacher experience. Programmes which are based on thought
alone and which fail to attend to the material conditions in which such
thought is located will become just one more instance of the failed
missionary work of sociology.[35] These proposals for transforming
teacher experience are fundamentally radical, for 'When the whole is at
stake, there is no crime except that of rejecting the whole, or not
defending it.'[36]

Investigations of strategic interaction and classroom decision-making processes can provide us with detailed ethnographic accounts of the school. Everyday realities must not be assumed or ignored by statements about structure. But there are limits to the explanatory power of strategic-interactionist models unless they are coherently integrated with considerations of structural constraints and the defining power of ideologically dominant value systems. To make such connections in a radical way not only allows meaningful understanding of the experienced present but also enables the delineation of a possible future.[37]

Transcript of a drama lesson

Key

T1		1st teacher
T2		2nd teacher
P		Pupil
M		Mimic
Ch		Charlie
∧		Upward intonation
∨		Downward intonation
1	T1	Right, all of you, sit on the carpet. C'mon.
2		(Pause)
3		Go sit on the carpet.
4		(Pause—children settle down on the carpet while
5		teacher & researcher talk)
6		Right. (Pause) What we're going to do this afternoon
7		is something that only very, very sensible people can
8		do. You'd better put your foot down, Terry Carter.
9		People who behave like Terry Carter
10		can't do it. Now then, without fussing (Pause)
11		without talking and shouting or whatever, I want you to
12		get into little groups of four. I said without talking,
13		so sit down again. Penny Dawson, sit down. When you're
14		in your groups, put your hands on your head so we can
15		see you're ready.
16		(Long pause—some noise as children organise into
17		groups)
18		Right, by the time I count five, I want you all sitting
19		with your hands on your heads without talking.
20		One (three-second pause)
21		Two (four-second pause)
22		Three—Who's got four? Which group has got four?
23		Right Pam, c'mon over here.
24		(Eight seconds pass after the word 'three' is uttered

25		and before the utterance below)
26		Four (class is now quiet—three-second pause)
27		Five.
28	Ch	We haven't got four.
29	T1	Right. Everybody's ready. Now then, what you're going
30		to do with your group. You can go anywhere in my area,
31		in the little corner or anywhere in Mrs H's area where
32		we can see you. You're going to get together and you're
33		going to think of something to mime. Now then, what
34		sort of things can it be?
35	P	Doing baking.
36	T1	Doing baking. ∧
37	P	At the shop.
38	T1	At the shop. ∧
39	P	Playing.
40	T1	Playing. ∧
41	P	Sewing.
42	T1	Sewing. ∧
43	P	Tidying up.
44	T1	Tidying up. ∧
45	P	Clearing up.
46	T1	Clearing up. ∧
47	P	Being the milkman.
48	T1	Yes. ∧
49	P	Going to school.
50	T1	Going to school. ∨ It can be anything you can think of.
51	Ch	Swimming!
52	T1	Sssshhhh. -er- If we see anybody being silly, you'll come
53		and sit down here and you won't take part in the lesson.
54		Are you listening, John Clarkson?
55		Now then, we'll give you about five minutes in which
56		to get (pause—looks at child talking to another child)
57		your mime ready. You do it without making a lot of
58		noise (raised voice), otherwise we won't bother. We'll
59		just come and sit down here and you'll get your reading
60		books. Are you listening? You're being very bad
61		mannered, Barry. And then when you've done it (pause—
62		look) you're all going to show us in your groups in
63		turns and we're going to see if we can guess what you've
64		been doing. So you've got to be very quiet because if
65		you stand over there and shout 'Oh, let's do this, let's
66		all be milkmen'—everybody'll know before you even
67		start. So you get together and you whisper very quietly
68		and then (pause—look) you work it out and you go
69		practise it—very quietly. When you're ready and when

70		I tell you, come and sit down and then we'll let you do
71		it in your groups. Right now, you've got to be really
72		sensible because if Mrs H sees anybody being silly or I
73		see anybody you will sit down. You won't take part in
74		it again this afternoon.
75	P	There's only two of us—me and Colin
76	T1	Well you can still do. . . .
77	P	We've got two
78	T1	There's two of you. Right, well you four join together
79		then.
80	P	Miss, there's only three of us.
81	T1	Well go (inaudible) then. It doesn't matter. Right,
82		very quietly, in your groups.
83		(Pupils now prepare their mimes. They are talking in
84		order to organise their mimes, but some are also
85		incorporating talk into their 'mime'.)
86	T2	Stop! Everybody stop! What's a mime? Nora? (pupil's
87		name)
88	N	It's when you don't speak.
89	T2	There is no speaking *at all* (raised voice). So it's no
90		good saying 'Well, I'll come and so and so to you and
91		you say such and such to me'. There's got to be no
92		talking at all. So really we shouldn't hear any sound
93		at all from you at all.
94		(Preparation continues)
95	T1	Right, now. (Pause) Now. Right. The people over there,
96		can you move over here so that whoever's doing it can
97		(Pause) be in front of you.
98		(Children move around)
99	T1	Don't be stupid.
100		(Long pause)
101	T1	Right, sit down on your bottoms, all of you.
102	P	(inaudible)
103	T1	On your bottoms, every single one of you. Now, people
104		round there can't see.
105	T2	There's plenty of space over here.
106	T1	Don't you dare move. You're liable to get your heads
107		chopped off.
108	T2	Look at that space there.
109	T1	Right. Now then. Which group would like to volunteer
110		to go first?
111		(Hands are raised)
112	T1	Ivy had her hand up first. Your group, c'mon, in this
113		space. Now then, you will have to be *really* quiet.
114		(Group moves towards front of audience)

Lines 75–77 are bracketed together with the annotation: (Complex interchange!)

115	T1	Sssshhhh! Sit *down*. Colin! David! Sandra! On your
116		bottom! They can't see for you. *You,* on your bottom
117		like everybody else. You can see through that gap as
118		well as anybody else. Right. You ready?
119		(Mime is now in progress. The particular mime is of
120		a situation involving poor table manners and the
121		offenders being placed up against a wall as
122		'punishment by their teacher'. The following
123		utterances occur whilst the mime is in progress.)
124	T2	You are talking.
125	P's	(inaudible)
126	T2	Now watch her. (Referring to the mime.)
127	T1	Remember, you've to guess what they're doing.
128	D	You've not to eat in school.
129	T2	Don't be silly about it, John.
130	T1	Have you finished? Right.
131		Well don't look at me. It's them you're asking.
132		(Addressed to the audience.)
133	P	Eating sweets in school and getting into trouble.
134	M	No.
135	T1	Does anyone know?
136		P. (Inaudible suggestion)
137	M	No.
138	P	Eating. . . .
139		T. Charlie?
140		P. . . . food (continuation of line 138)
141		T. Charlie?
142	Ch	Eating sweets and taking 'em off 'em. . . putting 'em
143		up at wall.
144	M	We're not eating sweets.
145	P	Eating bubbly gum.
146	M	(Shakes head)
147	Ch	Eatin' sausage roll.
148	P's	(slight giggles)
149	T2	We've already said they're eating sweets.
150	P	Being naughty.
151	M	No.
152	T2	You'll never guess.
153	Ch	Got fish and chips.
154	T1	Charlie!
155	P	They've both been bad mannered at table and been put in
156		t'corner.
157	M	Yes.
158	T1	That's right.
159	T2	Very good.

160	T1	That's fifteen team points for you, Matthew. You guessed
161		right. Now which group would like to go next?
162	T2	Sssshhhh.
163		(Hands are used to indicate who would like to go next.)
164	T1	(Selects a person) Is that the group who guessed it?
165	P	Yes.
166	T1	The group who guessed it. Right, Matthew, you, your group.
167		(Mime takes place. The subject this time is delivering
168		milk. Talk again takes place during the performance.)
169	T1	(Inaudible)
170	T2	Right, any silliness and you'll sit back down. (Addressed
171		to the mimics)
172	D	Yeah!
173	T2	Donald, are you in this? (Donald opted initially to be
174		excluded from the proceedings and has been drawing at
175		the side of the mimed performance but periodically moves
176		forward to observe the proceedings or to pass comment.)
177	D	No, Miss.
178	T2	Will you move toward the wall, then.
179		(Players are still on stage but have not yet started
180		the performance.)
181	M	Miss, Gary isn't here.
182	T1	C'mon, Gary. C'mon. Take your jumper off or is that
183		necessary. (Gary has a jumper tied round his neck.)
184		Right. Have you started (addressed to mimics)? Have
185		you started, Trevor?
186	M	Yeah.
187		(Performance now definitely under way.)
188	T1	I can't see what you're doing for Paul.
189	M's	(Much quiet giggling.)
190	T1	I think you're being a bit silly. Can you do it without
191		giggling, Terry?
192	M	Yeah.
193	T1	Donald, I suggest you go and sit down (Donald has moved
194		across to view proceedings again). Right, have you
195		finished?
196	M	Yes, Miss.
197	T1	Right, well don't look at me, ask them.
198	M	Charlie?
199	Ch	You're having a bag of chips.
200	M	No.
201	T1	Right, we're not going to ask Charlie in future 'cos he's
202		being silly.
203	P	Playing marbles.
204	M's	No.

205	P	(Inaudible)
206	M	What?
207	P	Meals on wheels?
208	M	No.
209	P	Playing about.
210	M	No.
211	P	Getting a drink o' water.
212	M	No.
213	P	Goin' to t'shop?
214	M	No.
215	P	Delivering milk?
216	M	Yeah.
217	T1	Well done. That's fifteen team points for you, Terry, and
218		your group.

(And so on after the tape has run out, with three
more mimes.)

Notes

1 Karabel and Halsey (1976).
2 In a case study which I conducted of two middle schools in suburban middle-class communities, instances of class teaching could be found even in the open-plan progressively organised institution. Groups of children were often addressed or taught as corporate units in French, at 'story time' and during periods of 'management' (e.g. commencing a new topic or arranging a school trip).
3 For a more detailed outline of the concept *coping strategy* in the context of progressive education see A. Hargreaves (1977b).
4 The choice of evidence from the small project rather than the major case study in two suburban middle-class middle schools is an act of deliberate selection on my part. The reason for my choice is that the salient features of policing and confrontation-avoidance are, I wish to argue, more clearly displayed in a school where the majority of the pupils are lower working class in origin.
5 See the final section for a more precise explication of this point.
6 Plowden Report (1967), p. 195.
7 This point is developed in the analysis of the transcript.
8 Parsons's assertion that such a conflation does not occur in secondary education now seems untenable in the light of subsequent research which has focused upon classroom interaction processes in secondary schools.
9 I use the term 'need' here in a psychologistic context-transcendent sense rather than a situationally specific one where needs would be seen as shaped by structural forms.
10 The question of the relationship between 'teaching' and social control is an urgent one and is of central importance to the sociology

of education. In this paper, I can offer only some brief comments which might aid clarification. One point I particularly wish to stress is that it should not be thought that it is somehow possible to devise a method whereby the polluting force of social control could be filtered out of the schooling process, and that the task of social science is to discover an efficient technique of filtration which would leave behind pure 'teaching'. The notion of pure teaching is as fallacious as that of undistorted communication when these processes are situated in hierarchical structures of power and domination. The conventional separations of education from politics and of task-based from non-task-based issues (Gibson, 1977) rests on a similar error.

There is a sense in which, in capitalist societies, education *is* social control in that it plays a preparatory and supportive role in reproducing the social relations of production, i.e. in perpetuating the structured relations of dominance and subordinacy in the society. My reference to social control in this paper is thus a narrower one and concerns its more explicit manifestation as a 'gentling of the masses'. This definition is probably closest to teachers' and educators' phenomenal awareness of social control as discipline and placation in circumstances where they are faced with such pressing matters as ROSLA or of the 'problems' presented by children in deprived areas, for example. Using social control in this sense, I would therefore argue that it is possible to distinguish it from something else which we might call teaching where the imparting and creation of school-relevant knowledge is considered the primary concern. Likewise, it is therefore legitimate, at this level, to distinguish between the cognitive and the moral components of schooling.

11 Explicit statements are those where the meaning is expressed literally. By literal meanings I refer to those which are least dependent on the social context for their sense.

12 By negotiative strategies, I mean those which must be implemented through and witnessed in on-going interaction. Negotiation here should not be taken to mean a process of reaching common agreement. Where interactional rights and power resources are distributed so unevenly, negotiative strategies could clearly not be part of a free bargaining procedure.

13 See n. 10.

14 P. 274.

15 Attempts to produce typologies of teacher behaviour proliferate in the sociology and social psychology of education. Interaction schedules invariably either seek to elicit or are predicated on different teaching styles (see Bennett, 1976). Some of the best attempts to produce lists of teaching styles which take into consideration the constraints within which such styles are framed are to be found in Waller (1932), D.H. Hargreaves (1972), and Woods (1977). Studies of particular coping strategies are too numerous and varied to mention. However, one exceptional and now classic study giving an account of the policing role of the teacher which is closest to the

one offered here is Webb's (1962) study of the secondary modern school teacher who is described as performing the role of drill sergeant.

16 Goffman (1970), p. 101—my stress.

17 P. 101.

18 See Goffman (1961, 1963).

19 The term 'avoidance of confrontation' is used in Hammersley's (1976) study of interaction in a secondary modern school (p. 109).

20 Goffman (1970), p. 91.

21 This information was given to me by the teachers.

22 For an account of the process of secondary adjustment see Goffman (1961), p. 172.

23 The indication through upward intonation that more participation is required does not always mean that pupil responses have been *accepted*. This is the case only where the teacher is eliciting alternative suggestions. Where she is after a 'right answer', then the signal for continued participation implies a *rejection* of previous contributions.

24 Indeed, the teacher's reply, 'We've already said they're eating sweets', could have been intended not only for Charlie's ears but for those of the whole class. (There are no grounds either in the transcript or in the original recording to assess how far this was true, however.)

25 Charlie now attends a residential school for the maladjusted.

26 This is despite the fact that ostensibly the teachers seek to *avoid* communicating this identity to the pupil.

27 P. 64.

28 The major difference is that, in classrooms, decisions are very much constitutive of the on-going flow of social interaction, whereas for Lukes, decisions are the *outcome* of debates and discussions about particular issues.

29 Bachrach and Baratz, quoted in Lukes (1974), p. 18.

30 *Ibid.*, p. 18.

31 *Ibid.*, p. 24.

32 The discussion here is necessarily brief and oversimplified. Ideology, hegemony and common sense are by no means synonymous expressions of the same process. For an account which deals with their relation both to one another and to the field of education, see A. Hargreaves (1977a).

33 Ellis *et al.* (1976), p. 94.

34 This conception of coping strategies thus represents a development from a definition which I have offered elsewhere (A. Hargreaves, 1977b). In that previous definition, the individually creative aspects of such strategies were perhaps overstressed and the significance of the parameters within which such strategies are situated a little underplayed.

35 See Fay (1975) and Bauman (1976) for examples of the idealist position, which holds that change will occur through a process of active self-understanding on the part of everyday members of the social world. In an otherwise excellent Marxist critique of the

schooling process in capitalist society. Michael Young and Geoff Whitty themselves seem to gravitate towards this position when they consider possibilities for radical change in education (Young and Whitty, 1976).

36 Marcuse (1964), p. 76.

37 Within the sociology of education, movements in this direction are just beginning which

'recognise that the practices which keep society going and hide the ideological dimensions of prevailing notions of knowledge from public view are not just those of the classroom but take place within a context as wide as capitalist society itself' (Whitty and Young, 1977).

Chapter 10

How teachers decide pupils' subject choices

Peter Woods

Commitment and accommodation

Teacher decision-making is subject to internal and external forces. The internal forces are to do with the degree and nature of the teacher's commitment to his job. This I have elaborated elsewhere as a process whereby the individual comes increasingly to identify with the institution (Woods, 1977). Thus, 'the individual who makes a cognitive-continuance commitment finds that what is profitable to him is bound up with his position in the organisation, is contingent on his participating in the system' (Kanter, 1968). The teacher's career is characterised by increasing investment in the system, accompanied by 'side-bets' (Becker, 1960). Together with this process of increasing integration of self and role goes one of differentiation from other possible job commitments. Like other highly skilled personnel in advanced industrial societies who have undergone a lengthy period of training, teachers are firmly and many irrevocably entrenched in their place in the occupational structure.

This, however, is becoming more difficult, for external forces increasingly constrain the teacher's autonomy. There are the perennial constraints of teacher-pupil ratio, the length of the teaching week, provision of resources, assessment, and compulsory education.[1] The leaving age has been raised and more examinations introduced, and it seems likely that the teacher-pupil ratio will increase, and resources in general diminish. Moreover, while such developments materially reduce the range of choices, a teacher none the less has to work within a climate of dynamic change, the product of the upsurge of interest in education since the Second World War. This continually urges him to orientate himself to new vistas, conceived idealistically and thus beyond his power to achieve. Instead of having a liberating effect therefore, much proposed reform is seen as a liability.

The product of the collision of internal and external forces, of commitment and constraint, is 'accommodation'. This refers to the solving or riding of problems thrown up by the organisation so as effectively to neutralise the threat to the actor's continuance in it. In everyday terms, it amounts to a large part of what is referred to as 'experience'. An 'experienced' teacher is one who has learnt how to teach his subject most effectively within the definitions imposed by the problems and structures of the system, which, as we have seen, are changeable. It is distinguished by a large element of adaptability and pragmatism. The classroom is no place for educational principles.

However, even experienced teachers are in difficulty today. Consider a teacher in the most besieged situation—strongly committed, but having to cope with a number of large, difficult classes; the whole basis of his commitment is under attack. The investments and sacrifices he has made, the side-bets he has laid down are all at risk. It is, in short, a survival problem. What is at risk is not only his physical, mental and nervous safety and well-being, but also his continuance in professional life, his future prospects, his professional identity, his way of life, his status, his self-esteem. There are only three alternative solutions—changing careers, becoming upwardly mobile (i.e. into higher education), or accommodating. Opportunities for the first two being relatively scarce, most teachers are forced to accommodate. They do so by developing survival strategies. Common ones that I have observed and, as a teacher, participated in, are 'domination', 'negotiation', 'fraternisation', 'absence' or 'removal', 'ritual' and 'routine', 'occupational therapy', and 'morale-boosting' (Woods, 1977). These do not always facilitate the teaching task but often transform it, so that survival masquerades as teaching, sporting an elaborate and convincing rhetoric. This strategic reaction can be seen at work within certain processes, such as subject choice, and it is this that I wish to analyse in the rest of this paper (Woods, 1976).

The importance of subject choice

In the English educational system, there is considerable variety among schools and, indeed, among teachers. Some are less 'constrained' than others. The particular secondary modern school where I worked, however, might be reckoned as having an extra burden. That is, it was about to become a comprehensive school, not uncontentiously in the area at large. This introduced extra problems of validation, for it was considered imperative by senior staff at the school that it be seen as 'working' by parents of erstwhile grammar school children. The traditional symbol of educational worthiness is examination results. A common device to 'improve' these is to present them in the form of percentages—that is, as proportions of those taking the examinations. Thus, a school might claim a '95 per cent success rate' or individual teachers '100 per cent' success, even though the teachers concerned might have sponsored only a few entrants. Clearly, all this throws the utmost importance onto one's selection processes. And since most examination courses begin in the fourth year, it would appear that third year subject choice, wherein pupils 'choose' the courses they wish to pursue for the next two years, is of crucial importance. In fact, it is imperative for the teachers that the pupils 'get it right'. It might save a lot of trouble if pupils were simply 'allocated' to courses, but this would be too revealing. The strategy is disguised behind a rhetoric of 'choice', wherein pupils sort themselves out by their own volition, with the professional guidance of their teachers. I should make clear that I am not suggesting that teachers necessarily do this deliberately or that they are lone operators in strategic action. It is a feature of modern society, and institutional life in particular; as such, the analysis applies to us all, whether we are in universities, hospitals, prisons, offices, factories, or schools. Equally, I do not want to suggest that it is beyond teachers' power to change things, but much depends upon individual head teachers here. In my study school, the head-master exerted great pressure on his staff to achieve results in the manner indicated, leaving them themselves, ironically, with little choice.

Teacher problems

Figure 10.1 illustrates the individual teacher's dilemma. The three blocks relate to three groups of children characterised by expectation of performance in the 16+ examination. The shaded areas are where adjacent groups overlap. For teachers, they can be high tension generators. Since they are not certain to pass the higher exam, the pupils in each shaded area represent a lot of hard work for the teacher,

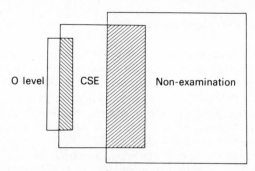

Figure 10.1 Examination/non-examination overlap

172

and at the same time, because some will doubtless fail and hence bring down his percentage pass rate, his labours stand to be misrepresented. The pressures therefore are great on the individual teacher to reduce the shaded areas as much as possible.

The major immediate repercussion of the process being cloaked in a democratic, liberal guise is illustrated in Figure 10.2, which shows an actual distribution of pupil choices for four main-line subjects (optimum number 30) and the resources cut-off point in relation to each. With subjects 1 and 2, there is no problem regarding resources, but with subject 3, 6 per cent need to be excluded, and with subject 4, 41 per cent.

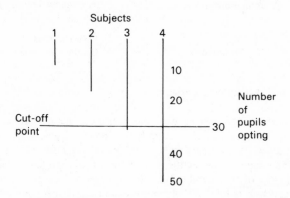

Figure 10.2 Subject choice overlap

It might appear that the teacher of subject 4 has the biggest problem, but this is not so. He can use the concomitant difficulties of lack of resources and dubious examination quality to cancel each other out, simply selecting the 'best'. The teachers of subjects 1 and 2 are likely to have a bigger problem, for they have no appeal to lack of resources. For this reason, the ground is often prepared well in advance.

Teacher tactics

The mass of tactics employed in the general strategy are revealed by teacher perceptions of subject choice as represented in Figure 10.3. This shows four basic types of choice from the teachers' point of view. The 'system acceptive' pupil is one who correctly interprets the school, its processes, and his relationship to it and hence the implications of the subject choice, be it for examination or non-examination subjects. The 'system disruptive' pupils, however, have misinterpreted the cues and made unrealistic choices, selecting examination subjects when they

173

should have chosen non-examination (by ability), or vice versa. The problem for teachers then becomes one of either persuading pupils of their 'rightful' designation beforehand or, in cases where that is not successful, removing those below the line to their 'rightful' places, pretenders to drop-outs and underbidders to academics.

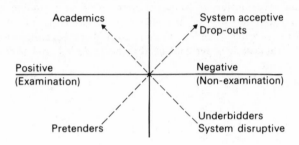

Figure 10.3 Attitudinal overlaps

It would indeed appear that the majority make realistic choices. After all, the whole of the school's teaching and assessment and, indeed, that of the primary school before it, culminating in the all-important examinations at the end of the third year, give most pupils a sound idea of their 'ability' at school subjects. Teachers' definitions of success and failure are paramount, and these are readily internalised by most pupils and parents (Beecham, 1973).

'We're not the brainy ones, *they* are.'
'How do you know?'
'Well, they are.'

Occasionally there is a spark of protest:

Amanda: They think because we're in a lower form they think we're dibby and we can't do it on our own. But then they never give us a chance to try do they, that's why we have gone off homework and don't like it, cos everybody thinks we're dibby and they don't give us a chance, you know, that's why we don't want to take exams and don't like teachers.
Me: Do you ever get called 'dibby' or anything like that?
Amanda: Well, they put it in a nice way. They say 'You're not as intelligent as all the others, and you ought to do so-and-so.'
Linda: Or they'll give you that strong impression, you know, talk to you like babies. One teacher goes over and over it so we understand, and he goes 'do—you—understand?' (mimicking a babyish, measured voice). And then when you say you don't he goes mad at you.

Interestingly, those who interpret teachers' behaviour towards them in this way are usually those who overreach themselves in subject choice and have to be corrected. To guard against this, a teacher might use special pre-option techniques. 'Scaring off' seems to be quite widely used. For example, the teacher of subject 4 in Figure 10.2, possibly anticipating a big redistribution problem, gave a talk which had the effect of cooling out several 'pretenders'.

Me: Why didn't you choose subject 4 in that group?
June: We'd get too much homework.
Mavis: Yeah! She don't 'alf put it on... 'you'll 'ave to work all the time'—an' homework! You think 'oh I can't do that—oh!' Talking about it made me feel ill.

Defining what counts as ability and devising and organising the measures to test it establish an eminently legitimate base from which to work. From there one can appeal to universal laws of 'rightness' and 'fairness'. There was much emphasis on 'fair procedures' at my study school. Thus the headmaster, in his talk to the third year pupils, announced that where there was competition for places, they could only resolve it by the fairest method—having a test to see who was the best. As if to underline the universality of this criterion, he asked then, rhetorically, 'That would be fair, wouldn't it?'

Some teachers go to a lot of trouble to be seen to be fair:

'A lot choose art, yes, and you know why don't you? I'm not fooled. I say to them "Why do you want to do art?" I say, "*I* know, but come on, you tell me", and they say, "Huh, I don't want to do old biology or whatever, all that homework" and so on. It's an easy option, and they go for it on both lines. My results this year were pretty poor, which rather proves my point. But what I do is this. I pick those with most artistic ability and I like it to be seen to be fair. I don't spring this on them either. I tell them all this at the beginning of the third year. I tell them they'll be judged on the quality of work that goes into their folders, and then towards the end of the year, I get them to lay it all out, so they can all see, and of course some are very good and some are pathetic. There's no other way, not if they want to take the exam. If they just want a skive they can do it somewhere else.'

Here is 'justice' being seen to be done, and opportunity given for pupils to make their cases. With its free and informal atmosphere and its different, non-exacting work task, the 'art' options are a natural attraction for the diffident counter-cultural chooser (Woods, 1977). But the art teacher is subject to the same forces as his colleagues, and the same criteria must apply.

The major factor against pre-conditioning is the pupils' understanding of the structure of the school, basically into two channels culminating in the final two years in examination and non-examination routes, and their understanding also of the unequal distribution of resources, favours, life chances and subsequently status between the channels. This inequality is solidly embedded in the traditions and everyday practices of the school. One of the functions of a subject choice system is to legitimate inequality by removing it from that plane of everyday reality and appealing on the one hand to a standard code of justice, as with 'fairness' above, and on the other to a broader, more pervasive reality which rests in society, outside school. This is an outflanking manoeuvre to head off 'pretenders' and to allay the stigma of the drop-out option. All this was evident in the headmaster's address to the third year pupils.

The 'choice' pupils made was represented as the most crucial decision they would make in their school career—indeed, as one of the most important decisions of their lives. Hitherto they had been merely 'getting a taste' for subjects, but the next two years were 'for real'. They counted for something in the world at large. This essential link with the occupational structure was emphasised in his advice on their approach to choice. They would obviously think in terms of 'what they wanted to do' after school. He gave examples, then warned against choosing subjects because they liked the teacher or 'environmental studies because they were interested in what goes on round the canals'. They were urged to think, first, if they were 'good at it' and second, 'what use was it going to be to them'. The importance and meaning of examinations were explained, and pupils needed (besides working hard when they got in an exam form) to ask themselves whether they were good enough in the first place to take an exam subject or if they ought to take a non-exam subject, in which of course there was 'nothing shameful'—people were needed for all sorts of occupations.

By these tactics, it is hoped pupils will make the 'right' choices. But a certain number still got through the net. Most of these were 'pretenders' from the lower streams (Woods, 1977). Whatever methods are used, they are unlikely to be 100 per cent effective as long as any semblance of choice is retained. But there are factors operating against them, such as parental knowledge of the system, the attraction of certain subjects, as with art, or the charisma of particular teachers, as with the teacher of subject 4 in Figure 10.2. How exactly do oversubscribed teachers arbitrate? The teacher of subject 4 employed three criteria— (1) the best ones; (2) those who seemed to have the 'right' attitude; and (3) from 3c, the three who seemed a 'cut above the rest'. It was no good having problem people like John Church. 'He's too lazy, he lays around, and if he gets his pen out, he lolls around saying "Oh Miss!" I can't take the risk, it spreads like a cancer. Who starts it, initiates it, I don't know.'

'It's cruel, I know, but what else can I do? I haven't time to motivate, inspire, correct for behaviour and so on, so you must cut out
all the miscreants and thickies. You just haven't got time. They do
drag you down. Now Sharon Brown, nice girl, parents didn't want
her in that form, I think once she gets out and in with this other lot,
they'll pull these three (from 3c) up.'

This teacher is articulating the system's rules, and by tidying up the
'misplacements' illustrates how the wedge is even more firmly driven
between two types of pupil. These two types, and who falls into them,
are clearly identified, as are their within-group influences. So also are
the criteria for success, which include, apart from past performance,
'attitude' and a 'cut above the rest'. The social undertones and divisiveness become explicit towards the end. Family background can be de-
cisive. It can rescue or condemn at the eleventh hour.

Overseeing the whole process and assuming responsibility for individual pupil programmes was the senior master. He told me that the
process worked like this: First, pupils filled in forms indicating their
first preferences; second, subject teachers were informed and asked if
they would accept those selecting their subjects; some 'thirty or forty'
were thus referred back and required to make second choices. These he
was 'able to give a fair amount of time to' and proceeded to 'negotiate
with teachers on their behalf'. He was also on the lookout for 'choices
for friendship' and 'correcting for career', which involved 'going
through the whole list'. However, though 'guidance was available, a
great deal of responsibility was placed on their shoulders'. No doubt
some individuals benefited from this advice and intervention, but
clearly it is operating within the severe constraints of the institutional
channelling current in the school; any scheme requiring a large amount
of self-responsibility surrenders decisions not to individuals, but to
group perspectives (Woods, 1977; Becker, 1961).

Teacher views

Some teachers, like the art teacher and the teacher of subject 4 above,
are aware of the main points of this analysis. They have read this, and
other accounts of the process of which they are a part, and have endorsed it. 'It's cruel, but true', said the latter teacher, and again, 'What
else can we do?' Others were not blind to the hypocrisy in the system
and wanted it scrapped and incorporated fully into their professional
jurisdiction. They would question, however, not the criteria of their
mediation, but the mechanics and the products of it. In other words,
they accepted their selection and allocation function and disputed
pupils' or parents' ability to make realistic judgments. They were the

only ones who knew which children 'stood a reasonable chance', yet this system put them under pressure from pupils, parents and head-teacher at both ends of the examination course. They 'bent over back-wards' to accommodate everyone, then when it came to homework, the pupils 'didn't want to know'. In other words, when they relaxed the strict application of their criteria for selection and enlarged the shaded zones in Figure 10.1, the pupils concerned failed to observe the norms required of the group. Another thought it 'ridiculous making these decisions before the third year examinations, and misleading parents in many cases about the actualities, encouraging them to think their kids are more capable than they really are'. Others blamed parents for not honouring implicit pledges to keep their children up to the mark.[2] These comments illustrate the invidious position many teachers find themselves in, subjected to conflicting and what some of them feel to be unnecessary pressures. Interestingly, from their point of view the headmaster is seen as opposition, for he not only wants his percentages but numbers too—it's a way of keeping his staff on their toes.

Summary and conclusion

Teachers are forced by the twin pressures of commitment and structural constraint to accommodate problems and develop survival strategies. This is true, in a sense, of all walks of life in modern society, but what makes institutions like schools interesting is that, at a certain point, such strategies cease to be acknowledged for what they are and become incorporated into policy. This act of incorporation is itself a survival strategy. I have applied this model of teacher action to the process of subject choice as observed in a secondary modern school. This was pre-sented by the teachers as 'guided choice' in which pupils were afforded a great deal of responsibility for choosing the subjects they wished to study in the fourth and fifth years, with teachers acting as professional mentors. In fact, teachers made most of the decisions, albeit by rather tortuous routes, which led some to protest and yearn for 'cleaner' de-cisions. Pre-choice tactics included communicating to pupils a 'proper' notion of their ability and of their 'rightful' place in the school struc-ture, heading off pretenders, encouraging underbidders (though this was not very evident—perhaps because unnecessary), removing the stigma of the drop-out choice, and extolling the fairness of selection tech-niques. Post-choice tactics include persuasion based on the criteria of ability and aptitude, which appears to have strong social class over-tones, and only in the last resort ruthless exclusion. The overall effect is to get the pupils to articulate the teachers' decisions. That they are prepared to go to such lengths instead of taking the easy way out shows just how far down the blind alley of pupil directed learning without any accompanying structual change we have come.

During my two year association with the school no other event struck me as being more important, more conflictual, more cataclysmic for the people involved than the process of subject choice. Also, no other was more revealing, both in terms of the school's relationship with wider society and in terms of individual teachers' actions and decisions. These, I suggest, are not always predicated on educational considerations or in the interests of the pupils. Nor does there seem much room for manoeuvre for individual teachers. Rather, they are caught up in an institutional mechanism which forces them to take certain decisions rather than others. 'What else can they do?' In all walks of life, survival comes first, and underneath the gloss, our educational system is still very primitive.

This analysis should not be seen as contributing to the 'blame the teacher' school of thought. On the contrary, it is more exculpating the teacher, in that it seeks to shift the basis of his decision-making from his own volition operating within a limitless panorama of free-ranging choice to the structure within which he works and to which he is committed. It is a precarious existence for any teacher who does not toe the line, as Duane, Mackenzie, Searle and Ellis, among others, have discovered. This does not mean that nothing can be done, but rather that it is to changes in the structure, and not simply teacher awareness, that we must look before real educational reforms can be enacted. Teacher commitment could be made more of a virtue and less of a millstone and the alienative impact of the headteacher removed at a stroke, if that office were abolished and schools run by a collective in which all teachers participated equally (Peters, 1976). Methods of assessment need radical overhaul to soften their association with the selection mechanism and to render decision-making less arbitrary. The teacher-pupil ratio could be improved and the same problem of coping with disaffected youth evaporated if the school leaving age were lowered and better provision made for post-school education. Alienative divisiveness could be further reduced by involving parents as active contributors to the educational function, as in community schools, rather than working for their separation.

Such reforms are possible within the present system and could lead to radical transformations in schools whereby the accommodatory shackles many teachers find themselves in would be removed and their educational aspirations, expertise and goodwill, sadly misused in our present system, would be given freer rein.[3] On the other hand, certain more basic changes which affect the school's aim, function and intake await changes in society. Inequalities there will always be, reflected in school. However, there is no reason to suppose that given more resources and less irritation, schools cannot in the long term make more of a contribution (Flacks, 1971; Musgrove, 1974; Hargreaves, 1974). At the moment, it is my contention that many teachers have been driven over the threshold that divides education from survival, teaching from accommodation, and preparing for a better society from a monotonous conformity to the old. There is nothing inevitable about that. It is the product of decisions made by us all.

Notes

1 The pressures and constraints and their effects are becoming increasingly acknowledged. See, for example, Sharp and Green (1975); H. Gracey, *Curriculum or Craftsmanship: Elementary School Teachers in a Bureaucratic System* (University of Chicago Press, 1972); C. Werthman, 'Delinquents in Schools: A Test for the Legitimacy of Authority', *Berkeley Journal of Sociology, 8,* no. 1, 1963, pp. 39–60; I. Westbury, 'Conventional Classrooms, "Open" Classrooms and the Technology of Teaching', *Journal of Curriculum Studies, 5,* no. 2, November, 1973.
2 These comments were freely made in informal conversations with six members of staff.
3 There are, of course, some outstanding examples of some of these reforms in action, e.g. Countesthorpe College, Sutton Community Centre.

Chapter 11

Towards a model of teacher activity

Martyn Hammersley

Introduction

It is a feature of our everyday experience that, intermittently, we face
dilemmas and have to decide what courses of action to adopt. Such
dilemmas can vary considerably in their intensity, as can the degree of
choice we have and the amount of deliberation we are able to engage
in. Decisions, then, are an everyday phenomenon, a feature of our experience in the world. What is not necessarily given in our experience,
however, is the origin of these dilemmas. Nor are we always conscious
either of the processes by which we make decisions or of all their
consequences. Not enough attention has been given in sociology to
decision-making; in general, we have relied on crude, unexplicated
models of action. In this paper I want to sketch the beginnings of a
more adequate model, with the explanation of teacher activity particularly in mind.

I shall begin by looking at one of the few explicit presentations of a
sociological model of decision-making, one which arose from the
rapprochement between structural-functionalism and empirical social
research in the late 1950s. Gross, Mason and McEachern (1958), along
with a number of other sociologists, argued that the original functionalist conception of roles as consensually defined must be modified to
take account of the existence of role conflict. In their research on the
school superintendent role they saw this conflict as arising from two
sources: among the expectations of the occupants of the *different* roles
in the school superintendent's role-set and among the expectations of
the multiple incumbents of any *particular* role in that role-set. Of
course, these various expectations were also backed up by differential
sanctions. Gross and his colleagues postulated three types of resolution
to such conflicts: according to perceived legitimacy (moral orientation);
according to the weight of sanctions on each side (expedient orientation);

181

or according to the 'net balance' of the two factors (moral-expedient orientation).

This role conflict model seems to be implicit in recent discussions of the dilemmas and inconsistencies involved in teacher activity, though with various modifications (Sharp and Green, 1975; Berlak *et al.*, 1975, 1976). However, while it is a considerable improvement on the consensus model, in its present form it still does not take account of a number of important features of social action. By developing this model further, we may be able to generate a more satisfactory conception of the nature of teacher activity.

Sources of dilemmas

In this model dilemmas arise solely from discrepancies among the expectations of other actors. Curiously, the actor himself seems to have no perspective on his role. All he can do is evaluate the legitimacy and expediency of conformity to others' expectations. Thus, the possibility of role conflict arising from discrepancy between his *own* definition of his task and the expectations of others is neglected. Furthermore, a number of authors (Schutz and Luckmann, 1974; Sharp and Green, 1975; Berlak and Berlak, 1976) have pointed to the existence of inconsistencies *within* actors' perspectives on their roles. This opens up two further sources of conflict: the teacher may find himself drawn to two mutually exclusive courses of action as a result of inconsistencies within his own conception of his task, and/or he may be faced by inconsistent demands from the *same* powerful other on different issues or occasions. Yet another form of conflicting expectations occurs among incumbents of the same role.[1] Thus, actors faced as a group with a particular problem may develop collective strategies for dealing with it. Often, the success of these strategies depends on solidarity and certain kinds of role performance—black-legging, rate-busting, being 'too soft' on pupils etc.—may be outlawed as a result.

Such elaborations of the sources of conflicting role definitions multiply the possibilities, but they do not exhaust them. Role definitions are not the only social phenomena among which there can be conflict. Besides having his own conception of his role, and reciprocally of those of others, an actor also has ideas about his *interests* and those of his clique, department etc.

Then again, others do not simply expect the teacher to perform his role in a particular way, they also have to provide him with the resources to do this. Discrepancies between the expectations of others and/or the actor's own goals *on the one hand* and the resources available *on the other* is a classic source of dilemmas (Merton, 1957). I suspect it is an endemic problem in most roles, but it is one which in the case of teaching at the present time may be worsening at both ends, expectations being heightened and resources cut.

Another source of dilemmas arises in connexion with the choice of means to achieve various expectations. The achievement of goals always relies on theories about how particular sectors of the world operate and there are often competing theories available and/or indeterminacies within theories. Even where theories are well developed, the amount and kinds of information available may be such as to make it difficult to decide what the consequences of different possible actions might be, in whose interests they are, and thus what the most appropriate and effective course of action is.

My argument, then, is that this model deals with only one kind of dilemma likely to face teachers. We need to explore others and modify the model accordingly.

Idealism and materialism in the sociology of education

In this section I want to examine the moral-expedient distinction, a distinction which underlies a current dispute within the sociology of education (see also Hargreaves, Hester and Mellor, 1975, ch. 8). One of the characteristic concepts of the 'new sociology of education' and of the 'new sociologies' in general is the notion of 'paradigm'. In the sense employed here the term is derived from the work of Thomas Kuhn, though Kuhn's usage of it is rather variable (Kuhn, 1970; Masterman, 1970). Esland, for example, postulates two teaching paradigms, two sets of contrary assumptions about the nature of curriculum, pedagogy, and evaluation, which he claims are institutionalised in different locales in the education system.[2] Commitment to one or other of these paradigms is a matter of belief in, or socialisation into, the paradigm assumptions, and, certainly in the case of the psychometric paradigm, these assumptions are conceptualised as self-fulfilling, as constituting a particular social world by their very use. This usage of the term 'paradigm' is characteristic of the phenomenological rather than the interactionist strand of the 'new sociology of education'. Thus, some criticisms of the latter for being idealist and neglecting material factors (Whitty, 1974; Sharp and Green, 1975) are accurate in the case of this strand, though they are not true of all phenomenological sociology,[3] and certainly not of interactionism.

The notion of a paradigm is implicit in Becker's early work on teachers, but it is used there in a rather different manner. In his article 'Social Class Variations in the Teacher–Pupil Relationship', Becker shows that a conception of an 'ideal pupil' underlies the teachers' descriptions of their pupils.[4] What we have here is the moral-expedient distinction in embryo. I have elsewhere (Hammersley, 1977a) sought to apply this distinction to teacher perspectives as a whole, postulating 'paradigmatic', or ideal world, and 'pragmatic', or realistic components of their perspectives. Dealing with pupils who deviate from the ideal, as all pupils do to one degree or another, may often involve teachers in practices which are deviations from their ideal model of teaching. Indeed, they may engage in practices under the auspices of the teacher identity which they define as non-teaching (Woods, 1977).

Unlike the phenomenological tradition, in which emphasis is given to the assumptions on the basis of which people make sense of the social world, interactionism, while sharing this theme, has also laid stress on the ways in which situations shape action. Also, rather than being concerned with deep paradigmatic assumptions informing all aspects of a person's behaviour, interactionists have generally focused on perspectives, social definitions generated by groups of actors to cope with particular situations they face.[5] In this manner, action is treated as context-specific. Thus, Becker (1964) has developed the notion of situational adjustment and used it as part of his explanation for patterns of teacher mobility in the Chicago school system.[6] In this concept is combined the interactionist stress on situation, interactionism's characteristic emphasis on process (since change in the situation will lead to changes in the actor's perspective), and the notion of contingencies, since implicit is a recognition that some features of the situation are beyond the actor's control.[7]

In fact, in my view, Becker's position is, if anything, over-materialist: he seeks to explain both change and stability of perspectives in materialist terms.[8] This threatens to eliminate the usefulness of any notion of a paradigmatic component of perspectives. Furthermore, it strikes at the heart of interactionism. The notion of paradigm—that actors always interpret the world through a perspective, that they don't simply respond to the world in an automatic fashion—has always been central to that theoretical approach, though it was never developed to the same degree or depth as in the phenomenological tradition.[9] This ambivalence within interactionism between the role of situation and that of actors' interpretations of situations is one version of an unresolved problem which permeates all social theory: determinism versus voluntarism. It is glossed in Marx's observation that 'circumstances make men just as much as men make circumstances' (Marx, 1970, p.59) and it has reverberated throughout the history of Marxism. In sociology as in Marxism there has been a tendency to swing periodically from one side of the equation to the other, without resolving the issue.

Up to now I have talked as though paradigms and pragmatic conceptions were entirely separate and unrelated components of teacher perspectives. In fact, while analytically distinct, in reality they are interrelated in complex ways. In any decision or role conflict situation, paradigmatic and pragmatic considerations of many kinds are usually involved on both sides. Rarely are actors faced with a decision between moral but *inexpedient* and *immoral* but expedient courses of action, even though this is the kind of situation which we often think of in connection with 'moral questions'. What is moral or expedient from one point of view will not be so from others. Thus, for example, the major carrier and reinforcer of paradigms, the reference group, is also a status group dispensing identities which are valued by the actor. It therefore also has pragmatic relevance. Similarly, there is often overlap between the members of an actor's reference groups and the incumbents of the role-sets in which he is involved, resulting in both paradigmatic and pragmatic considerations flowing along the same channels. This argument for the impurity and diversity of motivation is another characteristic of interactionism which is not shared by phenomenological sociology and which was largely absent from the 'new sociology of education'.

In summary, then, the moral-expedient distinction is best applied to components of teacher perspectives rather than to the orientations of particular teachers. Furthermore, the complex character of each of these components and of the relationship between them must be recognised.

Multiple dilemmas

Any decision-making situation usually involves multiple dilemmas, since dilemmas are not normally faced one at a time, in isolation from one another. Particular roles involve characteristic sets of dilemmas which permeate the folklore about the role. The dilemmas are, to one degree or another, ever present and ever relevant. Almost any teacher action, however apparently minor, is richly implicative: it can be interpreted by the various relevant publics—pupils, colleagues, parents etc.— as relevant to a number of different issues for which it can have important consequences. Take the identification and treatment of 'routine deviance' (Hargreaves, Hester and Mellor, 1975) in the classroom. The potential implications of a teacher's treatment of a 'deviant' pupil action are manifold. There are paradigmatically motivated considerations: upholding moral rules, teaching morality, teaching all pupils in an equal or universalistic manner etc. There are also more pragmatically based concerns: being *seen* to be fair and universalistic, preventing further deviance later by putting a stop to it now, ignoring deviance both in the hope that it will die down itself[10] and because to deal with it would interrupt the 'flow' of the lessons etc. Also relevant are considerations of identity: appearing 'tough', 'nobody's fool', 'kindly', 'fraternal' etc.; these identities may also be rooted in both paradigmatic and pragmatic concerns.

Negotiation

Gross, Mason and McEachern recognise the importance of power, but they deal only with perceived power. In the same way, they treat the whole process of decision-making as subjective, neglecting its inter-actional aspects.[11] Frequently, what we would describe as a decision[12] involves many sub-decisions which take place over a period of time and whose implementation involves interaction with others. Furthermore, often when we make decisions and implement them, things do not go as planned. In particular, our assessments of the expectations and power resources of other actors may be wrong. Indeed, we sometimes adopt lines of action in the *hope* that they will come off, recognising that there is a strong possibility that events will not turn out as we intend. In the event of our actions being unsuccessful, we must either decide on some new course of action shaped to the new situation or revise our original goals. Thus, the decision-making process, while partly subjective, also involves interactional phases.

A second important point arises out of this. The outcome of the interaction is, to one degree or another, uncertain. While we can make certain predictions as to outcomes on the basis of the availability of various power resources to different actors, *how* these resources are used will affect what happens. For example, as important as others' expectations and power resources is their access to information about the actor's role performances. And even where, as in the case of pupils' witnessing of the teacher's role behaviour, access is relatively unre-stricted, the presentation of appearances may play an important role. In this and other ways the decision-making process often involves strategic action and negotiation among actors over what they are and are not prepared to accept, and over what they can and cannot, will and will not do. Thus, interactionists have pointed to the importance of threat, bluff, persuasion, the exploitation of rules and expertise, and bargaining in the exercise of power (Strauss *et al.*, 1964; Goffman, 1969; Woods, 1977).

Routine decision-making

At the beginning of this paper I suggested that dilemmas and decisions, unlike their origins and consequences, were given to consciousness. I now want to throw doubt even on that. While, clearly, we are aware of dilemmas facing us and of decisions we take, I want to suggest that we are not consciously aware of *all* the dilemmas we face or of *all* the de-cisions we take.[13] Berger and Luckmann (1967) have pointed out the taken-for-granted character of much of our cultural knowledge; it be-comes conscious only when situations make it problematic. The notion of taken-for-granted knowledge is a necessary counter to the emphasis given by some interactionists and by ethnomethodologists to situational or contextual creativity in generating interpretations of, and strategies for dealing with, the social world. It is only on the basis of taken-for-granted knowledge, of both a formal *and* a substantive character, that situational perspectives can be generated; they do not emerge from nothing.

The distinction between awareness and non-awareness is not clear-cut; it is a continuum. Thus, I am not suggesting that subconscious routinised action—and much of teacher activity takes this form—is entirely automatic, that it is simply elicited by stimuli. Rather, the process of deliberation has itself been routinised, the number of options limited and the criteria on which they are selected simplified, the whole process thus being rendered subconscious. I am suggesting that dilemmas which when first faced are subjected to conscious deliberation come, over time, to be dealt with by routinised and subconscious reasoning.[14] This process is forced in the case of teaching by the 'immediacy' of the classroom situation, by the pressure of time and simultaneous concerns: there is often little time for conscious deliberation before a decision has to be made.[15]

The selection of different strategies and tactics can, however, still be described in terms of reasons rather than causes since this semi-routinised activity is the product of sedimented reflection or deliberation.[16] Thus, we can seek to explicate the theories underlying teachers' routine classroom actions: we can expect to discover interrelated theories about the capacities and likely actions of different kinds of pupils, the trajectories of different kinds of classroom process etc. However, the task of describing such sedimented theories is methodologically problematic, as indeed is the discovery of dilemmas.

Discovering dilemmas: a digression

I want to look briefly at the methodological problems raised by the detection of dilemmas. Obviously, this task is especially problematic if actors are not always conscious of the dilemmas that face them.[17] We can understand a person's actions only by reconstructing the perspective which motivates them; hence, we can only *begin* to recognise inconsistency, role conflicts and routine decisions once we have understood the internal relations of the perspective. I do not mean by this that each perspective has its own form of logic; by 'consistency' I mean strict, logical consistency. But the actual patterning and content of logical inferences will vary for different perspectives. Because of the limited sources of information available to any observer—the only access he has to perspectives is through their situational realisations, and he has to rely on typical, common sense lines of inference—purely logical inferences do not give sufficient leverage or narrow down the possibilities enough. Our typical, common sense lines of inference, plus the observation and interpretation of accounts and actions, provide us with hypotheses which can be tested in relation to further accounts and actions. However, they *must* be tested since we cannot assume an isomorphism between our own perspective and those of participants. There is always the danger that what appears as inconsistency from our point of view may, on further investigation, turn out not to be an inconsistency at all.

There has been little consideration in the literature of the methodological problems involved in recognising dilemmas. There has been a tendency on the part of some researchers to postulate idealised, thoroughly logical, models of decision-making, against which are contrasted the apparently inconsistent perspectives of teachers. The implication of such an approach is that the idealised model is an ideal state to which, ultimately, we are or should be moving.[18] I can see no grounds for making this assumption, though I do agree that inconsistencies in perspectives are important signs of dilemmas, useful clues to lines of investigation worth pursuing. I am arguing, then, following Schutz (1964) and Garfinkel (1967), that we must recognise a clear distinction between common sense and scientific rationalities—that is, between what is judged to be rational in scientific work and 'the rational' in everyday life; nor can we assume that the latter should, or is likely to, somehow move in the direction of the former.

The consequentiality of action

The theorising and decision-making of actors, then, are practical rather than scientific; they are tied to everyday concerns (Schutz and Luckmann, 1974). Actors' theorising is practical in another sense also: it usually provides the basis for action, often immediate action. This is of considerable importance. While, as noted earlier, actors recognise that there are features of their situation that cannot be changed, which they must adapt to, their actions do themselves affect the situation sometimes and, especially where the decision-making is routinised, without their being aware of it. Teacher adaptations, by acting back on the situation the teacher faces, often themselves give rise to further dilemmas or alter the shape of existing dilemmas. Thus, a dilemma which, it seemed to me, faced teachers in the classrooms of one school I studied lay between *generating* pupil attention and participation and *controlling* participation along 'official' channels (Hammersley, 1974). This dilemma is the product not of any distinct feature of the teachers' situation: it is not involved in other forms of classroom interaction, such as individual written work or group work. Rather, it is the product of a particular form of interaction, which I termed 'instruction', that is itself a routinised adaptation to the situations in which the teachers must work.[19] Because much of a teacher's working knowledge and actions are routinised, he tends to work within a framework which he takes for granted as 'how things are', but which is partly of his own making. This is not to deny that there are real and important constraints on what he can do; it is simply that these are mediated in their impact by the teacher's routine interpretations of his situation, his adaptations to those definitions of the situation, and the consequences of these adaptations.

Drift

Recognition of the richly implicative character of teacher action, the role of negotiation, the routinised, subconscious nature of much teacher activity, and the consequentiality of teacher adaptations leads us to a fourth feature of decision-making: what Matza has called 'drift' (Matza, 1964). The implications of any decision are not necessarily easily foreseeable and therefore are often unintended. As they work themselves out, further decisions are required which may also have unforeseen and unintended consequences. Hence, the situation in which the teacher is acting may change imperceptibly, yet he may continue to act on the basis of his earlier definition of the situation. Of course, this is not to suggest that the actor is simply at the mercy of this drift. Its direction may become perceptible at various points, and corrective action may be possible.

Actors, then, develop and come to take for granted certain adaptations to the dilemmas they face. These adaptations themselves lead to further dilemmas, a process involving drift. However, even when they are recognised, anomalies are usually explained away by various means so as to preserve the perspective. Adaptations are taken for granted until further notice, until anomalies are recognised *and* come to be judged as necessitating remedial action or perhaps reconsideration of the whole basis of action. Of course, some levels and kinds of anomalies will be judged to be unacceptable in paradigmatic and/or pragmatic terms, though just what the threshold is may be difficult to estimate analytically. Furthermore, this threshold may change over time as a result of various phenomena—for example, paradigmatic conversion on the part of the actor, moral crusades by others, or increasing resistance from incumbents of other roles.

Macro implications of the model

I shall turn now to some of the implications of this model of teacher action for conceptions of social structure. Structural-functionalism and Marxism[20] both recognise the existence of 'strains' and 'contradictions' and thus the potentiality for dilemmas in social life. However, *both* tend to treat these as factors leading to social change towards an equilibrium.[21] They do not seek to establish that social contradictions set up a dynamic which in turn resolves them: they *assume* it. In one case, this assumption is derived from homeostatic models in biology, in the other from Hegelian notions of dialectical development. However, there seems to be no good reason for assuming that these models are appropriate and much evidence for doubting it: contradictions are constantly being lived with, adapted to, compromised over etc.;[22] cases of societies 'dying' and of textbook revolutions are notoriously rare. All societies are normally characterised by some level of inarticulation among their parts, though there will be considerable variation in the level and nature of the contradictions or strains. Furthermore, these do not in any immediate or obvious sense threaten the breakdown of the society, nor can we *assume* that they lead to changes towards any kind of normal or ideal equilibrium or towards a new type of society.[23]

We can still ask how stability and change, the production and re-production of social forms, take place, of course; but we must not assume that what we have are overall societal patterns of cyclical or dialectical change towards equilibria. It seems to me that the impetus for social change stems not from teleological social systems but from the intended and unintended consequences of actors' attempts to realise their paradigms in pragmatically defined circumstances. And the socialisation of actors into particular paradigms and the structuring of the situations they face are the intended and unintended products of others' actions. Implicit in the conception of Western industrial societies being suggested here is the idea that they are characterised by fairly high degrees of functional autonomy (Gouldner, 1959) among, and within, various institutional sectors. We must investigate the levels and nature of the functional autonomy among institutions and how these change over time and also the ways in which this 'looseness' of structure produces dilemmas of various kinds at different social locations.

In conclusion, it is worth indicating the other side of the idea that institutional orders exercise a relatively high degree of functional auto-nomy compared to that implied by Marxist and functionalist macro-theories.[24] In contrast to naive conflict and pluralist macro-theories, on the model outlined here, the institutional orders of Western societies are mutually interdependent in various ways and, as a result, much of the work the different institutions perform in establishing, maintaining and reproducing *their* power bases serves to bring about the reproduction of the whole.[25] Indeed, it seems to me that the very existence of relatively high levels of functional autonomy among institutions means that there are multiple, partially independent, social control mechanisms operating towards the periphery as well as at the centre. The mass media, the education system, the work place, the family etc. all play a role in reproducing and changing existing social structures, though in ways which produce and reproduce all manner of contradictions and thus dilemmas.

Notes

1 Gross *et al.* (1958) deal with conflicting expectations among multiple occupants of *other* roles but not among fellow incumbents of the actor's own role.
2 See Esland (1971, 1972). In a more recent, slightly modified, version of his argument (1977), he suggests that the phenomenological paradigm has not been and cannot be fully institutionalised under capitalism because it is incompatible with the requirements of that mode of production. However, in none of the articles are we given any sound evidence for the accuracy of the paradigm descriptions or of the claims about their existence in the social world.
3 Since phenomenological sociologists such as Schutz and the ethnomethodologists are engaged in an enterprise very different from that attempted by the proponents of the 'new sociology of education'.
4 Becker (1952b). Keddie (1971) develops this notion of the 'ideal' pupil' through a distinction between teacher and educationalist contexts. She thus makes the important point that all accounts are socially situated and must be interpreted in their context. This may have important methodological implications for Becker's interviews.
5 Hence also the notion of 'definition of the situation', on which see Stebbins (1975). In contrast, McHugh's (1968) treatment of this concept is phenomenological and thus nicely highlights this difference between the phenomenological and interactionist traditions.
6 See Becker (1952b). There is a superficial similarity here between interactionism and ethnomethodology. However, whereas for the latter context-specific meanings are produced by underlying transsituational interpretive procedures, for Becker the situation *forces* change in the actor's perspective.
7 This illustrates that another of the recent criticisms of the 'new sociology of education', that it assumes that actors have complete freedom to act in any way they choose, is not applicable to interactionism.
8 He explains stability of perspective in terms of the concept of commitment. See Becker (1960, 1964).
9 See Blumer (1969). In fact, there has been a tendency to use the notion that the world is always perceived and interpreted through a particular perspective in an arbitrary manner; the perspectives of some groups, notably 'under-dogs', have often been treated as

though they were a reflection of the real conditions those groups face, whereas the perspectives of labellers have tended to be treated as independent of the situation in which they must act.

10 Either because it is endemic and has a known trajectory or because it is designed to intimidate the teacher into action.

11 Partly perhaps because of the methodological strategy they adopt, relying exclusively on interviews.

12 I am sidestepping all the problems involved in the definition of 'decision' here.

13 There has been considerable discussion in the role conflict literature over whether 'role conflict' is to be defined as conflicts perceived by participants or as conflicts detectable by the analyst. The idea of 'non-decision' as a crucial element in the exercise of power is also relevant here. For a discussion see Lukes (1974).

14 See Berger and Luckmann (1968), who derive this idea from Schutz.

15 On the 'immediacy' of the teacher's situation in the classroom see Jackson (1968), Smith and Geoffrey (1968), and Lortie (1975).

16 It may of course be affected by further reflection in the future: there is a continuing dialectic between reflection and routinised action.

17 Some may not be available to the actor even in reflection. This illustrates the need for sociological analysis, since the actor may not have a sociological theory adequate for detecting them.

18 There is a hint of this in the work of Sharp and Green (1975). The assumption relates to the idea of social equilibrium at the macro-level, which I shall discuss below.

19 The other forms of classroom interaction probably produce other dilemmas.

20 Of course, these two theoretical approaches are not internally homogeneous and my comments are not applicable to all versions of them. Broadly speaking, the position sketched here is a modified version of conflict theory. See in particular Lockwood (1964). For a similar approach, see Giddens (1976).

21 In the case of Marxism of course, social change leads to different forms of equilibrium, different types of society. For a useful discussion of equilibrium theory in the context of functionalism, see Guessos (1967).

22 Of course, both Marxists and structural functionalists recognise this in an informal or ad hoc manner.

23 This mirrors Schutz's position on inconsistencies in actors' perspectives.

24 And perhaps, compared also to the situation in East European societies, where control seems to come much more from the centre. Curiously, this seems in some ways to result in more fragile social structures.

25 Though we must remember that, as Giddens (1976, p. 102) has pointed out, '*All reproduction is necessarily production* however: and the seed of change is there in *every act* which contributes towards the reproduction of any "ordered" form of social life'.

Chapter 12

Curriculum development and social change: towards a reappraisal of teacher action　Denis Gleeson

In this paper, I discuss the phenomenon of curriculum development as part of the social reform movement in education in the 1960s and 1970s and, in the light of recent Marxist debate in the sociology of education, examine both the theory and practice of implementation which influenced such development.

It should be stated at the outset that it is not my purpose to dispute the thrust of much recent debate in the sociology of education, but rather to attempt to ground its critical formulations within the contradictions and struggle which tend to characterise school practice. While the recent growth of interest in Marxist perspectives has contributed significantly to our comprehension of the relationship between schooling and capitalism, these perspectives have generally failed to advance our understanding of the social space in which radical teachers and pupils may struggle for alternative conceptions of school practice. For, although it has now become commonplace to *describe* schools as 'State Apparatuses', 'Cultural Reproducers', 'Ideological Agencies', servants of 'Monopoly Capital' and so on, the use of such global terms, accurate or not, may well serve to obscure *explanations* of the ways in which schools, together with other agencies of cultural action, may act as important sources of critique and social change. In other words, what I am suggesting is that while theoretical debate may locate the dilemma of radical practitioners, it fails to recognise the potentialities of those repressive circumstances which may well provide the arena of social change. Therefore, although recent Marxist informed discussion in the sociology of education has enhanced our understanding of the system 'as it is', the discussion has largely ignored those circumstances of *intervention* and decision-making where practitioners may, through struggle, act to change that system. In order to understand how this situation has arisen *vis-à-vis* curriculum development, it would seem necessary to provide a brief outline of what I consider to be the

193

main Marxist critique of the educational reform movement.

The efficacy of achieving reform and hence social change through schooling has been attacked, not least of all on the grounds that such attempts ignore the political and ideological relations between capitalism and schooling. Althusser (1971), for example, questions the view that schools can ever be seen as agents of criticism or liberation since, he argues, schooling represents a powerful ideological state apparatus which 'functions' to safeguard capitalism by reproducing pupils with specific skills and appropriate thought processes, largely concerned with a respect for the existing social relations of production. Similar analyses have been re-stated by others, notably Bourdieu (1973), Baudelot and Establet (1971), Braverman (1975), Karier, Violas and Spring (1973) and Bowles and Gintis (1976). Broadly speaking, such theorists have sought to understand the educational system in the light of the social relationships of economic life and have posited a view of schooling as an integral element in the reproduction of the prevailing class structure of society. A significant feature of such a critique is that it highlights the contradiction of introducing reforms into existing structural processes designed to perpetuate class divisions and to extend institutional forms of control. Indeed, reformism has been attacked for sustaining such divisiveness both on the grounds that social policy identifies social problems as 'pathological' as well as on the grounds that the subsequent processes of amelioration obscure the underlying political and economic factors. Such a critique calls into question the hitherto accepted assumptions that education is a 'good' thing and that its extension necessarily leads to greater social mobility and improved life chances. However, while attempting to retain much of the radicalism of such a critique in analysing the curriculum development movement, I shall argue that ultimately such perspectives are less than helpful in considering alternatives at the grass-roots level.

It would seem, therefore, that before we may proceed to construct alternative forms of curricular change, there is a need to explore the issues arising from two inter-linked considerations: first, we need to know more about the ways in which the assumptions of curriculum development relate, or fail to relate, to the experiences and views of teachers; and second, we need to examine the ways in which teachers re-define their conceptions of school knowledge through working with curriculum development projects.

Transmission and reception

Curriculum development may perhaps be most aptly described as a product of its time, a product of affluence and expansion for which the expressed raison d'être was to reformulate and accelerate the transmission of knowledge from one sector of the educational system to another. Spurred on by economic crises and foreign competition, declining standards of maths and science teaching, not to mention the impending expansion of comprehensive education and the threat of ROSLA, curriculum development was born. It is not difficult to discern the issues underlying the professional response of curriculum developers, a response guided by a highly functional and pragmatic conception of the mechanistic relations which are assumed to exist between schooling and the 'problems' of society.

However, a major weakness of such a conception of curriculum innovation lies in its oversimplified view of the intricacies of classroom practice as well as of the social organisation of the school. Here, education is perceived as *the* most important rational mechanism for despatching messages from society to its youth. Such a functionalist model of curriculum development not only assumes consensus on the values to be transmitted to the various social groups through organised curricula, but also takes for granted the political desirability of such a transmission as a 'good thing'.

Perhaps the most significant weakness of the curriculum development movement was that it sowed within itself the seeds of its own destruction. For instance, those projects whose professed aims were to influence and challenge existing school knowledge were too often in conflict with the standard methods used to implement such 'radical' ideas in schools. More importantly, the effort to change the curriculum through such progressive concepts as active enquiry and teacher impartiality often met with strong resistance from teachers who experienced such innovations as externally imposed and irrelevant to their immediate problems. Unfortunately, much of the teacher 'reaction' against such innovations has been explained in terms of their conservatism; there has been little attempt to understand their reaction as a normal and critical response to pressure imposed by the functional models of curriculum development itself.

Another interpretation of teacher reaction might be that the assumptions of curriculum developers are not sufficiently grounded within the practitioners' frames of reference. Developers tend to assume that the educational system acts in a mechanised fashion, so that ideas once fed into it from the top (inputs: structured methods, materials and so forth) will be processed through various channels and arrive finally at the 'grass roots' at the bottom (output: school classrooms). Such a hierarchical conception of 'development' not only assumes a split between 'experts' and classroom teachers, but also implies a clear ascendancy of curriculum 'theory' over school 'practice'. Hence, Bartholomew (1976) argues that such unquestioned assumptions about hierarchy take the rationality of educational theory for granted, presupposing the superiority of its progressive and liberal status over the illiberal and inimical influences of school. In this way, educational 'theory' attains hegemony over practice, a hegemony which has no grounds in the contradictions and limitations of practice and which certainly ignores the ways in which such practice might inform theory. In other words, hierarchical conceptions of curriculum development may create disjuncture in the relations between theory and practice, thereby failing to consider the ways in which teachers may have important things to say about curricular innovation and change. Young (1976) raises a similar point where he criticises the Schools Council funding process, which confirms rather than transcends such disjuncture.

A related problem arising in centrally constructed curriculum developments is that persons tend to become separated from others in the course of the development programme. Planners and seconded teachers, for example, usually operate from the removed context of the university, evaluating ideas which are injected into selected trial schools. Although classroom teachers are certainly involved in such experiments, their participation is often of a token nature and is ultimately insignificant in decision-making. Indeed, an important feature of some projects is that induction into its methods and principles becomes a prerequisite of teacher involvement. In the case of the Humanities Curriculum Project (HCP, 1974), for example, induction became a crucial priority linked directly with evaluation and follow-up. Originally, HCP was considered to be one of the most radical of the early Schools Council projects because it sought to bring controversy into the classroom. That controversy, however, was ultimately neutralised because of the planners' emphasis upon impartiality and upon the thorough induction of teachers into the prescribed methods and principles of the project. The latter was seen to create an inflexibility which many teachers reacted against (Gleeson, 1976). Indeed, being inducted into a process often implies a passive role, rather than an invitation to question and influence decisions.

Shipman makes a similar point in his study *Inside a Curriculum Project* (1974), where he draws attention to the problem of 'innovation without change'. He indicates how teachers failed to participate in the Keele Integrated Studies Project, even though it was taking place in their own school. Shipman's book chronicles the events which led the Keele Project away from its initial concerns with facilitating integrative enquiry through grass-roots support towards the estrangement of the project team from the trial school. He describes how the project team, in their rush to produce work schemes and materials, failed to support teacher initiatives and began to dictate the terms upon which local support should operate. Inevitably, classroom teachers seriously questioned the nature of their involvement in the experiment and began to see their participation as peripheral to the real decisions being made elsewhere.

It would seem, therefore, that the normative model of curriculum development inevitably oversimplifies the problem of implementation. Moreover, teacher reaction against externally conceived ideas and methods suggests that schools are more complex places than hitherto realised. In other words, it is a misconception that schools do automatically adopt or passively respond to the engineered input of knowledge, even in circumstances where teachers support the general aims of curriculum projects—a misconception which may be seen to be largely responsible for the disappointing reception of both HCP and the Keele Integrated Studies Project.

In seeking to examine the apparent failure of those ventures, it is not my intention to reject out of hand the ideas upon which the projects were initially founded. On the contrary, some of their original aims and materials must be applauded because they sought to question much of the established nature of school knowledge. In different ways, both projects sought to influence and change accepted school organisation and practice so that alternative conceptions of humanities teaching might be implemented. Moreover, the advocation of such innovations as enquiry learning, team teaching, democratic participation and so on clearly raises important questions concerning the traditional authority structure of schooling. With varying emphases, both projects attempted to relate work in the humanities to the wider social context and held out the promise that learning could be 'for real', rather than a process of acquiring knowledge. Ultimately, they sought to blur the traditional distinctions between what goes on in school classrooms and in communities through the practice of active and open enquiry.

It is important that the radical significance of such ideas should not be overlooked, not least of all because they propose that schooling be a critical force in society. However, what I am suggesting is that the models used to implement such ideas ultimately served to neutralise their critical potential by imposing further constraints upon teachers in their already contradictory work. Teachers who seek to question existing social relations by introducing 'innovations' like integration, enquiry learning, participation, mixed ability and so on often find themselves alienated within their schools. Such teachers operate within politically vulnerable circumstances, in conflict and doubt, so that it is essential that curricular reform should support rather than frustrate them in their task. It would seem to be to this end that curriculum development programmes should be directed.

Alternatives

At the beginning of this paper, some reference was made to the contribution of Marxist perspectives in the sociology of education to-wards understanding why reformist policies have been less than success-ful. Such perspectives have offered critically significant insights into the ideological function of schooling which may be brought to bear on future attempts to formulate educational alternatives.

It is useful, therefore, briefly to outline the main Marxist criticisms of the reform movement of the late 1960s and early 1970s. Broadly speaking, from such a perspective, the educational system is seen to have two main objectives: the reproduction of labour power and the reproduction of the social relationships which facilitate the translation of labour power into profits. Thus, the educational system functions to *legitimate* rather than *transcend* economic inequality and the hier-archical division of labour. We may say, therefore, that such analysis not only highlights the process of schooling as a powerful mechanism of social control, but also points to the contradictory nature of the concept of reform within existing institutions. In other words, curri-cular reform movements which profess to seek greater social justice by re-arranging existing conditions within educational institutions are seen to be profoundly contradictory, since those very institutions act to extend the divisive social relations of capitalist production. Similar scepticism has been expressed concerning the 'child-centred' move-ment, which emphasises such concepts as participation, active enquiry and teacher neutrality. It has been suggested that such conceptions of teaching and learning ultimately mask the reality of schooling and, in particular, its hidden control (Sharp and Green, 1975; Dale, 1977). At another level, the 'progressive' movement has been criticised for sup-porting the status quo by alienating working class children from what is seen to be authentic knowledge. In other words, unless working class pupils gain control over what is accepted as school knowledge, they are likely to remain powerless in the wider social world (Young and Whitty, 1976).

What may be extracted from such analysis which is of relevance here is that efforts to improve or reform processes of teaching and learning will not of themselves render schooling a more 'critical' process. If schooling is to become instrumental in social change, we must look beyond the re-arranging of school knowledge and the liberalising of pedagogical relationships.

However, while welcoming such insights into the ideological aspects of educational reform, I wish to express reservations concerning their neglect of the conditions of practice from which, I would argue, viable alternatives may arise. In other words, what I am suggesting is that in many ways such 'long-term' critiques ignore the 'here and now' contra-dictions experienced by practitioners and with them their potential for change. Despite the theoretical efficacy of much Marxist-informed criticism of recent curricular innovation, and in the absence of immediate short-term alternatives, there is a need to examine the strengths and failings of curricular reform and to use that experience as a resource by which future developments may be informed. For, undeniably, the curricular reform projects of the 1960s, two of which I have briefly referred to (HCP and the Integrated Studies Project), were devised as a challenge to conventional patterns of school organisation; for that reason, we might be able to learn by their mistakes. Nothing intrinsic in such 'progressive' methods renders them, of necessity, forms of bourgeois control. Yet Marxist critiques of 'progressive' education have done little to extend the level of such debate. Rather, they have sacrificed the liberal 'middle ground' to the 'right' and in so doing have ignored the radical potential afforded by 'progressive' methods. Ironically, those same teaching methods are perceived by the 'right' as possible threats to the status quo.

In other words, 'progressive' approaches may represent more than novel strategies for facilitating the acquisition of conventional school knowledge and associated social relations; they may be used also as a means of enabling pupils and teachers to challenge existing authority structures both within school and without. As Frith and Corrigan (1976) point out, much depends upon where we wish to progress *to*. What I would argue is that while the Marxist critique of the relations between schooling and capitalism asks us, with justification, to re-examine the overall objectives of education, it fails to address the issues of everyday school practice and thus ignores possible strategies of intervention at the grass-roots level. In such a view of schooling, the institution itself is reduced to a static and reified abstraction of political economy. In other words, while describing the school as a conservative force (Bourdieu and St Martin, 1974) and examining the ways in which it reproduces existing social relations (Althusser, 1971; Bowles and Gintis, 1976), there is a tendency to ignore the actual conditions of practice. Moreover, this tendency to isolate education as a consumptive force and to ignore the contradictions in which individuals and groups work fails to recognise conflict and struggle as a possible point of intervention and change. Indeed, such problems as indiscipline, truancy and unemployment manifested by the lack of relation between qualifications and jobs may be interpreted as sources of potential change as opposed to reaction.

However, any serious consideration of struggle and change *within* education must recognise that such strategies are bounded by the limitations of what is possible. This does not mean that one accepts those limitations as 'given' or that one accepts as 'unproblematic' the contradiction of seeking to initiate radical change within reformist structures, but rather that one recognises that change must start *somewhere* and that waiting for the revolutionary conjuncture may ultimately mean doing nothing. However, according to recent debate in the sociology of education, to consider alternatives is to fall into the dreaded trap of reformism—the nemesis of revolution—and it is perhaps for this reason that Marxist-informed critique may be accused of confining itself to the level of theory. In short, what I would argue is that in seeking to avoid and condemn reformism, such theorising has failed to recognise the strategic implications for change within the reality of practical conditions.

Through analysing the contradictions within which teachers and pupils work, we may arrive at a realistic picture of the potentiality for educational and social change such conditions afford. Theorising which fails to recognise such imperatives adopts an idealistic position which smacks of disturbing elitism by assuming the ascendancy of theory over practice. Indeed, such a position permits the theorist to characterise those engaged in struggle as helpless ideologues subjugated to a system 'which is bigger than them and [which] crushes them' (Althusser, 1971). From this viewpoint teachers, social workers, coppers, shop-stewards and others who must 'negotiate' with the state by virtue of their class position may be dismissed as passive functionaries or agents of class control. Thus, despite the apparent radicalism of such a stance, its relevance at the level of practice is open to question. This situation arises not because the practitioners are unwilling or unable to understand the level of discussion but because such analysis is underdeveloped *vis-à-vis* intervention, struggle and action. It would seem that unless such issues are pursued teachers, not unlike social workers, will simply remain 'The dirty workers [who] are increasingly caught between the silent middle class which wants them to do the work and keep quiet about it and the objects of that work who refuse to continue to take it lying down' (Rainwater, 1974, quoted in Cohen, 1975).

At an initial level, therefore, teacher involvement in decisions which concern the conditions of their work is of paramount importance. In recent years we have witnessed a growing minority of teachers willing to challenge authoritarian structures both within and without school. Their involvement in a range of activities, curriculum change, examination reform, 'grass-roots' unionism and teacher education has been considerable. However, the structurally oriented nature of much Marxist-inspired sociology of education has either ignored the significance of such activities or caricatured them as 'piecemeal'—as if the practitioners engaged therein were unconscious of the political limitations of their actions. Clearly, educational equality and social change cannot take place through the educational system alone, but having said that, where does it leave us?

At a time when education itself no longer constitutes the great panacea, and when historically hard-won reforms are being 'cut', it seems a curious paradox that *academic* Marxists continue to be preoccupied with the ills of 'reformism' (and the curricular implications associated with it) and fail either to consider alternative programmes or to discuss the aims of critical education. While the air is thick with critiques of schools and teachers ('easy meat'), little attention has been paid to the ways in which existing 'contradictions' might inform future debate on educational *practice*. Perhaps this is why Cohen (1975) has suggested that, for the moment, action must remain a process of short-term intervention. Pursuing such strategies further, he writes:

> There are some very effective short term possibilities not just through humanitarian work but in conscious policies of raiding the establishment for resources, contributing to its crises, unmasking and embarrassing its ideologies and pretensions. Any such effectiveness can be lost by finishing. One must be able to live with ambiguity and refuse to accept what the *others*, the authorities demand—choice between revolution and reform.

Whilst any number of objections may be raised against such 'strategy', Cohen's remarks *do* address the limitations and parameters in which action can take place. Within the constraints imposed by economic recession and social reaction, few strategic avenues exist for critical teachers to innovate within educational processes. However, despite such limitations, much may be achieved within conventional frameworks by teachers acquiring more active involvement in curricular decision-making processes. Thus, at the risk of sounding naive, I see a need, at the institutional level, to establish closer working relations among classroom teachers, educationists, academics, teacher unions, administrators and researchers so that those agencies which presume to 'support' the school might understand something of the theoretical and practical contradictions which characterise its everyday practice. Although this may seem a familiar directive (James Report, 1971; Ford Teaching Project, 1975; Humanities Curriculum Project, 1974; Bartholomew, 1974; Young and Whitty, 1976) such collaborative relations have not been, and are unlikely to be, achieved within the present climate, where politicians, administrators and academics alike demonstrate antipathy towards the contradictions within which teachers and pupils work. Such collaboration not only implies the breakdown of hierarchical educational distinctions through which teachers may become more authentically involved in decision-making processes, but may also encourage 'educationists', Schools Council administrators, union leaders, politicians and others to learn from those who take active part in the teaching process. The Ford Teaching Project Team recognise the need for such teacher involvement when they write:

> With a few notable exceptions curriculum designers have failed to support teachers grappling with the problems that curriculum presents in the classroom. They have tended to underestimate the

stresses and strains which attend the necessary changes in role relationships. . .for both teachers and pupils, too easily assuming that changes in pedagogy can be brought about by merely changing content and materials (Elliott and Adelman, 1975).

Despite their tentative nature, such proposals illustrate the kinds of limited frameworks within which teachers work and from which radical forms of action and critique may be initially mounted. While it is too early to predict what kind of impact such strategies might have on developing alternative conceptions of school knowledge or on wider political questions, they do point to the need for collaboration *within* the learning context, as distinct from programmes which are grafted onto schools from 'outside'.

However, such proposals are not only concerned with the collaboration of practitioners, but seek to incorporate alternative conceptions of critical teaching and learning both *within* and *without* the classroom. It would be naive to suggest that such strategies of intervention might, of themselves, transform political inequality. They must form part of a movement, taking place alongside other forms of action outside education. However, what I have sought to explain is that radical theory must relate to struggle at the grass-roots level if it is to retain its critical potential. In other words, it is essential that there be engagement with teachers and pupils in their practical action and struggle (even though these are not always articulated in a uniform fashion). Moreover, there is a need to recognise the potential of the school as a critical force predisposed towards active cultural transformation. As Laing and Cooper (1971) have argued: Marx put his thought in very precise terms. If, for example, one wishes to act on or influence (*agir*) an educator, then one must act on or modify the factors which condition him.' Elsewhere (Erben and Gleeson, 1977), I have argued that 'The *one* can be the educator himself, other educators, or students or pupils acting within their own situation in a process of transformation.'

Conclusion

At a time when teacher 'autonomy' is under attack, there is a need to explore strategies for change which will enhance the teacher's right to influence the school curriculum. Alternatives cannot, of course, be plucked like rabbits from a magician's hat or stuck onto an exploited radical situation in a prescribed manner, but must be formulated through theoretical strategies fashioned in a critical awareness of the political consequences of schooling as well as of the conditions in which teachers work. The major problem is where to start such analysis. For the purpose of this paper, I have sought to examine curriculum development as a part of a more complex debate concerning teacher involvement in curricular change. Such questions may be of critical importance at a time when we have witnessed a carefully stage-managed 'Great Debate' about declining standards and the consequent questioning of teacher competency.

Chapter 13

Autonomy and organisation: a theoretical perspective on teacher decisions

George Mardle and Michael Walker

Whilst our knowledge of classroom processes is increasing, there are nevertheless substantial gaps, one of which concerns decision-making. In their daily activities teachers make many and varied decisions which range from immediate issues contingent upon teacher-pupil interaction, through decisions about planning, content and sequence of lessons, to long-term decisions about aims and objectives or the prospects of career advancement. As yet, we have no theoretical framework around which we might develop explanations about teacher decisions. It is suggested here that we should begin to develop such a framework and that a useful start might be made through a re-examination of decision theory developed in the context of organisational analysis.

Such an approach is not without problems. Theoretical models are normally constructed with a specific context in mind, and this context is likely to affect the nature of and solution to theoretical problems inherent in the model. Within organisational analysis itself, Silverman (1971, p.217) has shown how the overall theoretical orientation of a model varies according to the choice of major problem and the principal concepts employed. It would be naive to assume therefore that schools could be understood simply in terms of models constructed to explain large-scale industrial organisations. For this reason sociologists have, by and large, shown little interest in the application of organisational analysis to schools. Also, they may have been deterred by the heavily structural functional orientation and undertones of management ideology apparent in much of the work.

A more likely source for a theory of classroom decisions would seem to be in the interactionist, phenomenological or ethno-methodological traditions. Garfinkel's jurors, Bittner's policemen, Cicourel's law-enforcement officials and Silverman's bureaucrats (Garfinkel, 1967; Bittner, 1967; Cicourel, 1968; Silverman, 1974) all suggest models and modes of analysis ripe for application to the classroom. This kind of understanding of practical decision-making seems, however, to suggest a-theoretical conditions in which such a process takes place. Whilst it explores the nature of process, it offers little insight into the contextual limitations which may govern such a process. It suggests that the assumptions of human intentionality have no institutional or structural parameters.

What might be useful, therefore, is a theory which attempts to explain decisions in terms of both individual verstehen and the structural factors which contribute part of the determinants of that understanding: a theory of decisions which relates action to structure. Such a theory is available through a particular interpretation of the work of March and Simon (1958). Their work on decision theory attempts to bridge explanations of the individual and his socio-psychological understanding of decision-making, and the structural parameters encountered within the social or organisational context in which decisions are made.

In interpreting March and Simon, we shall look first at their assumptions about the nature of the individual and the subjective processes of decision-making, second at their assumptions about the nature of organisations, and third at the complex picture of individual action within the organisation. At each stage we hope to demonstrate that the theory being developed offers some purchase on existing data and to suggest some possible area for research.

Of central importance in the March and Simon theory is the notion of rationality. This is derived from a dissatisfaction with the conceptualisation of rationality in the 'economic man' of classical organisation theory. Economic man had knowledge of all alternatives from which to choose, he knew the consequences of his choices (albeit in degrees of certainty) and he had an unambiguous preference ordering of those alternatives. Thus, his rationality was manifest through deciding upon that alternative which led to the most preferred set of consequences. He made the optimal choice, the one best decision.

Following their logical criticisms of this model, March and Simon suggest that it is also substantively inadequate. Simply, men never have full knowledge of alternatives, consequences, or even preferences for that matter. At best, men can only be subjectively or intendedly rational. Choices can be made only far within the individual's frame of reference, limited by available knowledge. Furthermore, it is

> The organisational and social environment in which the decision maker finds himself [which] determines what consequences he will anticipate, what ones he will not, what alternatives he will consider, what ones he will ignore (Grusky and Miller, 1970, p.94).

Notwithstanding the unavailability of full knowledge, March and Simon suggest that men cannot handle even that limited knowledge which is available. Faced with the need to make a decision, their 'administrative man' constructs a simplified model of complex reality. The nature of this model will be determined by his biography and current perception of events. It will depend, in other words, upon his definition of the situation. However, few situations are unique, and this allows him to invoke solutions used on previous occasions, that is, routine responses. When routine responses are inappropriate he undertakes a limited search to find the first satisfactory solution. Whereas economic man sought optimal alternatives on the basis of perfect knowledge, administrative man seeks satisfactory alternatives on the basis of imperfect, simplified knowledge.

To what extent does the teacher, in the relatively confined context of the classroom or in the wider context of the school, resemble administrative man? Obviously, this is an issue of empirical concern about which we may only speculate here. However, there exist a number of somewhat diverse studies of classrooms, teachers, pupils and schools upon which we may draw as sources of data.

Taking the classroom context first: decisions about, for instance, the content of lessons or the degree of difficulty in the material have 'traditionally' been simplified by the organisational device of streaming. Teacher responses in the classroom could be seen as routinised in terms of the 'type' of child being dealt with. On this argument non-normal pupil achievement/behaviour would be problematic and demand search for a satisfactory solution. Now, the degree to which a teacher adopts satisfactory as opposed to optimal solutions is something which can only be ascertained empirically. However, Jackson (1968) claims that 'one study of elementary classrooms found that the teacher engaged in as many as 1000 interpersonal interchanges each day' (p.11). In another highly descriptive account of the teacher's day, Hilsum and Cane (1971) produce some data which may be revealing. From their observation of 129 teachers in 66 primary schools they identify teacher activity during lesson time in terms of eleven categories, of which, incidentally, decision-making is not one. What this suggests is a high diversity of observable activity. This is further evidenced by the finding that, for instance, in each lesson there were an average of 40 disciplinary incidents or 135 instances of organising pupils: 'It would seem that on average the teacher was involved in organising pupils about once every two minutes' (p.62) and this occupied only 15.5 per cent of lesson time. Obviously, these kinds of observations tell us nothing about the subjective processes employed by the teacher. But they do indicate the rapidity of change within the classroom. We would agree with Jackson that there is a 'here-and-now urgency' about classrooms, an immediacy which he sees as sustaining the 'spontaneous quality that brings excitement and variety to the teacher's work'. In our terms, this immediacy also prohibits the teacher's existential withdrawal in order to search for optimal solutions. Where routine activities are ineffective, satisficing follows.

Alternatively, we might examine a more progressive pedagogic perspective which does not assume grouping criteria based upon measured ability but attempts to work from the needs, interests and aptitudes of individual pupils. This presents teachers with a vastly more complex problem of 'knowing' individual pupils and structuring teaching, or rather, facilitating learning accordingly. This is precisely the problem experienced by Mrs Buchanan (Sharp and Green, 1975). Lamenting the fact that 'if she had more time and fewer children she would be able to do more', she says,

> I haven't got the time to keep following them up and making them sit down and read to me. . . .I would have to sit down with him for half an hour to get through to him, and I just haven't the time. . . . (p. 106).

Faced with the problem of 'getting through' to thirty plus individuals, the need to simplify would be acute.

Keddie (1971) encountered a similar situation: there was something in the 'teacher context' which prompted classroom decisions (about, say, the appropriateness of material) to be made on the basis of a simplified model of types of children rather than individuals. We shall argue later that this something is more than the teacher's incapacity to handle multiple phenomena; rather, it relates to the structure of the organisation itself. It is to this structure that we now turn.

Unlike other models (Socio-Technical Sytems, Structural Functionalist), the Simon and March model avoids reifying the organisation. It does this through beginning from assumptions about the social psychological characteristics of the individual and developing a model composed of such individuals. This is no mere social psychological reductionism, since the organisational structure is seen to act back, to limit the consciousness and actions of individual members. What might be seen as problematic is this very dependence of the organisation theory upon what amounts to assumptions about human nature.[1] Further, Perrow (1972) has argued that in order to come to terms with the complexities or organisations March and Simon oversimplify and neglect individual behaviour—'supposedly the real staff of organisational life'. Nevertheless, we have selected here five of March and Simon's characteristics of organisations which seem pertinent to an understanding of decision-making in schools.[2] These are:

1 A predominance of satisficing rather than optimising behaviour.
2 A high degree of routinised behaviour facilitated by the development of performance programmes which obviate the anomic uncertainty of continual optimising.
3 Specialisation in the division of labour, allowing the development

of perspectives focused upon restricted sets of values.

4 Training and socialisation which enable individuals to make the proper decisions.

5 The development of organisational vocabularies which canalise thought and direct attention to limited alternatives.

As with those assumptions concerning the nature of the individual presented earlier, these characteristics of organisations refer only to processes and not to content. (Could it be other in a general model?) In a specific application to schools we should need to examine content and context also. Why adopt this standard practice rather than that? Why this particular division of labour, these vocabularies rather than those? These are now familiar kinds of questions for those involved in the sociology of education. Answers have generally been couched in terms of power relationships and the ability of some to impose definitions upon others. Whilst it seems to us that March and Simon underplay the whole notion of coercive power, they are still aware of its pervasive influence. Perrow (1972, p.287), for instance, noted that:

> In March and Simon's view authority is not bottom up, emphasising the power of the subordinate to grant authority to the superior, or emphasising participation as in the human relations school. Instead the superior has the power or tools to structure the environment and perceptions of the subordinate in such a way that he actually sees the proper things in the proper light.

There is obviously a degree of ambiguity attached to 'power or tools' as used here, but we hope the essence of this position will be made explicit in our specific application to schools.

In applying the selected characteristics of organisations to schools we encounter an immediate problem. Much of the validity of the model presented depends upon the claim that in most instances individual, group or organisational decisions are based upon satisficing rather than optimising. And yet when applied to typically school decisions, this does not seem to be the case. Regardless of whether decisions are taken by the head, in consultation with senior staff, or by the whole staff we would expect something more than satisficing. On questions of school policy, to go open plan and team teach, to de-stream, to change examination boards, to develop a PTA, to abolish corporal punishment etc., we assume the availability of relatively full knowledge of alternatives and consequences. In addition, we would expect a relatively coherent philosophy which would facilitate preference ordering. Again these are questions for empirical study rather than assumption. To what degree do teachers have knowledge of such issues, how coherent is their philosophy?

Only by expanding the scope of the frame of reference employed could we see school decisions as satisficing. That is, if we conceive of the school as a unit within the wider organisational framework of the education system, then limited search for solutions might still hold. This would be to locate decisions on school policy within the routinised alternatives of the state system: that is, within the parameters set by current educational theorising, or political ideologies sustained through the local or national decisions of educational administrators.

This is an argument which would need developing and which foreseeably would strain the concept of organisation. It would seem more realistic at this stage simply to draw attention to the importance of school organisation and policy, however they are arrived at. What is important to stress here is that the mode of organising the school limits the extent and kind of search activity of the classroom teacher. But, school organisation is multi-dimensional. There are dimensions relating to pedagogic, administrative, academic, normative concerns, to which the teacher relates through his individual perspectives. Empirically we have no direct information about which of these perspectives assume relative importance for teachers or in which areas they satisfice. It would seem likely, however, that teachers could attempt to optimise along only one perspective, at the expense of others. That is to say that contradictions may occur within the organisational structure with which teachers cope via a range of satisficing strategies involving various degrees of 'play-off' among, for instance, subject, educationalist or career perspectives. These perspectives constitute the teachers' perception of competing organisational pressures.

Alternative interpretations of some empirical studies do seem to provide evidence of this. As was noted, Keddie's (1971) study may show how, in our terms, the classroom situation promotes satisficing on a teacher perspective rather than optimising on an educationalist perspective. Keddie interpreted this phenomenon as a discrepancy in theory and practice and explained it as the teachers' inability to distinguish between social and intellectual skills, which was again related to social class perception. We would argue that this particular discrepancy may be seen as one of many deriving from the impossibility of simultaneously optimising along several dimensions of school organisation.

Sharp and Green's (1975) study also presents some useful data. Their concern is to locate classroom interaction within a wider structural perspective. Thus, the social features of the school and classroom are structured

> not merely by language and meaning but by modes and forces of
> material production and by the system of domination which related
> in some way to material reality and its control (p.25).

Arguably, the 'some way' referred to here is inadequately explicated, which is hardly surprising, given the enormity of the task. This task may be rendered less onerous through a more systematic analysis of the mediating function of school organisation.

Both Keddie and Sharp and Green seem to understand their teachers as confused cultural dopes, unable to perceive the gap between rhetoric and practice. On the contrary, we understand teachers as attempting to satisfice within a set of organisational parameters which themselves may be contradictory. This is a notion which is recognised by Gracey (1976) in articulating the contradictory pressures experienced by (in this case) a progressive style teacher: '[The teacher] feels very strongly the discrepancy between her goal of individual instruction using material which is meaningful to the children, and organisational necessities of group instruction and the required curriculum. . . . [ultimately] The organisational structure of the school negates the key craftsman goal of individualised instruction' (p.84). These empirical examples touch only briefly upon an area as yet underdeveloped. What this indicates is a need for not only more studies of school organisation but studies which examine the precise nature of the relationship which teachers have to such an organisation.

Of the four remaining characteristics, none presents quite the same problem of applicability. Take the degree of routinised behaviour: a common sense understanding of schools sees them as highly routinised, rule governed, timetabled, bell punctuated, norm saturated institutions. Standard practices proliferate, evidenced by procedures for registration, wet playtimes, absent staff, treatment of persistent lateness or misbehaviour and so on.

Yet it would be easy to overemphasise the static rather than dynamic processes which produce this routinisation. Clearly, some forms of routine are features of rules set up by those in control of the organisation to facilitate its smooth running. Still others can be regarded as a product of negotiated interaction. That is, decisions about pupils (required by the teacher's professional mandate to be optimal) may be arrived at, in the first instance, through optimising. However, the degree of reflexivity required to maintain decisions at an optimal level in the day-to-day welter of classroom interaction necessitates routinisation.

Here again we have no real empirical data. Particularly, we have no longitudinal studies which might ascertain how far teachers, even within changed organisational circumstances, develop routine activities for classroom management which may dominate their daily activities. Significantly, what does seem in need of investigation is how far certain activities are open to negotiation and which of these activities are most highly routinised.

Specialisation in the division of labour would seem immediately apparent in two directions. The first is in the tight definition of roles related to subject specialisation. The second concerns the way schools as organisations have produced a wide variety of administrative structures over the past ten years.

Teachers, it is often suggested, teach subjects rather than children. As Esland (1971) points out, subject perspectives form a large part of the teacher's claimed professional knowledge, which is institutionalised within the organisation of the school. This institutionalised form can be seen as segmented across subjects and hierarchical within subjects.

Consequently, teachers, in terms of both the institutional context and career perspective, identify within given epistemic communities. Thus, the degree of negotiation over the knowledge component they are expected to transmit remains limited. Even the degree of flexibility in methods of transmission may be severely limited by the current state of thinking of legitimising agencies in subject development.

Such a division of labour therefore limits the degree of search patterns in which the teacher may be involved in developing his classroom practice. It also provides a basic insight into the means by which organisational control can operate through a system of vertical specialisation.

An interesting empirical study which can be understood in these terms is Shipman (1972). In looking at the development of the Keele Integrated Studies Project, Shipman suggests how the close identification of the teachers with subject areas and institutional form which supported such divisions produced severe strain in those asked to work on integrated material. This is perhaps a good example of routinised behaviour and a clear cut organisational structure providing the paramount frame of reference for teacher behaviour.

Variations in the administrative structures in schools, on which, again, one finds scant empirical evidence, illustrate another aspect of the division of labour. Recent developments in pastoral care, counselling systems and educational technology indicate a move towards a more fragmented administrative system. Here is an area where new job definitions abound. The lady with the key to the stock cupboard is now the media resources officer. A consequence of such fragmentation and demarcation may be not only to reinforce by renumeration certain defined key posts, but also to fabricate a more complex chain of decision-making.

It may well be a truism to claim that the professional training of teachers enables them to make proper decisions. This training, however, may in many instances provide such a tight frame of reference for the practice of teaching that appropriate stances to certain structures are already highly developed. In fact, many teacher responses could be seen to have origins before professional training. As Lortie (1969) indicates, teaching has a ready-made band of neophytes who have spent most of their lives in institutions for which they are now being trained to enter. Only a small proportion of teachers have any significant experience outside the education system and recourse to what Berger (1971) has called 'alternative plausibility structures'. College courses tend to polarise the theory of education and its practice—they in fact license the intending teacher on the appropriateness of his activities within the teaching practice classroom. Transgression from often implicit norms are 'cooled out' quickly, with an emphasis on propriety in the teacher's professional mandate, judgments and decisions.

The development of organisational vocabularies which canalise thought, focus attention and facilitate the construction of reality has been a fruitful area for sociologists. Much of the work in this area stems from the insights of Wright Mills (1940), and some of these have been applied to education (Cicourel and Kitsuse, 1963). In the context of our argument it is suggested that vocabularies may be viewed as aspects of organisational structure which facilitate interaction. That is, in complex organisations routine vocabularies are necessary for any form of regular unproblematic communication to take place, and part of the new member's initiation is to learn such vocabularies. On the other hand, the degree to which the vocabularies limit alternative constructions of reality is open to empirical investigation.

It is possible to argue that satisficing, routinisation, specialisation, socialisation and the development of vocabularies—that is, the structure of the organisation—effectively define situations in such a way as to determine what possible alternatives will come to mind and which in fact will be preferred. Hence, the individual is lost in the structurally overdetermined context of the organisation. But this interpretation would miss a fundamental point which March and Simon are making, namely that organisations are dynamic rather than static institutions, that negotiations and processes do exist within them but they are circumscribed within the organisational context in which they are made. What March and Simon point to are the kind of mechanisms which compose this context, the parameters within which sets of everyday negotiations are performed and the on-going nature of organisational life sustained.

The subtlety of their position is nowhere better illustrated than in their conceptualisation of control within the organisation. Conventional views of organisational control stem from Weber's bureaucratic model, where rules direct behaviour. March and Simon recognise that only a small proportion of behaviour is strictly rule governed. The rest, they suggest, is controlled through routinisation, socialisation, vocabularies etc. which effectively limit the content and availability of information, set up certain expectations as opposed to others, limit the search for alternatives etc. Thus, the structure of the organisation controls not decisions themselves but the premises upon which decisions are made.

However, even this insightful argument is not without its problems. In relying heavily upon normative socialisation and the ability to define situations through control and access to knowledge, it neglects hierarchy and power. Ability to impose definitions of the situation rests not simply upon possession of more or superior knowledge but also upon the control of resources and the capacity to apply sanctions. Further, we see it as a mistake to overplay the notion that if men define situations as real they are real in their consequences. There are occasions when regardless of whether men define situations as real they are nevertheless real in their consequences. In so far as teachers define school reality in completely different ways, they may, depending on many of the parameters we have looked at, still act on conditions which could be denied strongly at the level of consciousness.

In locating our model of analysis in what we consider to be an important 'middle area' we have argued for a more theoretical appreciation of the nature of school organisation and its effect on teacher activities in the classroom. We have argued against an over-socialised concept of man whilst still holding that the degree to which he can negotiate his own reality is severely limited by the institutional nature of the social world he inhabits.

We have outlined various aspects of this (school) world and argued that the lack of current empirical work in such areas may limit our appreciation of the decision-making process. We have advocated a model which places more emphasis on understanding the teacher as 'administrative' or 'organisational man' than viewing him traditionally as the 'autonomous professional'.

Finally, we hope to have gone some way towards providing an understanding of the conservative nature of schools as institutions, regardless of current, fashionable ideologies. This, we think, is a more realistic understanding of the function of schools as agents of social change. If, as we suggest, it is the organisational forms which decide the premises upon which we act and make decisions in schools, then conscious change becomes problematic unless such premises themselves are changed.

Notes

1 Arguably, it is impossible to start without some assumption about human nature. Basically, administrative man is a utilitarian pragmatist, which may be understood as an ideal type or as invalidating the whole argument.
2 Other characteristics such as 'stabilisation through sunk costs', 'minimal innovation' and 'incremental adaptation' could in fact be applied to schools in a more extensive framework, but time and space necessitate selection.

Bibliography

Adams, E.W., and Fagot, R. (1959), 'A Model of Riskless Choice', *Behavioural Science*, 4, 1–10.

Adams Weber, J.R. (1969), 'Cognitive Complexity and Sociality', *British Journal of Social and Clinical Psychology*, 8, 211–16.

Allen, D.W., and Fortune, J.C. (1965), *An Analysis of Micro Teaching: A New Procedure in Teacher Education*, Stanford University Press.

Allen, D.W., and Ryan, K. (1969), *Microteaching*, New York: Addison-Wesley.

Allen, V.L. (1975), *Social Analysis: A Marxist Critique and Alternative*, London: Longman.

Althusser, L. (1971), 'Ideology and Ideological State Apparatuses: Notes Towards an Investigation' in *Lenin and Philosophy and Other Essays*, London: New Left Books.

Althusser, L. (1972), 'Ideology and Ideological State Apparatuses', in B. Cosin (ed.), *Education: Structure and Society*, Harmondsworth: Penguin.

Apple, M. (1977), 'Power and School Knowledge', *Review of Education*, 3, no. 1, January–February.

Apter, D. (ed.) (1964), *Ideology and Discontent*, New York: Free Press.

Argyle, M., and McHenry, R. (1971), 'Do Spectacles Really Affect Judgements of Intelligence?', *British Journal of Social and Clinical Psychology*, 10, 27–9.

Argyris, C. (1965), *Organisation and Innovation*, Illinois: R.D. Irwin.

Asch, S.E. (1946), 'Forming Impressions of Personality', *Journal of Abnormal and Social Psychology*, 41, 258–90.

Bachrach, P., and Baratz, M.S. (1962), 'Two Faces of Power', *American Political Science Review*, 56, 947. Also in F.G. Castles (ed.) (1971).

Barnard, C. (1938), *The Functions of the Executive*, Cambridge, Mass.: Harvard University Press.

Barnes, D., Britton, J., and Rosen, H. (1969), *Language, the Learner and the School*, Harmondsworth: Penguin.

214

Bartholomew, H. (1976), 'Schooling Teachers: The Myth of the Liberal College', in G. Whitty and M.F.D. Young (eds.) (1977).

Bartholomew, J. (1974), 'Sustaining Hierarchy through Teaching and Research', in M. Flude and J. Ahier (eds), *Educability, Schools and Ideology*, London: Croom Helm.

Baudelot, C., and Establet, R. (1971), *L'Ecole Capitaliste en France*, Paris: Maspéro.

Bauman, Z. (1976), *Towards a Critical Sociology: An Essay on Commonsense and Emancipation*, London: Routledge & Kegan Paul.

Bealing, D. (1972), 'The Organisation of Junior School Classrooms', *Educational Research*, 14, no. 3, June 1972, 231-5.

Becker, H.S. (1952a), 'The Career of the Chicago Public Schoolteacher', *American Journal of Sociology*, 57, 470-7.

Becker, H.S. (1952b), 'Social Class Variations in the Teacher-Pupil Relationship', *Journal of Educational Sociology*, 25, 451-65. Also in B.R. Cosin *et al*. (eds), *School and Society*, London: Routledge & Kegan Paul, 1971; 2nd ed., 1977.

Becker, H.S. (1960), 'Notes on the Concept of Commitment', *American Journal of Sociology*, 66, 32-40.

Becker, H.S. *et al*. (1961), *Boys in White*, University of Chicago Press.

Becker, H.S. (1964), 'Personal Change in Adult Life', *Sociometry*, 27, 40-53.

Becker, H.S. (1971), *Sociological Work*, London: Allen Lane.

Beecham, Y. (1973), 'The Making of Educational Failures', *Hard Cheese Two*, March.

Bellaby, P. (1974), 'The Distribution of Deviance among 13-14 Year Old Students', in J. Eggleston (ed.), *Contemporary Research in the Sociology of Education*, London: Methuen.

Bellaby, P. (1975), 'Attitudinal Measurements', unpublished PhD thesis, University of Cambridge.

Bellaby, P. (1977), *The Sociology of Comprehensive Schooling*, London: Methuen.

Bendix, R. (1970), *Embattled Reason*, Oxford University Press, p. 12.

Bennett, N. (1976), *Teaching Styles and Pupil Progress*, London: Open Books.

Berger, P.L. (1971), *A Rumour of Angels*, Harmondsworth: Penguin.

Berger, P.L., and Luckmann, T. (1967), *The Social Construction of Reality*, Harmondsworth: Penguin.

Berlak, A. *et al*. (1975), 'Teaching and Learning in English Primary Schools', *School Review*, 83, 215-43. Reprinted in M. Hammersley and P. Woods (1976).

Berlak, H., and Berlak, A. (1976), 'Towards a Political and Social Psychological Theory of Schooling', *Interchange*, 6, no. 3.

Bernbaum, G. (1977), *Knowledge and Ideology in the Sociology of Education*, London: Macmillan.

Biddle, B.J., and Ellena, W.J. (1964), *Contemporary Research on Teacher Effectiveness*, New York: Holt, Rinehart & Winston, p. 2.

Bieri, J., Atkins, A.L., Briar, S., Leaman, R.L., Miller, H., and Tripodi, T. (1966), *Clinical and Social Judgement*, New York: Wiley.

Bibliography

Bilski, R. (1973), 'Ideolcgy and the Comprehensive Schools', *Political Quarterly*, 44, 2, p. 197.

Bishop, A.J., and Whitfield, R.C. (1972), *Situations in Teaching*, London: McGraw-Hill.

Bittner, E. (1967), 'The Police on Skid Row: A Study of Peace Keeping', *American Sociological Review*, 32, 699–715.

Bjerstedt, A. (1969), 'Critical Decisions on Video-Tape: An Approach to the Exploration of Teachers' Interaction Tendencies', *Didakometry and Sociometry*, 1, 54–76.

Bligh, D.A. (1972), 'Teaching Decisions with Small Groups in Large Classes', *London Educational Review*, 1, 67–74.

Blumberg, P. (1968), *Industrial Democracy: The Sociology of Participation*, London: Constable.

Blumer, H. (1969), *Symbolic Interactionism*, Englewood Cliffs, New Jersey: Prentice-Hall.

Bonarius, J.C.J. (1965), 'Research in Personal Construct Psychology', in B.A. Maher (ed.), *Progress in Experimental Personality Research*, vol. 2, New York: Academic Press.

Bourdieu, P. (1973), 'Cultural Reproduction and Social Reproduction', in T. Brown (ed.), *Knowledge, Education and Cultural Change*, London: Tavistock.

Bourdieu, P., and St Martin, M. de (1974), 'Scholastic Excellence and the Values of the Educational System', in J. Eggleston (ed.), *Contemporary Research in the Sociology of Education*, London: Methuen.

Bowles, S., and Gintis, H. (1976), *Schooling in Capitalist America*, London: Routledge & Kegan Paul.

Boyson, R. (1975), *Parental Choice*, London: Conservative Political Centre.

Braverman, H. (1975), *Labour and Monopoly Capitalism*, New York: Monthly Review Press.

Bronfenbrenner, U., Harding, J., and Gallway, M. (1958), 'The Measurement of Skill in Social Perception', in D.C. McLeland, A.L. Baldwin, U. Bronfenbrenner and F.L. Strodtbeck (eds), *Talent and Society*, Princeton: Van Nostrand.

Brown, R. (1969), 'Some Aspects of Mass Media Communicators', in P. Halmos (ed.), *The Sociology of Mass Media Communicators*, *Sociological Review Monograph 13*, Keele: University Press.

Bruner, J.S., Shapiro, D., and Tagiuri, R. (1958), 'The Meaning of Traits in Isolation and in Combination', in R. Tagiuri and R. Petrullo (eds), *Person Perception and Interpersonal Behaviour*, Stanford University Press.

Brunswick, E. (1956), *Perception and the Representative Design of Psychological Experiments*, Berkeley: University of California Press.

Buchanan, J.M. (1969), *Cost and Choice: An Inquiry in Economic Theory*, Chicago: Markham Publishing.

Campbell, D.P. (1971), *Handbook for the Strong Vocational Interest Blank*, Stanford University Press.

Campbell, U.N. (1960), 'Assumed Similarity, Perceived Sociometric Balance and Social Influence: An Attempted Integration within one

Cognitive Theory', unpublished PhD dissertation, University of Colorado.

Camus, A. (1953), *The Rebel*, London: Hamish Hamilton.

Cancian, F. (1975), *What are Norms? A Study of Beliefs and Action in a Maya Community*, Cambridge University Press, p. 26.

Carchedi, G. (1975), 'On the Economic Identification of the New Middle Class', *Economy and Society*, 4, no. 1, 361–417.

Castles, F.G. (ed.) (1971), *Decisions, Organisations and Society*, Harmondsworth: Penguin.

Cattell, R.B. (1957), *Handbook of the 16 PF Questionnaire*, Champaign, Illinois: IPAT.

Cattell, R.B. (1967), *The Sixteen Personality Factor Questionnaire*, Champaign, Illinois: IPAT.

Chanan, G. (ed.) (1972), *Research Forum on Teacher Education*, NFER.

Cicourel, A.V. (1968), *The Social Organisation of Juvenile Justice*, New York: Wiley.

Cicourel, A.V., and Kitsuse, J.I. (1963), *The Educational Decision Makers*, Indianapolis: Bobbs-Merrill.

Cohen, S. (1975), 'It's All Right for You to Talk', in R. Bailey and M. Brake (eds), *Radical Social Work*, London: Edward Arnold.

Collingwood, R.G. (1946), *The Idea of History*, Oxford University Press.

Collins, R. (1972), 'Functional and Conflict Theories of Education Stratification', in B. Cosin (ed.), *Education: Structure and Society*, Harmondsworth: Penguin.

Cook, W.W., Leeds, C.H., and Callis, R. (1951), *Minnesota Teacher Attitude Inventory (Form A)*, New York: Psychological Corporation.

Cope, E., and Raab, C.D. (1976), 'Administrators as Researchers: Collaboration in the Scottish Regions', Centre for Educational Sociology, University of Edinburgh.

Coulson, M.A. (1972), 'Role: A Redundant Concept in Education? Some Educational Considerations', in J.A. Jackson (ed.), *Role*, Cambridge University Press, pp. 119–22.

Crawford, D.G., and Signori, E.I. (1961), 'An Application of the Critical Incident Technique to University Teaching', *Canadian Psychologist*, 3, 153–72.

Cyert, R.M., and March, J.G. (1963), *A Behavioral Theory of the Firm*, Englewood Cliffs, New Jersey: Prentice-Hall.

Dahl, R.A. (1958), 'A Critique of the Ruling-Elite Model', *American Political Science Review*, 52, June, 463.

Dale, R. (1977), 'Implications of the Rediscovery of the Hidden Curriculum for the Sociology of Teaching', in D. Gleeson (ed.) (1977).

Dale, R., Esland, G., and Macdonald, M. (eds) (1976), *Schooling and Capitalism: A Sociological Reader*, London: Routledge & Kegan Paul.

Delamont, S. (1976), *Interaction in the Classroom*, London: Methuen.

Dember, W.M. (1969), *Psychology of Perception*, New York: Holt Saunders.

Department of Education and Science (1965), *The Organisation of Secondary Education*, DES Circular 10/65, London: HMSO.

Department of Education and Science (1977), *Introducing the Assessment of Performance Unit*, pamphlet, London: DES.

Dettre, J.R. (1970), *Decision Making in the Secondary School Classroom*, Scranton: Intext, Educational Publishers.

Deutscher, I. (1965), 'Words and Deeds; Social Science and Social Policy', *Social Problems*, 13, 233–54.

Dill, W.R. (1964), *Decision-making in Behavioral Science and Educational Administration*, 63rd Yearbook NSSE, University of Chicago Press, pt 2.

Driver, G. (1976-7), 'Ethnicity, Cultural Competence, Social Power and School Achievement: A Case Study of West Indian Pupils Attending a Secondary School in the West Midlands', *New Community*, Winter.

Dunkin, M.J. (1976), 'Problems of Design in Research in Teaching', *BERA Research Intelligence*, 1, no. 2, Stirling Proceedings, 10–12.

Eastman, G. (1967), 'The Ideologising of Theories: John Dewey's Educational Theory: a Case in Point', *Educational Theory*, 17 no. 2, p. 107.

Eggleston, J. (1975), 'The Hidden Conflict in Education', *British Journal of Teacher Education*, 1 no. 3, 305–10.

Eggleston, J. (1977), *The Sociology of the School Curriculum*, London: Routledge & Kegan Paul.

Eggleston, J.F., Galton, M.J., and Jones, M.E. (1976), *Processes and Products of Science Teaching*, London: Schools Council/Macmillan.

Ehrlich, H.J. (1969), 'Attitudes, Behavior and the Intervening Variables', *American Sociologist*, 4, 29–34.

Elliott, J., and Adelman, C. (1975), 'Teacher Education for Curriculum Reform: An Interim Report on the Ford Teaching Project', *British Journal of Teacher Education*, 1, no. 1, 105–14.

Ellis, T. *et al.* (1976), *William Tyndale: The Teachers' Story*, Writers and Readers Publishing Co-operative.

Erben, M., and Gleeson, D. (1977), 'Education as Reproduction: Notes Towards a Critique of Some Aspects of the Work of Louis Althusser', in M.F.D. Young and G. Whitty (eds).

Esland, G. (1971), 'Teaching and Learning as the Organisation of Knowledge', in M.F.D. Young (ed.).

Esland, G. (1972), 'Pedagogy and the Teacher's Presentation of Self', in The Open University, E282, School and Society, Unit 5.

Esland, G. (1977), 'Schooling and Pedagogy', in The Open University, E202, Schooling and Society, Unit 6.

Eysenck, H.J., and Eysenck, S.B.G. (1963), *Eysenck Personality Inventory*, University of London Press.

Eysenck, H.J., and Eysenck, S.B.G. (1964), *Manual of the Eysenck Personality Inventory*, University of London Press.

Eysenck, H.J., and Eysenck, S.B.G. (1969), 'Scores on Three Personality Variables as a Function of Age, Sex and Social Class', *British Journal of Social and Clinical Psychology*, 8, 69–76.

Fay, B. (1975), *Social Theory and Political Practice*, London: Allen & Unwin.

Finn, D., Grant, N., and Johnson, R. (1977), 'Social Democracy, Education and the Crisis', in *On Ideology – Working Paper,* University of Birmingham, Centre for Contemporary Studies.

Finn, J.D. (1972), 'Expectation and Educational Environment', *Journal of Educational Research,* 42, no. 3, 387–410.

Fitzgerald, R.T., Musgrave, P.W., and Pettit, D.W. (1976), *Participation in Schools?,* Victoria: Australian Council for Educational Research.

Flacks, R. (1971), *Youth and Social Change,* Chicago: Markham.

Flanders, A. *et al.* (1968), *An Experiment in Industrial Democracy,* London: Faber & Faber.

Flanders, N. (1970), *Analysing Teacher Behavior,* New York: Addison-Wesley.

Flynn, J.C. (1959), 'Construct Complexity and Construct Constellations as Antecedent Conditions of Role Variability', unpublished MA thesis, Ohio State University.

Foulkes, D., and Foulkes, S.H. (1965), 'Self Concept, Dogmatism and Tolerance of Trait Inconsistency', *Journal of Personality and Social Psychology,* 2, 104–10.

Frankenberg, R. (1974), 'Functionalism and Actor', *International Journal of Health Services,* 4 no. 3, 411–27.

Frith, S., and Corrigan, P. (1976), 'The Politics of Education', in M.F.D. Young and G. Whitty (eds).

Garfinkel, H. (1967), *Studies in Ethnomethodology,* Englewood Cliffs, New Jersey: Prentice-Hall.

Garfinkel, H., and Sacks, H. (1970), 'On the Formal Properties of Social Action', in J.C. MacKinney and E.A. Tiryakin (eds), *Theoretical Sociology,* New York: Appleton-Century-Crofts.

Geertz, C. (1964), 'Ideology as a Cultural System', in D. Apter (ed.), pp. 52–7.

Gibson, R. (1977), 'Bernstein's Classification and Framing: A Critique', *Higher Education Review,* Spring, 9, no. 2, 23–45.

Giddens, A. (1976), *New Rules of Sociological Method,* London: Hutchinson.

Gintis, H. (1974), 'Welfare Criteria with Endogenous Preferences: The Economics of Education', *International Economic Review,* 15 no. 2, 415–30.

Gleeson, D. (1976), 'Experiencing a Curriculum Project', in G. Whitty and M.F.D. Young (eds).

Gleeson, D. (ed.) (1977), *Identity and Structure: Issues in the Sociology of Education,* Driffield: Nafferton Books.

Goffman, E. (1961), *Asylums,* Harmondsworth: Penguin.

Goffman, E. (1963), *Stigma,* Harmondsworth: Penguin.

Goffman, E. (1969), *Strategic Action,* London: Blackwell.

Goffman, E. (1970), *Strategic Interaction,* London: Blackwell.

Gouldner, A. (1954), *Patterns of Industrial Bureaucracy,* New York: Free Press.

Gouldner, A. (1959), 'Reciprocity and Autonomy in Functional Analysis', in L. Cross, *Symposium on Sociological Theory,* New York: Peterson; reprinted in A. Gouldner, *For Sociology,* Harmondsworth: Penguin, 1975.

Gracey, H. (1976), 'The Craftsmen Teachers', in M. Hammersley and P. Woods.

Gramsci, A. (1971), *Selections from the Prison Notebooks*, London: Lawrence & Wishart.

Gretton, J., and Jackson, M. (1976), *William Tyndale: Collapse of a School or System*, London: Allen & Unwin.

Gross, N., Mason, W., and McEachern, A. (1958), *Explorations in Role Analysis*, New York: Wiley.

Grusky, O., and Miller, G.A. (eds) (1970), *The Sociology of Organisations: Basic Studies*, New York: Free Press.

Guessos, M. (1967), 'A General Critique of Equilibrium Theory', in W.E. Moore and R. Cook, *Readings on Social Change*, Englewood Cliffs, New Jersey: Prentice-Hall.

Guilford, J.P. (1956), *Fundamental Statistics in Psychology and Education*, New York: McGraw-Hill.

Habermas, J. (1971), *Towards a Rational Society*, London: Heinemann.

Hammersley, M. (1974), 'The Organisation of Pupil Participation', *Sociological Review*, August, 22 no. 3, 355–68.

Hammersley, M. (1976), 'The Mobilisation of Pupil Attention', in M. Hammersley and P. Woods.

Hammersley, M. (1977a), 'School Learning—The Cultural Resources Required by Pupils to Answer a Teacher's Question', in M. Hammersley and P. Woods.

Hammersley, M. (1977b), 'Teacher Perspectives' and 'The Social Location of Teacher Perspectives', in The Open University, E202, Schooling and Society, Units 9, 10 and 12.

Hammersley, M., and Woods, P. (eds) (1976), *The Process of Schooling*, London: Routledge & Kegan Paul.

Harding, J., Kutner, B., Proshansky, H., and Chein, I.E. (1969), 'Prejudice and Ethnic Relations', in G. Lindzey and E. Aronson (eds), *Handbook of Social Psychology*, vol. 2, Cambridge, Mass: Addison-Wesley.

Hargreaves, A. (1977a), 'Ideology and the Middle School', unpublished paper delivered to the Middle Schools Research Group, University of Liverpool.

Hargreaves, A. (1977b), 'Progressivism and Pupil Autonomy', *Sociological Review*, 25, no. 3, 585–621.

Hargreaves, D.H. (1972), *Interpersonal Relations and Education*, London: Routledge & Kegan Paul.

Hargreaves, D.H. (1974), 'Deschooling and New Romantics', in M. Flude and J. Ahier (eds), *Educability, Schools and Ideology*, London: Croom Helm.

Hargreaves, D.H. (1976), 'Learning to Be Deviant in School: Aspects of the Hidden Curriculum', in T. Roberts (ed.), *The Circumstance of Education*, Manchester University Press.

Hargreaves, D.H., Hester, S.K., and Mellor, F.J. (1975), *Deviance in Classrooms*, London: Routledge & Kegan Paul.

Harrod, P.M.F. (1977), 'Talk in Junior and Middle School Classrooms: An Exploratory Investigation', *Educational Review*, 29, no. 2, 97–106.

Hartnett, A., and Naish, M. (eds) (1976), *Theory and Practice of Education,* vol. 2, London: Heinemann.

Herbert, N., and Turnbull, G.H. (1963), 'Personality Factors and Effective Progress in Teaching', *Educational Review,* 16, 24–31.

Hilsum, S., and Cane, B.S. (1971), *The Teacher's Day,* Slough: NFER.

Hirst, P.H. (1971), 'What is Teaching?', *Journal of Curriculum Studies,* 3, no. 1, 5–18.

Hoffman, P.J. (1960), 'The Paramorphic Representation of Clinical Judgement', *Psychological Bulletin,* 57, 116–31.

Homans, G.C. (1958), 'Social Behavior as Exchange', *American Journal of Sociology,* 63, 596–606.

Horrocks, J.E., and Jackson, D.W. (1972), *Self and Role: A Theory of Self Process and Role Behavior,* Boston: Houghton Mifflin, p. 96.

Hovey, K.H. (1977), 'An Analysis of Change in Teachers' and Pupils' Perceptions Following an Out of School Visit', unpublished dissertation, University of Keele.

Humanities Curriculum Project: An Introduction (1974), London: Heinemann; also HCP, University of East Anglia (1972).

Husen, T. (1968), 'Educational Research and the State', in W.D. Wall and T. Husen, *Educational Research and Policy Making,* Slough: NFER.

Hyman, R.T. (1971), *Contemporary Thought on Teaching,* Englewood Cliffs, New Jersey: Prentice-Hall.

Ichheiser, G.H. (1949), 'Misunderstandings in Human Relations', *American Journal of Sociology,* 55, no. 2, 395–9.

Illich, I. (1973), *Deschooling Society,* Harmondsworth: Penguin.

Illich, I. (1975), *Medical Nemesis,* New York: Calder & Boyars.

Ingleby, J.D., and Cooper, E. (1974), 'How Teachers Perceive First Year Schoolchildren', *Sociology,* 8, 464–73.

Jackson, P.W. (1968), *Life in Classrooms,* New York: Holt, Rinehart & Winston.

James Report (1971). *Teacher Education and Training,* London: HMSO.

Jaspars, J.M.F. (1964), 'Individual Cognitive Structures', *Proceedings of 17th International Congress of Psychology,* Amsterdam.

Jenks, C. (1975), *Inequality: A Reassessment of the Effects of Family and Schooling in America,* Harmondsworth: Penguin.

Jenks, C. (1973), 'A Question of Control: A Case Study of Interaction in a Junior School', MSc thesis. University of London Institute of Education.

Kanter, R.M. (1968), 'Commitment and Social Organisation', *American Sociological Review,* 33, 499–517.

Karabel, J., and Halsey, A.H. (1976), 'The New Sociology of Education', *Theory and Society,* 3, no. 3, 529–52.

Karier, C.J., Violas, P., and Spring, J. (eds) (1973), *Roots of Crisis: American Education in the Twentieth Century,* Chicago: Rand McNally.

Katz, D. (1960), 'The Functional Approach to the Study of Attitudes', *Public Opinion Quarterly,* 24, 163–204.

Keddie, N. (1971), 'Classroom Knowledge', in M.F.D. Young (ed.).

Keirstead, B.S. (1972), 'Decision-taking and the Theory of Games', in C.F. Carter and J.L. Ford (eds), *Uncertainty and Expectations in Economics*, Oxford: Blackwell.

Kelly, G.A. (1955), *The Psychology of Personal Constructs*, New York: Norton.

Kelvin, P. (1969), *The Basis of Social Behavior*, New York: Holt, Rinehart & Winston.

Kerr, J.F. (1964), *Practical Work in School Science*, Leicester University Press.

Kerry, T. (1977), 'The Teacher Education Project', *Research Intelligence*, 3, no. 2, 30–1.

Killcross, M.C., and Bates, W.T.G. (1968), 'The APU Occupational Interests Guide: A Progress Report', *Occupational Psychology*, 42, 119–22.

Kogan, M. (1971), *The Politics of Education*, Harmondsworth: Penguin.

Krause, E.A. (1969), 'Functions of a Bureaucratic Ideology: Citizen Participation', *Social Problems*, 162, 127–413.

Kuhn, T. (1970), *The Structure of Scientific Revolutions*, University of Chicago Press.

Kyriacou, C., and Sutcliffe, J. (1977), 'Teacher Stress: A Review', *Educational Review*, 29, no. 4, 299–306.

Kyriacou, C., and Sutcliffe J. (1978), 'A Model of Teacher Stress', *Educational Studies*, 4, no. 1, 1–6.

Laing, R.D., and Cooper, D.G. (1971), *Reason and Violence: A Decade of Sartre's Philosophy 1950–60*, 2nd edn, London: Tavistock.

Lemert, E. (1951), *Social Pathology*, London: McGraw-Hill.

Linard, M. (1973), 'Effects of T.V. Feedback on the Learning-Teaching Process in a Small Group Situation', unpublished PhD thesis, University of Paris (Nanterre).

Lockwood, D. (1964), 'Social Integration and System Integration', in G. Zollschan and W. Hirsch (eds), *Explorations in Social Change*, London: Routledge & Kegan Paul.

Lortie, C. (1969), 'The Balance of Control and Autonomy in Elementary School Teaching', in A. Etzioni (ed.), *The Semi Professionals and their Organisation*, New York: Free Press.

Lortie, D. (1975), *Schoolteacher*, University of Chicago Press.

Lukes, S. (1974), *Power—A Radical View*, London: Macmillan.

Lunsford, T.F. (1968), 'Authority and Ideology in the American University', *American Behavioral Science*, 11, 5–14.

Lyman, S., and Scott, M. (1970), *Sociology of the Absurd*, New Jersey: Appleton-Century-Crofts.

Lynch, J. (1975), 'The Legitimation of Innovation: An English Path to "Open Education"', *International Review of Education*, 21, 447–64.

McDonald, B. (1975), *Ford Teaching Project*, University of East Anglia.

McHugh, P. (1968), *Defining the Situation*, Indianapolis: Bobbs-Merrill.

McPhail, P. (1967), 'Adolescence: The Age of Social Experiment', unpublished paper presented at a meeting of the British Psychological Society.

March, J.G., and Simon, H.A. (1958), *Organisations*, New York: Wiley.

Marcuse, H. (1964), *One Dimensional Man*, Kent: Abacus.

Marx, K. (1970), *The German Ideology, 1846*, London: Lawrence & Wishart.

Masterman, M. (1970), 'The Nature of a Paradigm', in I. Lakatos and A. Musgrave (eds), *Criticism and the Growth of Knowledge*, Cambridge University Press.

Matza, D. (1964), *Delinquency and Drift*, New York: Wiley.

Merton, R. (1957), *Social Theory and Social Structure*, New York: Free Press.

Miller, G.A. (1956), 'The Magical Number Seven, Plus or Minus Two', *Psychological Review*, 63, 81–97.

Mills, C.W. (1940), 'Situated Actions and Vocabularies of Motive', *American Sociological Review*.

Mills, C.W. (1970), *The Sociological Imagination*, Harmondsworth: Penguin.

Minar, D.W. (1961), 'Ideology and Political Behavior', *Mid-West Journal of Political Science*, 4, p. 323.

Monks, T.G. (ed.) (1970), *Comprehensive Education in Action*, Slough: NFER, pp. 173–6.

Moscovici, S. (1972), 'Society and Theory in Social Psychology', in J. Israel and H. Tajfel (eds), *The Context of Social Psychology: A Critical Assessment*, New York: Academic Press, p. 55.

Murphy, R.F. (1971), *Dialectics of Social Life*, New York: Basic Books.

Musgrave, P.W. (1968), *The School as an Organisation*, London: Macmillan.

Musgrove, F. (1971), *Patterns of Power and Authority in English Education*, London: Methuen.

Musgrove, F. (1974), *Ecstasy and Holiness: Counter-Culture and Open Society*, London: Methuen.

Naish, M., Hartnett, A., and Finlayson, D. (1976), 'Ideological Documents in Education: Some Suggestions Towards a Definition', in A. Hartnett and M. Naish, pp. 55–117.

Nash, R. (1973), *Classrooms Observed*, London: Routledge & Kegan Paul.

Neave, G. (1975), *How They Fared*, London: Routledge & Kegan Paul.

Nuthall, G., and Snook, I. (1973), Chapter 2, in R.M.W. Travers (ed.), *Second Handbook of Research on Teaching*, Chicago: Rand McNally.

Oberschall, A. (1972), *The Establishment of Empirical Sociology*, London: Harper & Row.

Oliver, R.A.C., and Butcher, H.J. (1968), 'Teachers' Attitudes to Education', *British Journal of Educational Psychology*, 38, 38–44.

Osgood, C.S., Suci, G.J., and Tannenbaum, P.H. (1957), *The Measurement of Meaning*, University of Illinois Press.

Parlett, M., and Hamilton, D. (1972), *Evaluation as Illumination: A New Approach to the Study of Innovatory Programs*, Occasional Paper 9, Centre for Research in the Educational Sciences.

Parsons, T. (1959), 'The School Class as a Social System', *Harvard Educational Review*, Fall.

Passow, H.A. (1966), 'The Maze of Research on Ability Grouping', in A. Yates (ed.).

223

Pateman, C. (1970), *Participation and Democratic Theory*, Cambridge University Press.

Payne, G. (1976), 'Making a Lesson Happen', in M. Hammersley and P. Woods (eds).

Perrow, C. (1972), 'The Neo-Weberian Model; Decision Making Conflict and Technology', in G. Salaman and K. Thompson (eds).

Peters, R.S. (ed.) (1976), *The Role of the Headteacher*, London: Routledge & Kegan Paul.

Plamenatz, J. (1970), *Ideology*, London: Pall Mall.

Plowden Report (1967), *Children and their Primary Schools*, Central Advisory Council for Education, London: HMSO.

Preece, P.F.W. (1977), 'Problems of Discipline of Teaching Practice: A Model Based on Catastrophe Theory' in *Research Intelligence*, 2, no. 2, 22–3.

Purvis, J. (1973), 'Schoolteaching as a Professional Career', *British Journal of Sociology*, 24, 43–57.

Rainwater, L. (1974), *Social Problems and Public Policy: Deviance and Liberty*, Chicago: Aldine: cited in S. Cohen.

Rokeach, M. (1960), *The Open and Closed Mind*, New York: Basic Books.

Rosenshine, B. (1971), *Teaching Behaviour and Student Achievement*, Slough: NFER.

Rosenthal, R., and Jacobson, L. (1970), *Pygmalion in the Classroom*, New York: Holt, Rinehart & Winston.

Ryans, D.G. (1960), *Characteristics of Teachers*, Washington: American Council on Education.

Ryle, G. (1949), *The Concept of Mind*, Harmondsworth: Penguin.

Salaman, G., and Thompson, K. (eds) (1973), *People and Organisations*, DT352, Unit 5, London: Longman for Open University Press.

Sallach, D. (1974), 'Class Domination and Ideological Hegemony', *Sociological Quarterly*, 15, 78–93.

Sarbin, T.R., Taft, R., and Bailey, D.E. (1960), *Clinical Inferences and Cognitive Theory*, New York: Holt, Rinehart & Winston.

Schutz, A. (1971), 'The Stranger: An Essay in Social Psychology', in B. Cosin *et al.* (eds), *School and Society*, London: Routledge & Kegan Paul; 2nd ed., 1977.

Schutz, A., and Luckmann, T. (1974), *The Structure of the Lifeworld*, London: Heinemann.

Science Teacher Education Project (STEP) (1974), written materials, 8 vols, London: McGraw-Hill.

Seaman, J.M., and Koenig, F. (1974), 'A Comparison of Measures of Cognitive Complexity', *Sociometry*, 37, no. 3, 375–90.

Shackle, G.L.S. (1961), *Decision, Order and Time in Human Affairs*, Cambridge University Press.

Shackle, G.L.S. (1976), *Time and Choice*, London: The British Academy.

Shaffer, J.A. (1968), *Philosophy of Mind*, Englewood Cliffs, New Jersey: Prentice-Hall.

Sharaf, M.R., and Levinson, D.J. (1957), 'Pattern of Ideology and Role

Definition among Psychiatric Residents', in M. Greenblatt *et al.* (eds), *The Patient and the Mental Hospital,* London: Free Press.

Sharp, R., and Green, A. (1975), *Education and Social Control,* London: Routledge & Kegan Paul.

Shavelson, R.J. (1973), 'What is the basic teaching skill?', *Journal of Teacher Education,* 144-51.

Shavelson, R.J. (1976), 'Teachers' Decision-making', in N.L. Gage (ed.), *The Psychology of Teaching Methods,* NSSE 75th Yearbook, University of Chicago Press.

Shepard, R.N. (1964), 'On Subjectively Optimum Selections among Multi-Attribute Alternatives', in M.W. Shelley and G.L. Bryan, *Human Judgements and Optimality,* New York: Wiley.

Shipman, M. (1968), *Sociology of the School,* London: Longman.

Shipman, M. (1972), 'The Role of the Teacher in Selected Innovative Schools in the United Kingdom', in *The Changing Role of the Teacher and Its Implications,* Paris: OECD.

Shipman, M. (1974), *Inside a Curriculum Project: A Case Study in the Process of Curriculum Change,* London: Methuen.

Silverman, D. (1971), *The Theory of Organisations,* London: Heinemann.

Silverman, D. (1974), 'Accounts of Organisation', in J. McKinley (ed.), *Processing People: Case Studies in Organisational Behavior,* New York: Holt, Rinehart & Winston.

Simon, H. (1957), *Administrative Behavior,* 2nd edn, New York: Free Press.

Simon, H.A. (1957), *Models of Man,* New York: Wiley.

Sinclair, J. McH., and Coulthard, M. (1975), *Towards an Analysis of Discourse,* Oxford University Press.

Slater, P. (1965), *The Principal Components of a Repertory Grid,* London: Vincent Andrews.

Smith, A. (1975), 'Secret Lie Detector in the Lab', *New Scientist,* **67**, no. 964, 476-8.

Smith, L., and Geoffrey, W. (1968), *The Complexities of an Urban Classroom,* New York: Holt, Rinehart & Winston.

Stebbins, R. (1975), *Teachers and Meaning,* Leiden: Brill.

Steiner, I.D. (1954), 'Ethnocentrism and Tolerance of Trait Inconsistency', *Journal of Abnormal and Social Psychology,* **67**, 388-91.

Steiner, I.D., and Johnson, H.H. (1963), 'Authoritarianism and Tolerance of Trait Inconsistency', *Journal of Abnormal and Social Psychology,* **67**, 388-91.

Stern, G.C., Masling, J., Denton, B., Henderson, J., and Levin, R. (1960), 'Two Scales for the Assessment of Unconscious Motivations for Teaching', *Educational and Psychological Measurement,* **20**, 9-29.

Stones, E., and Morris, S. (1972), *Teaching Practice: Problems and Perspectives,* London: Methuen.

Strauss, A. *et al.* (1964), *Psychiatric Ideologies and Institutions,* New York: Free Press.

Sutcliffe, J., and Whitfield, R. (1976), 'Decision Making in the Classroom', *Research Intelligence,* **2**, no. 1, 14-19.

Sutton, C. (1975), 'Resources for Professional Studies', *British Journal of In-Service Education*, 1, no. 2, 41–8.

Taylor, M.T. (1976a), 'Teachers' Perceptions of Their Pupils', *Research in Education*, 16, 25–35.

Taylor, M.T. (1976b), 'What Is a Personal Construct?', *Psychology Teaching*, 4, no. 2, 184–8.

Taylor, P.H., and Reid, W.A. (1971), 'A Study of the Curricular Influence System of the English Primary School', *Scandinavian Journal of Educational Research*, 16, 1–23.

Taylor, T.R., Aitchison, J., and McGirr, E.M. (1971), 'Doctors as Decision Makers: A Computer Assisted Study of Diagnosis as a Cognitive Skill', *British Medical Journal*, 3 July, 35–40.

Television Education Debate, chaired by Robin Day, BBC2, 4 February 1977.

Thompson, B. (1975), 'Nursery Teachers' Perceptions of their Pupils: An Exploratory Study', in J.M. Whitehead (ed.), *Personality and Learning*, vol. 1, London: Hodder Educational.

Thorndike, E.L. (1920), 'A Constant Error in Psychological Rating', *Journal of Applied Psychology*, 4, 25–9.

Todd, F.J., and Rappoport, L. (1964), 'A Cognitive Structure Approach to Person Perception: A Comparison of Two Models', *Journal of Abnormal and Social Psychology*, 68, 469–78.

Turner, R.H. (1971), 'Sponsored and Contest Mobility and the School System', in E. Hopper (ed.), *Readings in the Theory of Education Systems*, London: Hutchinson.

Walker, R., and Adelman, C. (1975), *A Guide to Classroom Observation*, London: Methuen.

Waller, W. (1932), *The Sociology of Teaching*, New York: Wiley.

Warr, P.B., and Knapper, C. (1968), *The Perception of People and Events*, London: Wiley.

Warr, P.B., and Simms, A. (1965), 'A Study of Co-judgement Processes', *Journal of Personality*, 33, 598–604.

Warwick, D. (1974), *Bureaucracy*, London: Longman.

Watts, J. (1977), *The Countesthorpe Experience*, London: Allen & Unwin.

Webb, J. (1962), 'The Sociology of a School', *British Journal of Sociology*, 13, 264–72.

Weber, M. (1947), *The Theory of Social and Economic Organisation*, New York: Free Press.

Wegmann, R. (1976), 'Classroom Disciplines: An Exercise in the Maintenance of Social Reality', *Sociology of Eduction*, 49, 71–9.

Werthman, C. (1971), 'Delinquents in Schools: A Test for the Legitimacy of Authority', in B. Cosin *et al.* (eds), *School and Society*, London: Routledge & Kegan Paul; 2nd ed., 1977.

Whitfield, R.C. (1975), 'Teaching as Decision Making for and in the Science Room', in P.L. Gardner (ed.), *The Structure of Science Education*, Melbourne: Longman.

Whitty, G. (1974), 'Sociology and the Problem of Radical Education Change', in M. Flude and J. Ahier (eds), *Educability, Schools and Ideology*, London: Croom Helm.

Whitty, G., and Young, M.F.D. (eds) (1977), *Explorations in the Politics of School Knowledge*, Driffield: Nafferton Books.

Wicker, A.W. (1969), 'Attitudes vs. Actions', *Journal of Social Issues*, 25, 41–78.

Wilenski, H.L. (1967), *Organisational Intelligence: Knowledge and Policy in Government and Industry*, New York: Basic Books.

Williams, G. (1961), *Criminal Law: The General Part*, 2nd edn, London: Stevens.

Willis, P. (1977), *Learning to Labour: How Working-Class Kids Get Working-Class Jobs*, Saxon House.

Wilson, C., and Alexis, M. (1962), 'Basic Frameworks for Decisions', *Journal of the Academy of Management*, 5, in W.J. Gore and J.W. Dyson (eds) (1964), *The Making of Decisions*, London: Collier-Macmillan, pp. 180–95.

Wishner, J. (1960), 'Reappraisal of "Impressions of Personality"', *Psychological Review*, 67, 96–112.

Woods, P. (1975), 'Showing Them Up in Secondary School', in G. Chanan and S. Delamont (eds), *Frontiers of Classroom Research*, Slough: NFER.

Woods, P. (1976), 'The Myth of Subject Choice', *British Journal of Sociology*, June.

Woods, P. (1977), 'Teaching for Survival', in P. Woods and M. Hammersley (eds).

Woods, P., and Hammersley, M. (eds) (1977), *School Experience*, London: Croom Helm.

Yamamoto, K. (1969), 'Images of the Ideal Pupil Held by Teachers in Preparation', *Californian Journal of Educational Research*, 20, no. 5, 221–33.

Yates, A. (ed.) (1966), *Grouping in Education: A Report Sponsored by the UNESCO Institute for Education, Hamburg*, New York: Wiley.

Yntema, D.B., and Torgerson, W.S. (1961), 'Man Computer Co-operation in Decisions Requiring Common Sense', *IRE Trans Human Factors Election HFE 2*, 20–6.

Young, D. (1976), 'Comprehensive Schools—The Danger of Counter Revolution', *Comprehensive Education*, 5, 6.

Young, M.F.D. (ed.) (1971), *Knowledge and Control*, London: Collier-Macmillan.

Young, M.F.D., and Whitty, G. (eds) (1976), *Society, State and Schooling*, Brighton: Falmer Press.

Index

For full bibliographical details or works referred to in the index by author, see the bibliography.